Longing for the End

Longing for the End

A History of Millennialism in Western Civilization

Frederic J. Baumgartner

palgrave

LONGING FOR THE END
Copyright © Frederic J. Baumgartner, 1999. All rights reserved. No
part of this book may be used or reproduced in any manner whatsoever
without written permission except in the case of brief quotations
embodied in critical articles or reviews.

First published 1999 by
PALGRAVE™
175 Fifth Avenue, New York, N.Y.10010 and
Houndmills, Basingstoke, Hampshire RG21 6XS.
Companies and representatives throughout the world.

PALGRAVE is the new global publishing imprint of St. Martin 's Press
LLC Scholarly and Reference Division and Palgrave Publishers Ltd
(formerly Macmillan Press Ltd).

ISBN 0-312-21092-2 hardback
ISBN 0-312-23834-7 paperback

Library of Congress Cataloging-in-Publication Data

Baumgartner, Frederic J.
Longing for the end : a history of millennialism in western civilization /
Frederic J. Baumgartner.
    p.   cm.
  Includes bibliographical references and index.
  ISBN 0–312–21092–2 (hardback)
  ISBN 0–312–23834–7 (paperback)
    1. Millennialism—History. 2. Civilization, Western. I. Title.
BT891.B38   1999
336'.9—dc21   99–14214
                                                                    CIP

A catalogue record for this book is available
from the British Library.

Design by Letra Libre, Inc.

First paperback edition: February 2001
10 9 8 7 6 5 4 3 2 1

Printed in the United States of America.

CONTENTS

Five pages of illustrations appear between pages 212 and 213.

PREFACE

WHEN I WAS A SMALL CHILD, my parents took me to the site of a Marian apparition at Necedah, Wisconsin. I remember little of the day, yet I have never forgotten it. It created in me a curiosity about such events that has never left me. In due course I became an academic historian studying the Reformation, an era as loaded with millennial and apocalyptic anxiety as the current one. The idea of studying millennialism as a distinct topic did not occur to me, however, until I had the opportunity several years ago to develop a fourth-year seminar in millennial cults. It rekindled my interest in endtime beliefs and led to this book.

This book is restricted to Christian groups and those heavily influenced by Christianity. Buddhism and Taoism have eschatological beliefs that have given rise to a number of apocalyptic movements in Asian countries. Some became violent: for example, White Lotus, involved in the Taiping Revolt in China; Hoa Hao in Vietnam; and most recently Aum Shinrikyo in Japan. I will not devote space to them since their Christian element is superficial, if present at all. I will give some attention to several non-Christian eschatologies, for example, the Norse and the Aztec, that have had an impact on Western history. Islamic and especially Judaic messianic beliefs have influenced Christian millennialism, and both will be given limited discussion. Even within Christianity the number of millennial groups is overwhelming; some are not discussed and others are given very limited attention.

There are many synonyms for the events of the endtime; frequently scholars use them with specific shadings of meaning but there is no established pattern of usage. Please see the glossary for definitions of how I use them in this book. I have used the New Revised Standard Version of the Bible (Nashville, 1989) for biblical citations and quotations. It contains the Deuterocanon and Apocrypha, and the translation is in a modern and dignified English. The King James Version's archaic English, for all its eloquence and tradition, is becoming ever more difficult for many people to understand, and only a minority of the millennialists studied in this book used it. The notes are limited to citations for direct quotations, and there is a brief bibliography of my major sources, most of which are easily accessible in large public libraries. There is also a short list of Web sites that proved informative on recent cult activities.

Without the dedicated help of the Interlibrary Loan librarians at Newman Library, I could not have written this book. I wish also to thank my colleagues David Burr and William Ochsenwald for their advice and constructive criticisms, April Cheek and Paul Grady for their invaluable services as my research assistants, Jimmy Harrison for his insights into how a millennial cult works based on his experience in one, and the students in History 4074, whose curiosity and enthusiasm for this subject helped to persuade me that writing this book was a worthy project. Michael Flamini and his excellent staff at Palgrave also have my appreciation for their hard work and skills in seeing this book to print. And I thank my wife Lois who has always supported my efforts at being an author.

GLOSSARY OF TERMS

Many of the following words are difficult to define because scholars use them with specific shadings of meaning but with no established pattern of usage. These definitions reflect what I sense are the most common meanings of the words as they are used today and indicate how I use them in this book.

amillennialism: From the Greek words for *not* and *thousand.* It refers to the Christian view of the endtime that emphasizes God's unknowable will in setting its date and opposes efforts to determine its coming from historical and current events.

antinomianism: From the Greek words for *against* and *law.* It refers to the belief that human law does not bind those who are among the saved because they have a higher law to follow.

apocalypse, apocalyptic: From the Greek word for *revelation,* the first word in the Greek text of the Bible's Book of Revelation. The terms refer to a violent and catastrophic endtime brought about by the deity or another outside force. I use them also for the Judaic and early Christian literature that proclaimed the imminent, violent end of the world.

chiliasm: From the Greek word for *one thousand.* It is used specifically for the belief in the imminent return of Christ and his thousand-year reign on an earth that will become a material paradise. It includes the sense that violence is deemed necessary on the part of believers to make the return happen.

church: An organized, long-established group of believers, conventional in its beliefs and behavior, usually used in reference to Christianity.

cult: From cultivate. A small group, usually short-lived, that defines itself as separate and distinct from a larger religious tradition by attaching particular importance to a leader, a belief, or a practice, and often all of these.

denomination: From the Latin word for *name.* A recognized division within a larger religious tradition. Generally used for the established sects within Protestant Christianity.

discomfit, discomfiture: To frustrate or disconcert. In the context of millennialism, it refers to a loss of faith in a prophet because of the failure of a prediction for the endtime.

dualism: From the Latin word for *two.* It refers to the theological or philosophical belief in the existence to two supernatural powers, one good and one evil, that are in constant conflict for control of the world and human beings.

eschatology: From the Greek word for *last things.* It refers to the study of what will happen in the last days. It has the broadest meaning of the words for the end of the world, referring to the endtime regardless of how it will come about or what will happen during or after it. I also use it to refer to endtime beliefs of religions other than Christianity, Islam, and Judaism.

heresy: From the Greek word for *choice.* It refers to a theological position condemned as erroneous by the dominant group within a religious movement.

messiah, messianism: From the Hebrew word for *anointed.* Originally the term Messiah referred to the expected savior of the Jews and later was applied to Jesus Christ. It has come to mean any leader who will fulfill the fervent desires of a group. I use messianism in reference to Judaic and Islamic endtime beliefs.

millennialism: From *millennium.* Originally, it referred to a belief in the 1,000-year reign of Christ after his Second Coming; it has come to mean a belief in the complete transformation of the world at the endtime. I use it to refer to Christian beliefs about the last days and, more broadly, to those found in Western civilization. I do not use the term *millenarianism,* a synonym for millennialism, in this work.

millennium: From the Latin word for *one thousand.* Capitalized, it refers specifically to the 1,000 years during which Christ will reign on earth as foretold in Revelation 20; more broadly, it can refer also to any period of peace and transformation of human society for the better. Lowercased, it refers to a period of 1,000 years.

myth: A traditional story intended to explain some aspect of the universe and human life whose true explanation is obscure, or to express a culture's moral values in human terms.

orthodox: From the Greek words for *straight* and *thought.* It refers to a theological position defined as correct by the dominant element in a religious movement. Capitalized, it is used to designate the Eastern Christian church or a branch of Judaism.

parousia: From the Greek word for *coming.* It refers to Christ's Second Coming.

perfectionism: The theological concept that it is possible for human beings to become flawless and sinless while still in the world.

postmillennialism: The belief that Christ will return only after the Millennium, during which time humanity will prepare for him by achieving perfection.

premillennialism: The belief that Christ will return before the Millennium to save the saints from the time of trial prior to his reign on earth.

rapture: The belief that Christ will take a chosen few bodily from earth prior to or during the time of trial that precedes the Millennium.

realized eschatology: The belief that Christ has already returned to earth and established his kingdom.

schism: From the Latin word for *cut.* It refers to a division in the leadership of an organization, usually a church.

sect: From the Latin word for *follower.* It refers to a religious division that has split off from a larger body over doctrinal differences while retaining much of the original group's belief and practice.

I

INTRODUCTION

THE BELIEVERS HAVE MASSED at the chosen site in a state of both incredible anticipation and dread. Many are on the verge of hysteria; others are serene and peaceful. They await the return of a man who left their world a long time ago. His return will signal the end of time as they know it and usher in a new world far different from and better than the present one, and they alone, his faithful followers, will have a place in it. Who is this man? Quetzalcoatl? Maitreya Buddha? Jesus Christ? The Mahdi? Where is the place? Tenochtitlan? The Forbidden Mountain? Mount Zion? Jerusalem?

That this brief description of the world's end fits equally well for Aztecs, Buddhists, Christians, and Muslims serves as powerful evidence of the near universality of eschatology in human cultures and religions. Confucianism alone among the world's major systems of thought, and most minor ones, lacks an eschatological myth. Not every religion expects the return of a deity to mark the end of time, nor do many believe that the world itself will be entirely destroyed. Eschatology often predicts the end of a particular people only or the transformation of the world into a different one. It is also true that many eschatological myths are not explicit on how or when the present world will end, but most agree that at some point in the future the world will be radically changed for the better. In some of the myths, the endtime will be peaceful and serene, but in most it will be cataclysmic and violent, usually through fire. Only a few of these myths look for the world's or humanity's complete destruction. In most the result will be a new world, a paradise, for the faithful remnant, the gathered few who have believed in the truth of the eschatological myth and endured the trials and terrors of the last days, which are the final tests of their faithfulness.

Eschatology involves a specific view of history: At some point a deity or some other extranatural force will bring an end to time, often through the agency of a messiah who has a special mission to punish the wicked and reward the faithful. Eschatology fosters a linear view of history: The divine power that created the present world in the distant past will end it sometime in the future. After the last days those in divine favor, the chosen people, will live in an unchanging and unending state of bliss in which there will be no time. This idea of history contrasts with the cyclical view of history: History is made up of a series of cycles, perhaps endless, in which essentially the same pattern is repeated again and again. For both the ancient Greeks and the Confucianists the repetition of the cycles will not result in any significant change in human society. Some Greeks were convinced that the dead would live the exact same lives in the next cycle. Although eschatology has been largely absent in traditional Chinese thought, Taoism has spawned several violent eschatological groups.

Eschatology, however, is not entirely incompatible with cyclical history. In both Hindu and Buddhist thought, history consists of immensely long cycles of time lasting millions of years. The cycles begin with the world in a state of near perfection that slowly degenerates until a catastrophic destruction is followed by a rebirth of the world. In societies without a sense of the incredible length of history found in Indian thought, the theme often is the return of the golden age that existed in the past and will reoccur in the future. Whether the cycle will be repeated is not a matter of much consideration; the primary concern is the urgent desire for the return of the golden age since the current world is in a state of decay and decadence. For example, the Roman eschatological myth called for six ages of the world and then a lasting golden age identical to the first age. The poet Virgil, writing about 40 BC, believed that the world was about to enter that golden age. In his *Fourth Eclogue* he predicted that the land would bear fruit without labor, men would put down their plows, and the oxen would be released from their yokes. What he had in mind was the universal domain being created by Rome, but one can hardly fault early Christians for thinking he was referring to Christ's coming.

The Judaic, Christian, and Islamic views of history, and the Zoroastrian tradition of Persia from which they may have drawn inspiration, are strongly linear. Time passes from the creation to its end according to the will of God, with specific events as mileposts along the way, although for many in those traditions there is still a sense of the cyclical: The postapocalyptic paradise will involve a return to the Garden of Eden. The period from beginning to end is brief compared to those of the Eastern traditions. More important in explaining the strength of eschatology in the three great monotheistic religions is the sense that the end will occur soon, perhaps even in the lifetime of the people now alive. In comparison to Hindu eschatology, for example, in which the catastrophic end is incomprehensibly far in the future, it is immediate in Jewish and Islamic messianism and Christian millennialism. Jews, Muslims, and Christians face the possibility that they will have to suffer the terrible events of the final days and get to enjoy the reward of those who endure them faithfully. This gives a deep urgency to the eschatological myth for many in the three religions. It also helps to explain the prevalence of millennial cults in the history of Christianity. If the endtime is likely to occur in one's lifetime, then it makes sense to prepare for it by becoming a member of the faithful remnant. And if the expected immediate return of Christ is delayed, then it becomes plausible, as one reaction to the failure of the end to occur, to believe that the faithful remnant must act to bring about the return, perhaps by violently purging the world of sinners. Millennialism often inspires violence in its adherents but even more frequently it inspires violence in others against them.

Another key difference among the three monotheistic religions and several other religions, especially those originating in India, is that latter's belief in reincarnation. While reincarnation does not preclude a belief in eschatology (Buddhism has a strong endtime myth), it is difficult for persons to think of the next world when they expect their souls to live again in other bodies. The Indian religions also believe that every soul will eventually complete its cycles of existence and reach union with the divine. In the monotheistic religions, however, one does not know the soul's fate after death, and the consensus among them is that not all souls, perhaps very few, will enter paradise. While these religions regard souls as unique to each human, they also have a sense of collective salvation: All souls of those in the group will be saved. It is a crucial element in millennial cults.

The eschatological myth has had the most impact on Christianity out of all the world's religions. No other religion has an eschatological text as powerful or as deeply ingrained within it as the Book of Revelation. The decision by the early Christian Church to include it as one of the books of the Bible's New Testament ensured that millennialism would be a major part of Christian doctrine and, therefore, of the history of Western civilization. For nearly 2,000 years the vast complex of ideas, symbols, and emotions—Antichrist, 666, the Four Horsemen, Armageddon—that make up millennialism has continually spawned religious groups. Some have endured to become thriving Christian denominations; others quickly disappear or self-destruct, as did Heaven's Gate. Some have perpetrated extraordinary violence as they prepared for Christ's return and have been destroyed by the violent response of the society around them. Others have quietly and passively waited for the Second Coming, most dissolving when it failed to occur as predicted, a few lasting for centuries. The range in beliefs, practices, and size of these groups throughout history has been enormous. If it is true that secular ideologies, like Marxism, National Socialism, and many anticolonial movements in the Third World owe a great deal to Christian millennialism, then the impact of Revelation and of the texts in the Hebrew Scriptures that helped to inspire it extends beyond the realm of religion into politics.

While Christianity has always been pervaded with millennialism, since the 400s the sense that the world's end is at hand has been subsumed for the average Christian in the effort to save one's soul and attend to one's personal endtime. Although no main-line Christian church has repudiated either millennialism or the texts in the canon of the Bible that support it, it has been unusual for mainstream Christians to give special attention to the immediacy of the Christ's Second Coming. Strongly millennial groups, which arose in Christianity within a century after Christ, have usually been deemed heretical. Human nature always finds it difficult to accept differences of opinion in any aspect of human activity but especially regarding religion. If society at the time is relatively tolerant and the millennial beliefs are not too different from those of the mainstream, the millennial group will organize a sect. When the authorities punish people with deviant beliefs, it is more likely that those so punished, rather than returning to orthodoxy, will withdraw, forming a secret cult. The history of millennialism in Western Civilization is replete with sects and cults since there are myriad ways to interpret the many millennial texts in the Bible, and many interpretations are diametrically opposed to the orthodox positions of the main-line churches.

Millennial cults and sects are natural occurrences in Christianity. Jesus and his band of disciples serve as the prototype of such groups, which have been often the products of conscious efforts to imitate his example and follow the Scriptures. Max Weber, who coined the term "charismatic leader," based the concept largely on Jesus the anointed one. Today most Christians are reluctant to apply to Jesus and his disciples the connotations that "cult leader" currently implies and are not likely to understand how Jesus could serve as a model for men like Jim Jones or David Koresh. The significance of identifying Jesus as a charismatic leader of a millennial cult and his disciples as its members lies in how it helps to explain the perennial presence of similar groups in the history of Christendom. The very model for a successful cult lies open in the Gospels, Christianity's primary documents. Once Christianity became the established religion of the Roman Empire, there was a strong need to downplay the Bible's millennial message and dampen the millennial expectations of the first generations of Christians, which St. Augustine did most successfully in the early fifth century. Hence, millennialism has been kept to a minimum in mainstream Christian churches, but in times of stress—whether economic, political, religious, or often simply personal—one has only to read the Gospels to find a blueprint for a millennial cult. Early Christianity is the prototype, the template of millennial cults, which, consciously or not, follow the pattern Jesus established. Except for the Jewish movements that predate Christ, it is rare to find eschatological cults rising out of religions that Christianity did not influence to a considerable extent.

Of the many attempts to define a cult's characteristics, the most successful is still that by sociologist Werner Stark.[1] His key features of cults are

1. The cult depends, initially if not entirely, on the inspiration and authority of a leader who can be defined as a charismatic leader.
2. It begins as a protest against the real or perceived economic or societal repression of one group by the larger society.
3. It rejects the view of reality taken for granted by the establishment and presents an alternative vision of human society and law.
4. It is a voluntary association. Members are not born into it; they accept belief by conversion.
5. It is egalitarian. Except for the leader, all members have the same status regardless of their place in society before they joined the cult.
6. It offers acceptance and love within the group. Members believe that outside the cult there is neither.
7. It demands full commitment from its members. Shunning, in a few cases even death, is the punishment for those who join but are unwilling to give that full commitment. A millennial cult, then, is a group that combines these features, or at least most of them, with a conviction that the cult members are living on the verge of the end of the evil world, and that only they will be saved from the destruction of the world and given life in the new world to come.

Millennial cults offer their members several psychological benefits: a group to which they are fully committed where they can find a sense of love and belonging, the certainty of a truly happy fate, the expectation of vindication against those who have oppressed them, and of seeing their oppressors tormented and punished. The motive of vengeance is often very powerful in such groups. Millennial cult members define themselves as different from other people since they are or will become the new people of the new age. Thus, their behavior will often be sharply distinct from the norms concerning sex and family, violence, property, and dress. For some the belief that they are a new people, chosen to live in the New Kingdom, leads to a sense that the laws of the old society do not apply to them because they are above that law. The term *antinomian* (against the law) is used for the extremes of that belief.

Another way that millennial cults have often differed from the broader societies in which they arise is the larger role of women. The case can be made that both leadership and membership in these movements serve as compensation for a lack of opportunities in the larger society. That argument also helps explain the predominance of people from lower economic classes and those who have failed in other endeavors among both cult leaders and members. Also in many societies, there is a sense that women are more in touch with the spiritual, which is one reason women have been more often accused of witchcraft. It perhaps also explains why women make up the majority of spiritualists. Women frequently have been the prophets and visionaries who have sparked the formation of a millennial cult, although they often have conceded or lost leadership to men.

Cults founded by women have differed from those founded by men in several respects. They are quietist, not militant. They often see the Deity as a union of male and female and seek to achieve the same in humans as well, requiring celibacy as the means of reaching that goal (but possibly also reflecting the dangers of childbirth before modern medicine), while men have led all those cults notorious for sexual deviancy. Women-led cults depend more heavily on visions and new revelations while male-led cults often insist on a literal interpretation of the millennial texts. Reflecting the imperative of reproduction, attitudes toward sex have been a key aspect of nearly every cult. Few cults have had the same attitude toward sex as the society from which they came. Most are restrictive, and many expect celibacy from members, although the leaders sometimes have sexual access to their followers. Some, however, are entirely antinomian about sex, claiming that flouting the mores of the society around them is proof of their special status as the people of the New Kingdom.

Millennialists of all kinds are intoxicated with the coming new age; they look into the future and find it good. As one historian of a millennial group says, "They would destroy the present as fast as possible in order to usher in the longed-for future, to hasten the end. They are victims of what Montaigne called 'the frantic curiosity of our nature which is pleased to become absorbed with future things as if it did not have enough to do in digesting the present ones.'"[2] From the historian's point of view, a major problem with that attitude is that millennial groups tend to have little interest in keeping a record of their past. They are firmly focused on the future and care not a whit that future historians might not have reliable sources to describe their beliefs and acts accurately since there will be no time and no history in the New Kingdom. It is true also that many groups lack historical records because of their secretive nature. As a consequence much of what is known about many millennialist groups discussed in this book, especially those in the early chapters, comes from hostile sources, compiled by religious and civil authorities who regarded them as deviant or worse. Because most information about the early movements has come from their enemies, who, it is assumed, have presented them in the worst possible light, modern scholars have often discounted such sources; yet the beliefs and behavior of recent cults make these reports seem plausible. There is no way around the problem except to understand that much of the history of millennialism is based on hostile witnesses who felt no need to be sympathetic or even impartial to groups they despised and feared.

Certainly millennial groups usually have beliefs that strike most other people as strange, and they act in ways considered bizarre. If, however, we refuse to understand those beliefs and acts as products of a religious tradition older than Christianity, we stand to alienate the millennialists until the conclusion they reach is that the world will not listen. If we choose to ignore or dismiss their worldview, then we will allow more tragedies like Jonestown and Waco. The best way to protect society from the destructive acts of zealots like Jim Jones or David Koresh, which in turn will prevent such cult leaders from bringing out the worst in society, is through a serious inquiry into the history of millennialism. We cannot abandon the field to those for whom the end will not come soon enough.

II

THE JESUS CULT

MILLENNIALISM PERVADES THE HISTORY of Christianity because the religion began as an apocalyptic cult. It is entirely plausible to see Jesus himself as the archetypal charismatic leader, creating within Judaism a cult that became the world's largest religion. Christianity came out of a society that had a powerful apocalyptic vision. Racked by Hellenistic and Roman occupations for three centuries before Christ, the Jews had created a vast apocalyptic literature that had a powerful influence on Christian millennialism. Many of the key ideas of the Jewish apocalyptic, however, may not have originated in Judaism but in an earlier Persian religion, Zoroastrianism.

Our knowledge of Zoroaster (Greek for Zarathustra) is so limited that we are not even certain of the era in which he lived. Although the standard Persian sources place his life around 600 BC, there is reason to argue for a date 400 years earlier. Tradition states that he was trained as a priest in the archaic Persian religion but abandoned it at about age twenty because of his dissatisfaction with its tenets and the behavior of its priests. Ten years later he received a revelation that unveiled the truth about the universe. It came from Ahura Mazda, the Wise Lord, the source of all truth and good, the creator of angels and the human race. In stark contrast with this Supreme Good Being is Angra Mainyu, the Adversary, who is the source of all the world's evil, including death. Like Ahura Mazda, he has existed from all time, but he is less powerful, lacking knowledge of the future. Angra Mainyu created a host of demons to spread evil in the world and within human hearts. The conflict between good and evil in Zoroastrianism is not between spirit and matter but between two opposite forces present in every aspect of the universe. Zoroastrian dualism does not contrast the good human spirit with the evil human body; rather, it sees the conflict as taking place within both at the same time.

The cosmic battle between Ahura Mazda and Angra Mainyu has both a beginning and an end; time in Zoroastrianism is linear, consisting of four periods of 3,000 years each. During the first trimillennium, Angra Mainyu was locked away in a bottomless pit of darkness; at the end of it he escaped and introduced evil into the world. Ahura Mazda, unprepared for the onslaught of evil, was forced to make a truce with Angra Mainyu: Ahura Mazda would rule the world for 3,000 years; then his foe would rule. During his period of dominance, Ahura Mazda created the human race and endowed it with free will to choose between good and evil. When Angra Mainyu took over the world in the third trimillennium, the present era, he introduced natural evils such as earthquakes and volcanoes and took advantage of human free will to seduce mankind into wickedness.

The final period of 3,000 years will see the cosmic showdown between the two gods. It will begin with the public ministry of Zoroaster, to whom Ahura Mazda has given the truth in order to prepare humanity for the events of the cosmic battle about to occur. Mankind, however, will ignore Zoroaster's teaching and degenerate into total corruption over a period of a thousand years. Then the first of three saviors, all direct descendants of Zoroaster a thousand years apart, will come to reverse Angra Mainyu's success. Truth will begin to prevail, more so after the second savior, and will be victorious at the time of the third. At the end of this trimillennium, all the dead will arise, be purified by walking through molten metal, and be given immortality. Meanwhile, Angra Mainyu will assemble his forces for a final showdown with Ahura Mazda in a truly horrendous war. Ahura Mazda's victory will result in the fiery destruction of Angra Mainyu, his demons, and the present world. In apocalyptic scenarios fire is the usual choice for destroying the world. Then Ahura Mazda will transform the world, leveling the mountains and filling the valleys, and he and human souls will live forever, united in bliss.

The similarities between Zoroaster's eschatology and that of Revelation and other apocalyptic works in Judaism and early Christianity are obvious, but whether Judaic and in turn Christian apocalyptic authors knew of the Persian tradition and drew from it is less certain. The fact that the key Zoroastrian eschatological text was compiled only after Christ complicates determining cross influence. Certainly the Jews at the time of the Babylonian captivity had the opportunity to become acquainted with Zoroastrianism. The ruling Achaemenid dynasty of the Persian empire that conquered Babylon in 539 BC had embraced Zoroastrianism and promoted it as a state religion, although the Persians were unusually tolerant of other religions. Cyrus I allowed the Hebrew exiles to return to Palestine in 538 and rebuild the Temple. That act made him one of the most praised persons of the Old Testament: "I am the Lord . . . who says of Cyrus 'He is my shepherd and he shall carry out my purpose'" (Isaiah 44:28). The scholars who have studied the question of Zoroastrian influence on Judaism are divided between those who conclude that it occurred and those who argue against it. Zoroastrianism remained the dominant religion of Persia until the Arab conquest in the mid-seventh century AD and thus continued to have an impact on religious thought in the Middle East through the formative years of both Christianity and Islam. Today, there are a few thousand Zoroastrians in Iran and a somewhat larger community, the Parsees, based in India.

There is little eschatology in the early books of the Bible. The early Hebrews gave limited thought to the question of what would happen to the world in the distant future. The trauma of exile in Mesopotamia and the destruction of the Temple, followed by the triumphant return and the Temple's rebuilding, and perhaps Zoroastrian influence, encouraged a sense of history as the playing out of God's will. From then on, the Jews had a keen sense of eschatology and also began to develop a doctrine of life after death. One of the first, if not the first, piece of apocalyptic literature in the Bible is the Book of Ezekiel, which, it is generally agreed, was written largely by a priest who was among the exiles. He sought to explain why God condemned the Israelites to the agony of exile, and he revealed the divine promise of their return to the Promised Land. The prophet described the restored land of Israel as one that "has become like the garden of Eden" (Ezekiel 36:28–37). This theme frequently appears in millennialism: God will renew nature, and it will become so abundant that all want will disappear. A second vision revealed "the valley of the dry bones," where God will raise up the dead and restore them to Israel.

Ezekiel's importance in the history of millennialism lies especially in the next two chapters, in which the invasion of Gog from the land of Magog is prophesied. (Here, Gog is a ruler; Magog is his realm; in Revelation, both are nations.) Magog is described as being located in the remotest north, the direction from which most of the invasions of Palestine came. Gog will lead an enormous horde of mounted warriors against Israel. When the mighty army arrives, God will destroy it and the land of Magog as well. Gog's army is so huge and the number of casualties so vast that it will take seven months to bury the dead and seven years to burn their weapons. The prophet then describes in detail the temple that will be rebuilt after God's victory. These last chapters of Ezekiel, anticipatory of the last chapters of Revelation, are also suggestive of Zoroastrianism. That the author of the first 37 chapters does not appear to be familiar with the Persian religion is one reason, along with differences in content and context, for the view that the last part of Ezekiel was written perhaps a half-century later by someone else. The hypothesis that the apocalyptic chapters were inserted later fits what would become a standard feature of Judaic apocalyptic literature: the appropriation of the name and authority of a recognized man of God by an apocalyptic author.

The best example is the Book of Daniel. Many of the symbols and images used in later apocalyptic literature come from Daniel, reappearing, either unchanged or expanded, in Revelation. The scholarly consensus is that Daniel contains a collection of stories about events during the Babylonian captivity involving a heroic Jew named Daniel, to which was added an apocalyptic vision written about 165 BC by an unknown author. The apocalyptic chapters of Daniel describe a time of persecution. Alexander the Great's death had placed Palestine under the rule of the Seleucids, descendants of one of his generals. The Seleucids were very interested in spreading Greek culture throughout their realm. When Antiochus IV became king in 175, he took the policy of Hellenization well beyond his predecessors and deeply antagonized the Jewish population. Their resistance led Antiochus to strike at the core of Jewish identity, their religion. He forbade the observance of Jewish practices and made the Temple a site for the cult of Zeus, which probably was the "abomination of desolations" so abhorred by Daniel (9:27). The Jews led by the Maccabees revolted and succeeded in restoring the Temple in 164. Antiochus died at the end of 164, and the Jews gained a century of self-rule under the Hasmonean high priests, the descendants of the Maccabees, until the Roman conquest.

The apocalyptic vision of Daniel takes the form of a revelation from the angel Gabriel to Daniel, supposedly in the sixth century BC, accurately foretelling the events prior to and during Antiochus IV's reign. Daniel, however, is wrong on the circumstances of the king's death, which suggests the book was written shortly before it occurred. This format allows the author to assume the authority of having infallible knowledge of the future, especially the certainty of the evil king's destruction. Twice Daniel is told that he must keep the revelation secret until the appointed moment at the endtime, which will occur after Antiochus's destruction. Many of the key symbols of later millennialism appear: the four beasts, representing the four great empires to be destroyed before the coming of the eternal kingdom, which will be the fifth monarchy of God and the saints; the beasts' horns, symbolizing rulers; and the metals—gold, silver, bronze, and iron—representing the four ages of the world. Among Daniel's symbols, the most potent are his numbers: "a time, two times, and half a time" (three and a half), the 1290 days, and the 70 weeks, all used to indicate the time before Jerusalem and the Temple will be cleansed and rebuilt. Those numbers later became the source of intense endtime calculation. Equally significant are the prophecies of a period of anguish just prior to the end of time; the coming of the Messiah, "one like the son of man" (7:13); the bodily resurrection of some of the dead—the righteous receiving everlasting life on earth, evildoers everlasting shame—and the coming of the kingdom of God, an everlasting earthly realm where the righteous will rule with God. An obvious part of Daniel, and of most millennial works, is the thirst for vengeance against those who are oppressing the people with whom the author identifies.

The Book of Daniel largely established the genre of apocalyptic literature as it flourished over the next four centuries in Judaism. Some of the books date to the Maccabean period, but most come from the era of Roman rule that began in 63 BC. Although in Palestine the Romans practiced their usual toleration of the religions of their subject peoples, the Jews chafed badly under their rule and heavy taxes. Most fervently longed to reestablish an independent Jewish kingdom purified of the pagan Romans, which would have the dominant place in the world or, according to some, the only one. Its king would be either David himself returned to rule, as proposed in a few works, or, more commonly, a messianic figure from the house of David. The apparent hopelessness of this overwhelming desire to oust the Romans and recreate the Davidic Kingdom led many Jews to the conclusion that there was nothing they could do make it happen; God in his own good time would, through a messianic figure.

The idea that God has determined the events of history is one of the characteristics that define noncanonical works, such as the Book of Jubilees or the Book of Enoch, as apocalyptic. Enoch "walked with God; then he was no more, because God took him" (Gen. 5:24); he was an important figure in many apocalyptic works because he was expected to return to earth before the endtime. Usually paired with Enoch was the prophet Elijah, who was taken to heaven in a fiery chariot (2 Kings 2:11). His expected return was based on Malachi (4:5): "Lo, I will send you the prophet Elijah before the great and terrible day of the Lord comes."

Another characteristic is the use of pseudonyms, whereby the authors attributed their visions of the future to a prophet or hero of the Hebrew past; we have no idea who the authors of these books really were. They receive their visions from an angel or spirit, who usually charge them to keep them secret until the proper time, and they use the literary device of foretelling the past to establish credibility for their prophecies of the future. That future involves the decline of the world into a state of near total depravity except for the faithful remnant of Israel. Nature will also reflect the downward spiral of humanity with natural catastrophes and a drastic decline in fertility. A profoundly evil ruler will appear, provoking the final showdown between good and evil, which will take the form of a hugely destructive war. The good will ultimately prevail through the agency of the Messiah, God's chosen one. The new Davidic kingdom will be established, and the righteous who have survived will be admitted to it. The dead will rise and be judged. The righteous among them will be rewarded with a place in the New Kingdom; the evildoers, among the living and the risen, will be doomed to eternal punishment. Time as it has existed will come to an end. Although some of these authors take off on flights of mysticism, astrology, and magic in addition to their eschatology, they all reveal a strong sense of dualism, attributing evil to the agency of an enormously powerful spirit, Satan, not quite the equal of God. Jewish apocalyptic also has a twofold division of time: the present age, full of evil and sorrows but certain to end at God's will; and the future one, timeless, eternal, full of goodness and justice.

As much as the Jews hated Roman rule, most of them, including the priests, found that they could accommodate themselves to it in order to carry on daily life while maintaining their hope of the Messiah. The Essenes, however, were moved by their apocalyptic vision to reject any cooperation with Rome: The faithful remnant of Israel must not defile itself by any contact with Satan's hordes. The Essenes, who had started as a group opposed to the high priests of the Hasmonean dynasty, were convinced that they lived on the verge of the final days. In order to prepare themselves for the great war between the sons of light and the sons of darkness and for the new life that would follow, they withdrew into their own communities to live the life of the future kingdom in the present. The most celebrated was the one at Qumran, the source of the Dead Sea Scrolls that provide so much information about their life. Although there is no evidence conclusively identifying the group at Qumran as Essenes, the similarities are strong enough to make it probable. The scrolls speak of a charismatic leader called the Teacher of Righteousness, who led the group in its withdrawal from the world, following the words of Isaiah (40:3): "In the wilderness prepare the way of the Lord." His foe was the Wicked Priest, probably the Hasmonean high priest Alexander Jannaeus (d. 76 BC), whose alleged transgressions of the law led the teacher to remove his followers from Jewish society. The Essenes followed a strict interpretation of Mosaic law but added their own rules, practiced celibacy although probably not in every community, ate communal meals in anticipation of the great messianic banquet, and handed over all property to the community after a year-long probation. They believed that within their present lifetime, the sons of light, led by the son of God, would enter into a war lasting 40 years against the sons of darkness. All the non-Jewish nations and many Jews as well would join the army of evil, but the sons of light, with the help of angels, would be victorious and emerge as the sole inhabitants of the world. They would then return in triumph to Jerusalem, and the faithful remnant would take part in a communal meal of bread and wine. From then on all would perfectly observe the Mosaic Law, and eternal peace would reign.

Although Rome was not the original enemy of the Essenes, it took center stage in their eschatology after 63 BC. The revolt that broke out in 66 AD and led to the destruction of the Temple had been simmering for a long time and involved more Jews than just the Essenes; there is little question, however, that they played a major role in the revolt. Not enough is known of the final band of rebels who held out in the fortress at Masada to identify them as Essenes or to conclude that their eschatology motivated their collective suicide, but eschatalogical beliefs are more likely to lead to such an act than any other form of thought. In 132 the Jews revolted again, led by Simon bar Kosiba, better known as Bar Kokhba, which has a messianic meaning, "son of the star," referring to Numbers (24:17): "A star shall step from Jacob." What little is known about him suggests that he proclaimed or was the focus of the messianic hope of liberating Jerusalem and rebuilding the Temple. He assembled a good-sized force that probably held the city for a time and took the Romans three years to crush. Judea was devastated, and messianism largely disappeared as an activist element in Judaism. Despite frequent persecution to the present century, since Bar Kokhba, Jews have rarely resorted to violent messianism as a response, although men claiming to be the Messiah have often appeared at times of crisis in Jewish communities.

Although messianism was declining in Judaism, it found a new and permanent home in a new religion, Christianity, which began as a messianic cult within Judaism. Shortly after Jesus' birth a Galilean named

Judas led an agrarian revolt against Rome. It was serious enough that the Romans replaced the system of client kings who governed for them with Roman governors. This led to greater interference in Jewish society—for example the introduction of Roman coins with pagan engravings—and caused even deeper resentment of Roman rule. The urgency of the Messiah's coming became far greater, as did the sense that the endtime had to be close at hand. Nonbiblical sources such as the Roman-Jewish historian Josephus note the appearance of a number of men who claimed or were deemed to be the Messiah, although they do not mention Jesus. Someone Josephus does mention, John the Baptizer, plays a significant role in the Gospels. John lived in the wilderness, dressed in camel's hair, and baptized in the Jordan, an act symbolizing purification. This description suggest some affinity with the Essenes, although John is a loner when he appears in the Gospels. His message was apocalyptic: He is the precursor of one who is to come, who will lay the ax to the roots of the trees and separate the wheat from the chaff, gathering the good grain in his granary while burning the chaff. John's message was an urgent call for the people to repent before the day of the Lord comes so that they might join the Lord in his great victory. Like many later millennial prophets, John was executed by the temporal power he attacked.

According to the three synoptic Gospels, Jesus was John's "one who is to come," a phrase with messianic overtones. In the past century great effort has gone into trying to ascertain which Gospel passages are authentic, and many recent scholars have concluded that they are very few. Some are especially eager to deny the authenticity of the apocalyptic passages in order to undermine recent violent millennialism. Yet there is no good reason to deny Jesus' apocalypticism; apocalyptic thinking pervaded Jewish society of his time. As there will never be a good solution to this authenticity question or the one of whether there was an original gospel, known as the "Q" source to biblical scholars, the only recourse is to take the Gospels at face value and study Christ as a messianic prophet while recognizing that it may have been his disciples who were responsible for much of the messianism in them. In truth, it matters little, if at all, for the history of millennialism whether Jesus said and did the things the Gospels attribute to him since Christians have always accepted them as truly his. It is precisely those with a powerful millennial vision who have the least doubt about the authenticity of the Gospels and take Jesus and his disciples as the model of how to live and behave.

When Gabriel gave Mary the name at the Annunciation, he told her that her son would be called the Son of the Most High and that he would sit on the throne of David and rule over the House of Jacob forever (Luke 1:32–36). These titles tie directly into Judaic messianism, especially as it is characterized in the Dead Sea Scrolls. Probably no Jew of the first century would have failed to recognize them as messianic. The genealogies of Jesus in the Gospels indicate another messianic characteristic, descent from David. Although a carpenter's son was not in the Jewish elite, a craft placed him a level up from most of his disciples, such as the first four apostles, all fishermen. His authority did not come from any established sources either Jewish or Roman; it was the *charisma* (favor) of God. Jesus excited crowds by his teaching, created enemies by challenging the morals of Jewish religious leaders, criticized the old religion and proposed to purify it, and provided a new vision of the proper relationship to God. There is no hint in the Gospels that Jesus' appeal came from his physical appearance or verbal eloquence; it was the content of his message and the conviction with which he presented it that attracted people. His miracles helped to affirm that he had God's favor, the essence of charismatic leadership.

Jesus' first public words, "Repent, for the kingdom of God is at hand" (Matt. 4:17), are apocalyptic. It is possible to point out dozens of Jesus' statements with apocalyptic overtones in the synoptic Gospels, but there are few in John. He uses the apocalyptic idea of a secret revelation when he tells his apostles that he will reveal to them the secret of the kingdom of God but everyone else must be taught in parables (Mark 4:11). Even the Lord's Prayer has strong apocalyptic content: One prays for the coming of the Kingdom and the time when God's will is done on earth as well as in heaven, the coming of the new age, and avoiding the time of trial. Jesus' acts of healing, exorcising, and performing other miracles also define him as the figure of the endtime. So, too, does his conflict with Satan the Tempter, the evil one who controls the world; Jesus must vanquish him to restore divine order to the world and bring about the New Kingdom. Jesus' last meal with his apostles has greater resemblance to the Essenes' messianic banquet of bread and wine than to the Passover meal. He pledges that he will not "drink of the fruit of the vine until that day when I drink it new in the Kingdom of God" (Mark 14:27).

The key messianic passage is the "Little Apocalypse" in Mark (13:3–37), the most eschatological of the Gospels, with versions in Matthew and Luke. After Jesus says that not a stone of the Temple will be left on another, several apostles ask him privately to explain when and with what signs the endtime will come. He answers that there will be false prophets, wars and rumors of wars, earthquakes and famines, and persecution of his disciples, but the end will not come before the good news has been proclaimed to all the towns of Israel. Jesus speaks of the abomination of desolations as the sign that the time of troubles of the endtime has begun. Believers will flee to the mountains; Jerusalem will be destroyed; signs will appear in the heavens; and finally the Son of Man will come on a cloud in glory and power. With a trumpet he will summon the elect to eternal life from the four corners of the world; at that time one of two people standing in a field will be taken and the other left, the event later called Rapture. Jesus concludes with the warning that none knows the day or the hour, but in Mark, as in Luke, he makes it clear that it will happen to those listening to him: "This generation will not pass away until all these things have taken place" (Luke 21:32). That these statements promising an imminent fulfillment of Jesus' prophecies were kept in texts that did not reach their final form until at least fifty years later lends authenticity to them. If there had not been a strong tradition that they were Jesus' words, they would have been changed to reflect the passing of the first and several more generations.

There can be no doubt that Jesus had a powerful sense of messianism, but can we call him the charismatic leader of a millennial cult? Let us look at how Jesus and his disciples fit the key elements that constitute a millennial cult. Jesus and his followers expect the immediate end of the world and feel an overwhelming need to prepare themselves for it by breaking with their families and occupations. When he calls his first disciples, they leave their nets and families to follow him (Matt. 4:18–22). When one disciple wants to go and bury his father, Jesus tells him to let the dead bury the dead (Matt. 8:21–22). He says that anyone who loves family members more than him is not worthy of him (Matt. 10:34–39). "Whoever does the will of God is my mother and brother and sister" (Mark 3:35). In regard to sex and marriage, Jesus comes down strongly on the side of abstinence: "There are eunuchs who have made themselves eunuchs for the sake of the kingdom of heaven" (Matt. 19:12). When asked about the sex life of the dead who will be raised, he replies that there will be no marriage in the new age; the risen will be like angels, without sex. His followers must take up the cross and follow Jesus, even cut off a hand or pluck out an eye if it causes any wavering in their commitment. The obligation to shun members who do not live up to the demands of the community is only hinted at in the Gospels—the salt that loses its savor and the yeast that does not leaven must be thrown out—but is made clear in several of Paul's epistles. Regarding violence, Jesus is a pacifist: He tells his followers to turn the other cheek and put up the sword. While Jesus expects the end of Roman rule and the coming of the Kingdom of God, it will happen through God's intervention, not human agency.

To what extent was Jesus's movement a protest against repression? Key to seeing Jesus as leading a protest movement is what sociologists call relative deprivation, the sense among a people of being repressed, rather than hard evidence that such repression is necessarily real. There is no debate that most Jews of that era harbored a deep sense of being harmed by Roman occupation since Roman taxation compounded the taxes of the Jewish authorities. The hope that the New Kingdom preached by Jesus would overthrow Roman rule is manifest throughout the Gospels. While that motivation might have been enough in itself to create a movement, Jesus also addressed the resentment of the Jewish peasants toward their own religious elites. He seems to have been addressing largely the rural population since his parables use mostly agrarian examples. Whether or not he sought to attract the rural discontented, their support for his cause is clear enough that a biblical scholar has called it the "greatest agrarian protest in all history."[1] Jesus attracted outcasts in the society, such as lepers, tax collectors, and prostitutes, but he also appealed to some persons of a higher status.

Women also had reason to feel repressed at the time of Jesus. Few societies have been as rigidly patriarchal as Roman society was, and

Jewish society of that era was only slightly less so. In contrast, early Christianity gave women wider opportunities and came close to granting them equal status. In regard to divorce, Jesus emphasizes the rights of both partners, thus placing himself in opposition to Mosaic law, which emphasizes the rights of the husband. The initiative of women in going to Jesus for help and becoming involved in the community is clear in the Gospels of Mark and Matthew and is stronger in Luke. Luke has many instances where women receive special divine favor; most importantly women are the first to learn of the Resurrection. Jesus' definition of the family includes mother and sisters, whereas a Roman one was restricted to father and brothers. At Pentecost, Peter cites the statement of the prophet Joel (2:28–29) that women will prophesy and receive the Spirit. Jesus was not modern enough to place women among his apostles, but the role of women in the leadership of the early Church in Jerusalem as described in the Acts of the Apostles is unique for that era.

There is no doubt that Jesus and his followers demonstrated another characteristic of a cult: rejection of the established view of society in favor of an alternative vision. Jesus has come to proclaim his message to the poor and the meek, not the rich and mighty. The Beatitudes are intended as an indictment of established society and a description of the new one. Jesus proposes that his followers lead a lifestyle later called apostolic poverty, which means living without regard for sowing or reaping. As he does for the ravens and the grass in the field, God will provide for those who strive for his kingdom. Jesus says, "Sell your possessions and give alms" (Luke 12:22–33). When he feeds 5,000 with five loaves and two fishes, he shows what will happen in the New Kingdom. A communal life of shared property and wealth was in place among his followers by the time of his death. If the present world with its economic injustices is coming to an end, then it is not necessary to prepare for the future. Early Christianity contains a radical critique of riches, a demand for a detachment from the goods of this world, and an elimination of the barriers between the rich and the poor through the agency of the Christian community. In regard to established law, Jesus proclaims his respect for the Law of Moses, declaring that he has not come to abolish it, but he allows his disciples to break many of its rules. When, for example, his disciples violate the rules of the Sabbath by plucking and eating grain from a wheat field, Jesus justifies it by saying that the Son of Man is the lord of the Sabbath (Matt. 12:1–8). He presents different rules that his followers must obey to be righteous. They take it on his word that he speaks for God in presenting the new law.

In respect to egalitarianism, another feature of a cult, despite the special status of the twelve apostles, Jesus makes strong statements about the equality of all: "The first will be last, and the last will be first!"(Mark 10:31) "Let the little children come to me, and do not stop them, for it is to such as these that the kingdom of heaven belongs" (Matt. 20).

Some twenty years later, Paul writes, "There is no longer Jew or Greek, slave or free, male or female" (Gal. 3:28). There could not be a more powerful statement undermining the rigid Roman division of society into male/female and free/slave. Largely because of Paul's statement, Christian cults have emphasized egalitarianism. When someone enters the community of the cult, the roles and status of the outside world fall away, and everyone stands equal before God and the cult leader. Not everyone finds that attractive, but for many, especially those whom the outside world deems of little value, it is most appealing. Even some with high status outside of the cult find it appealing and give up their high place in the world to join.

Understanding Jesus as the leader of a millennial cult provides insight into the reason for his death. Cults and their leaders have always earned the suspicion of the authorities; in any circumstances, Jesus and his disciples would have been kept under a watchful eye. In 30 AD the situation in Palestine was very tense. Several rebellions against Roman rule had erupted in the previous decades, and both Jewish and Roman authorities were expecting further outbreaks. The Jewish authorities had been keeping track of Jesus for some time. When he entered Jerusalem at the head of a crowd shortly before Passover, the feast of liberation from oppression, the significance of his act was obvious although it was not threatening enough to provoke an instant reaction. The high priests, who had previously overlooked the radicalism of his challenge to traditional Judaism, felt obliged to take action before he upset the uneasy peace with the Romans.

The fate of John the Baptizer made it obvious to Jesus what would happen to him if he continued to proclaim the New Kingdom with its challenge to both Roman and Jewish authority. Faced with the threat of death before the high priests and Pontius Pilate, he refused to back down from his proclamations. Firm in his belief that he was the Son of Man, he went to his crucifixion, the mode of death the Romans used for rebels who were not Roman citizens. The death of the charismatic leader, a common event in the history of millennial groups, is a moment of unprecedented crisis, but it has rarely meant their end. Those who have committed themselves to a cult leader have so much invested in him psychologically that they cannot accept the death as breaking the faith of the group. One explanation for the Resurrection is that it came out of the refusal of the Jesus cult to accept the finality of his death.

Whether one believes that the Resurrection is fact or artifact, it is, short of the end of the world itself, the ultimate millennial event. Jesus's victory over death defeated Satan and sin, Satan's tool for subjugating the world, since it is through sin that death entered the world (Romans 5:12). The Resurrection is the promise of the New Kingdom where all the righteous who have died will return to life and be given a place. As both proof and pledge of eternal life, the Resurrection not only gave Christianity its most appealing belief, it also ensured that millennialism would have a permanent part in the religion. Those who died in the course of the war against Satan would be ensured an eternal place in the New Kingdom.

Forty days after the Resurrection, a second major event for Christian millennialism occurred. Prior to ascending from Mount Olivet, Jesus commissioned his disciples to be his witnesses to the ends of the world but warned them that only the Father knew when he would return to restore the kingdom to Israel. As they looked up to the heavens, two angels appeared, who announced that Jesus would return in the same way as they saw him taken up. Thus, the Christian community had an unambiguous promise of Christ's Second Coming, the Parousia, at which time the New Kingdom would be fulfilled. The timing of this wonderful event was left unspecified although all were convinced it would be soon.

Absolutely convinced that they were the ones who would have a place in the New Kingdom and facing taunts for believing in a leader who suffered the humiliating death of crucifixion, the disciples formed a tightly knit community that broke bread together and shared all property in common. They also shared a truly powerful missionary zeal. Jesus probably did mandate them to spread the good news at least to all of Israel, but it has been argued that a millennial cult, faced with a crisis of belief such as the death of the charismatic leader, often responds by seeking to convince others of their vision.[2] The belief of others serves to ratify the truth of the vision. The apostles and disciples preached about Christ and the coming of the New Kingdom to anyone who would listen. Their proselytizing included letter writing, and the non-Pauline epistles have two key statements for millennialism. Peter reassures those who ask why the Parousia has not yet happened: For the Lord a day is like a thousand years (2 Peter 3:10–13). He admonishes his readers to lead lives of godliness, "waiting for and hastening the coming of the day of God." When it does come, like a thief in the night, "the heavens will pass away with a loud noise, and the elements will be dissolved with fire." Then will appear "new heavens and a new earth." The First and Second Epistles of John have the only biblical mention of Antichrist. In 1 John (2:18) the evangelist speaks of antichrists as those who deny that Jesus is Christ and seek to deceive the faithful. Their coming is a sign of the last hour.

While Jesus proclaimed that the end would come very soon, he recognized the need to provide for the leadership of his community by identifying the twelve apostles and, after his resurrection, naming Peter to lead them. It is common in cults, however, that the blessing of the original leader is not enough to pass the mantle of leadership. Frequently an outsider enters the group and appropriates charismatic authority. To a large extent that is what happened with Paul. He was not among those who were with Jesus when he was alive, but because of his vision on the road to Damascus, he became equally convinced that Jesus was the one "who will return to defeat every authority and power and even death" (1 Cor. 15:24). Paul was more important than Peter in setting the agenda for the believers after Jesus' death. In the long-term survival of any cult, the second-generation leader is as important as the original leader. Regardless of the charisma or popular success of the cult founder, the group is not likely to endure for long without a strong, effective second leader who can codify the message and provide an organizational structure. (The third-generation leader occasionally provides that service.) Paul, not Peter, was that effective second-generation leader for Christianity.

Paul's concept of the New Kingdom, where the faithful will put on spiritual bodies and bear "the image of the man of heaven" (1 Cor. 15:24–49), is more truly a spiritual realm than any found in the Jewish apocalyptic literature or among his Christian contemporaries. He had a major role in formulating the Christian vision of the reward that the faithful will receive at the endtime. He also helped to create the image of what will then happen: "In a twinkling of an eye . . . the trumpet will sound" (1 Cor. 15:52). Paul was convinced that the endtime would be very soon, within his lifetime, although he came to believe that it would take place only when the full number of Gentiles had come into the faith. Paul became the Apostle to the Gentiles and helped to infuse in Christianity a zeal for proselytizing stronger than that in any other major religion.

Paul's strongest apocalyptic statements, found in his epistles to the Thessalonians, were written to a community suffering persecution at the hands of the local Roman authorities. His purpose was to defuse an explosive millennial situation. Some converts believed that the Parousia was so near at hand that they were proclaiming their freedom from traditional sexual mores and the need to work. It is noteworthy that antinomianism in Jesus' name appeared already in the first generation of Christians. They were also confused about the deaths of believers before the Parousia and what would happen to them when Christ returned. Paul affirmed that Jesus would soon return "like a thief in the night"; then those who had died in the Lord would rise from the dead. "Then we who are alive, who are left, will be caught up in the clouds together with them to meet the Lord in the air, and so we will be with the Lord forever" (1 Thess. 4:16–17). This is the second key text for the Rapture. Paul spoke of the "man of sin," who was deceiving them and leading them into antinomianism, but he did not use the term *Antichrist*. He regarded the man of sin as a religious leader, not a political tyrant. The man of sin was already active but only until one who restrained him would be removed. "Then the lawless one will be revealed, whom the Lord Jesus will destroy with the breath of his mouth" (2 Thess. 2:8).

The primary millennial work in Christianity, the Revelation of John of Patmos, also was a product of persecution in the form of exile, to which he refers in his introduction. Far from dampening millennial expectations as Paul sought to do, John was clearly intent on inflaming them, producing the most controversial and difficult book of the New Testament. Among the controversies surrounding it are the questions of dating and authorship. Two different time frames around the years 69 and 95 AD are plausible based on the internal evidence suggesting that the seven-headed beast (Rev. 13) is a Roman emperor sixth in a sequence of imperial reigns—either Galba, Nero's successor, or Domitian. Neither date was a time of severe persecution for Christians in Asia Minor, but exile has a way of building up resentment and breeding radicalism. The author's mindset when he wrote the book, therefore, may not have reflected Christianity's situation at the time. The argument for the earlier date rests largely on chapter 11, where the author seems to be unaware of the destruction of Jerusalem and the Temple in 70 AD. The case for the later date is based in large part on the word of several Christian authors of the next century.

Unlike the Judaic apocalyptic literature, which is all pseudonymous, Revelation's author states his name several times: "I, John." The only personal information he provides, however, is that he was exiled for the sake of the word of God to the island of Patmos off Asia Minor, where he received the visions presented in the book. Early on he was identified, by Irenaeus of Lyons among others, as the Apostle John, the author of the Fourth Gospel and three canonical epistles. If one accepts 95 as the book's date, the apostle would have been about 85 years old, quite aged for the fevered energy that pervades Revelation. Yet its Greek style, sharply different from the learned Greek of the Johannine Gospel and epistles, suggests the author was someone whose native tongue was not Greek, a point that makes its attribution to the apostle stronger than for the other books attributed to him. In the mid-third century, Dionysius of Alexandria attacked the tradition of apostolic authorship on both stylistic grounds and internal evidence. His criticism had little impact on the Western Church, which accepted Revelation as part of the canon of the Bible; the Third Council of Carthage in 397 made the definitive statement on the matter. Only after 800 was it accepted in the Eastern

Church. Modern scholars, inclined to agree that the apostle wrote none of the books bearing his name, prefer to attribute Revelation to a Christian prophet named John from western Asia Minor. Scholars, however, cannot remove the book from the canon, where it was placed largely on the premise that its author was the apostle.

John of Patmos was thoroughly versed in Jewish apocalyptic. He proclaims that he had a revelation from God in his first words: "The Revelation of Jesus Christ," 'αποχαλιπσισ, hence the title The Apocalypse, by which it has been known in Catholicism. A detailed account of its themes and symbolism would fill a book in itself, but it is necessary to describe briefly the key elements since they reappear constantly down to the present. There is little in Revelation, however, that was new; it amplified the millennial ideas already present in Christianity and provided a Christian interpretation for images, numbers, and symbols largely taken from Daniel. These ideas have inspired and agitated Christians ever since.

In the prologue John seeks to assure his readers that he has suffered persecution as they have and that the revelation he is unveiling is of divine origin. Then come letters to seven churches of western Asia Minor. In the letters to Ephesus and Pergamum, John sharply attacks a group that was allowing Christians to eat the food sacrificed to idols. This indicates the continued importance to the author of Judaic ritual purification, which would become a major emphasis for some later millennial groups. The church in Laodicea is condemned for being lukewarm, which serves to justify the red hot zeal of later millennialists. Only the church in Philadelphia receives praise for its faithfulness and a promise to be kept from the hour of trial coming soon; hence, some millennial groups use the name for themselves.

The author is then transported to heaven, a common event in apocalyptic literature, where he watches the endtime unfold before him. The one seated on the throne of God holds in his hand a scroll with seven seals. Only the Lamb that has been slaughtered is worthy of opening the seals, which it proceeds to do. With the opening of the first four seals appear four horsemen. The first, riding a white horse, represents the conqueror; the second, on a red horse, represents war; the third, on a black one, denotes famine; and the fourth, whose horse is pale green, represents death. They are given authority to kill a fourth of the world. The opening of the fifth seal reveals the martyrs for the word of God, who are given a white robe and told to wait a little longer for the number of martyrs to be complete. The sixth seal produces natural disasters and signs in the heavens. John then sees that there are 144,000 elect from the twelve tribes of Israel (excluding the tribe of Dan), who have the seal of God on their foreheads. With them is a great multitude of faithful from every nation, who have been washed in the blood of the Lamb.

With the opening of the seventh seal, there is a period of silence in heaven; then seven angels appear, bearing trumpets. Six of the trumpets sound, each unveiling a catastrophe—fire, hail, falling stars, locusts, war, plague. Before the seventh trumpet, there is an interlude in which two witnesses are given authority to prophesy for 1,260 days (precisely three and one-half years in the lunar calendar) until the beast from the bottomless pit rises up to kill them. They lie unburied for three and a half days, until God brings them back to life and takes them to heaven. When the seventh trumpet does sound, the action shifts from manmade and natural disasters on earth to cosmic warfare in the heavens. First appears the woman clothed with the sun who is about to give birth to a son. She and her son are attacked by the seven-headed dragon aided by the beast with ten horns and seven heads, which is given power over the entire world for three and one-half years. Next comes the two-horned beast, who will exercise the authority of the first beast and persuade the multitudes to worship it. This second beast marks its subjects with 666, a number that represents a person. General agreement over the centuries has been that the number signifies Nero Caesar when each letter of his name in Hebrew is given a numerical value.

Meanwhile, John sees the Lamb standing on Mount Zion surrounded by 144,000 men (apparently not the 144,000 elect of Israel), the first fruits from mankind for the Lamb. They are marked with the Lamb's name because they are virgins. Seven angels appear who carry seven bowls containing seven plagues, that they inflict on the earth. The seventh bowl produces an earthquake that destroys the evil city Babylon (that is, Rome). An angel then reveals to John the judgment against the Whore of Babylon, who is seated on a scarlet beast and dressed in scarlet and purple. The angel also reveals the meaning of the seven-headed beast. Its heads represent five rulers who have fallen, one who is now, and one who is yet to come whose reign will last a short while only. The ten horns represent ten kings who are yet to come and will unite with the beast against the Lamb.

After a long song decrying the sins of the Whore and rejoicing in her fall, John goes on to describe the great battle at Armageddon, where the armies of the beast have assembled. The Word of God, appearing as a rider on a white horse, leads the forces of heaven in a great victory over the beast, "who is the Devil and Satan," and throws him into the bottomless pit along with the false prophet, locking them there for a period of a thousand years. Those who have been martyred for the Word of God will reign with Christ for the millennium. At its end Satan will be released from the pit to do battle one last time with God. He will gather the nations of Gog and Magog and march on the camp of the Lamb and the saints, but fire will come down from heaven to consume the evil army. Satan will be thrown back into the pit to be tormented forever. When the final judgment takes place, those not in the book of life will be thrown into the lake of fire; but the elect join God in the holy city, the new Jerusalem, which will come from heaven, and everything will be made anew. A new Garden of Eden and River of Life will be found in the city, but it will not have a new Temple because the presence of God and the Lamb will be the Temple. Time and history will come to an end.

Millennialists have had an enormous range of ideas and symbols to draw out of Revelation, but some that they use most extensively receive less emphasis in the book than might be expected while others do not appear at all. The word *Antichrist* is not used, and the beast/false prophet who usually is taken to be Antichrist has a relatively minor role. The Rapture is not mentioned. On the other hand, the thirst for revenge on the great Babylon for persecuting the saints is palpable. The God in Revelation, like the God in all the apocalyptic texts, is not a merciful God but an avenger, one who does not blink at the enormous misery, carnage, and terror of the last days. Many numbers and lengths of time are tossed around, providing millennialists a feast of material for predicting the Second Coming. The key number is seven, which is the perfect number because it is the sum of three, the number of heaven, and four, the number of earth. Three and one half is half of seven; hence it is the symbol of evil and the time Satan will be allowed to dominate the world. The number 666 is also evil because each digit is one less than seven. The theme running through these fevered descriptions of the endtime is that it will all take place very soon. The one revealing these things to John says, "Surely I am coming soon." John answers, "Amen. Come, Lord Jesus."

This synopsis suggests more structure and form than the book possesses. At first reading Revelation comes across as a labyrinth of ideas, images, and symbols. A cynic has said that one cannot long preoccupy the mind with it without jeopardizing sanity. Part of its appeal and power is that the reader must come up with a personal interpretation. The sense that everything has hidden meaning is overwhelming, providing vast opportunity for those who claim that they have fathomed the depths of the book's secrets or that God has revealed to them their meaning. Finally, the book excels as drama. The contest and contrast between Good and Evil have never been more effectively represented. Little wonder that it continues to elicit so powerful a response two millennia later.

III

MILLENNIALISM IN EARLY CHRISTIANITY

P ROBABLY NO ASPECT OF THE FIRST GENERATIONS of Christians is more obvious than their utter conviction that the Parousia would occur in their lifetimes. To what extent did millennialism play a role in the success of Christianity in winning converts, surviving Roman persecution, and becoming the dominant religion of the Roman empire? Recent studies of the social origins of early Christians before 313 downplay the previous emphasis on their being drawn from a Roman proletariat, but all the evidence still indicates that despite the presence of some wealthy Romans, they came largely from among petty merchants, artisans, and laborers. It is easy to see how attractive millennialism can be for people who live on the margin or, perhaps more importantly, perceive themselves that way. Soon they, the chosen few, will be rewarded beyond all comprehension, and those they see as their oppressors will suffer unimaginable punishment. Even for some among the elite, the millennial vision can have its appeal since there are other ways besides economic deprivation to feel marginalized. The fact that the fastest growing Christian denominations of our time—Mormons, Jehovah's Witnesses, and Seventh-day Adventists—emphasize millennialism suggests something of its power today even among modern middle-class persons.

Once Romans became Christians, they found themselves in a small minority facing scorn and, often enough, violent persecution and martyrdom. Millennialism explains why such is the lot of the saints; it turns the status of being a despised, persecuted minority into a mark of God's unique favor. For its first three centuries, millennialism was an important factor in Christianity's growth, but it also had a negative effect by creating factionalism. Many of the disputes renting the early Church involved the proper understanding of the Parousia. One dispute was over which apocalyptic books to include in the Bible. Among the many apocalyptic works that appeared in the first two centuries, the Apocalypse of Peter and the Apocalypse of Thomas had high standing in the Christian community, and they joined John's in the Bible among some early Christians. The strength of millennialism in the early Church is made clear in those books. Unlike Revelation, their authors hid behind the names of apostles, putting them more in the tradition of apocalyptic works. The common threads found in them include a major role for Antichrist, a deep sense of the present as the time when the final crisis has begun, and a strong emphasis on the afterlife. In regard to Antichrist, these texts establish the tradition that the Man of Sin would be a Jew from the tribe of Dan, said to have remained in Babylon after the captivity. Thus, Antichrist's origins in Dan would satisfy the prediction that he would come from the east. It has been suggested that the killing of Christians who refused to join the Jews in the Bar Kokhba revolt, as reported by Eusebius, was behind the identification of Antichrist as Jewish, one of many ways in which Antichrist would parody Jesus.[1]

The Christians also reworked a number of Judaic apocalyptic works to give them the Christian message; the most important were the Sibylline Oracles. The sibyl was a Greek seer with a high reputation in the Hellenistic world for the accuracy of her predictions about the destruction of kingdoms and cities. Hellenized Jews in Egypt had appropriated her name for several apocalyptic works that emphasized God's rule over history; Christians also used her name. The Christian Sibyllines reveal a deep hatred of Rome for persecuting the saints. In the Middle Ages several Christian Sibylline text were mistaken as pagan in origin and therefore praised for their foreknowledge of Christ. For this reason the medieval funeral dirge, the *Dies Irae* ("Day of Wrath"), has a reference to the sibyl's prophecy of the last judgment.

Several of the Christian apocryphal apocalypses espoused Gnosticism. Influenced by the Platonic emphasis on ideas as the true reality,

Gnostics believed there was a radical separation between the divine and the human, the spiritual and the material, the eternal and the temporal, the perfect and the corrupt. Human souls came from the divine sphere but had been trapped in human bodies by the evil power, where they have been subjected to the awful corruption of the material world. God sent a messenger to the world to bring to souls the knowledge they needed to free themselves from their bodies and return to heaven. Gnostics could be pagans, Jews, or Christians, but they were in accord with the idea of Christ as the divine messenger. The Gnostics are regarded as contributing significantly to establishing the doctrine of his divinity. Gnostic attitudes conformed to the opposition to the material world found in the Gospels. The Gnostics regarded sex as the worst corruption since it created new bodies to trap souls. Remaining a virgin was the best means of purifying the soul so that it could rejoin God in eternal union. The key Gnostic virtue was martyrdom, through which one renounced the body to the point of being willing to sacrifice life for the sake of truth. Gnostics were attracted to the Christian doctrines of the immortality of the soul and the resurrection of the glorified body; by making these doctrines more explicit, they helped to reinforce them among Christians.

Gnostic Christians soon found themselves at odds with the developing mainstream of Christianity since the Gnostic view of Christ emphasized his divinity to the point of denying his humanity. The major Gnostic movement was Manichaeism. Mani was born in Mesopotamia about 215 AD to a prominent Iranian family that belonged to a Judeo-Christian sect. He traveled as far as India and founded a movement that incorporated elements from the major religions of western Asia, including Zoroastrianism and its belief in the dualistic cosmos. For Mani, good or light and evil or darkness were more equal in power than they were for Zoroaster, and he saw the material world, including the human body, as products of evil. Trapped in each human being is a spark of light that wishes to be freed from the body and returned to the world of spirit, a process achieved through knowledge of the cosmic battle taking place and understanding of how to fight lust and envy. Jesus, who only appeared to have a human body, and other prophets such as Buddha were God's messengers who helped men

gain that knowledge. For the Manichaean elect, there were strict pro-
hibitions against work, sex, drinking wine, and eating meat; at their
deaths their spark of light rejoined the Good. A second class of
Manichaeans, the hearers, were allowed those things in moderation,
and at their deaths, their souls transmigrated to other bodies until finally they joined the elect. As befits a religion that drew from several
apocalyptic religions, Manichaeism had a powerful eschatology.
When all but a minute portion of the light has returned to the Good,
a cosmic battle will ignite a conflagration lasting for 1,468 years,
which will destroy the entire material universe. Evil and Darkness
will be locked into the abyss for eternity while Good and Light will
reign for ever.

Mani suffered martyrdom at the hands of the Persians in 276, and
martyrdom became one of the signs of his followers. They had numerous opportunities to achieve it since few other movements have had as
large a proportion of its believers suffer at the hands of so vast a range
of rulers professing nearly every other religious affiliation. They had a
missionary zeal even stronger than the Christians; Mani took Paul as his
model and deemed himself "the Apostle through the will of Jesus."
Manichaean communities appeared from western Europe to China, and
the movement had influence in Europe to the end of the Middle Ages.

Gnosticism had a broad influence on Christianity, but some in the
early Church reacted against its condemnation of the human body and
the material world. One of the most outspoken opponents was Irenaeus,
a native of Asia Minor and bishop in Gaul, who died about 200. His
Against Heresies is a valuable history of the doctrinal problems that
plagued the early Church, including the many interpretations of the endtime. It is a sympathetic source for the views of Papias, a Christian Jew
of the early second century, who fled from Palestine after the Bar
Kokhba revolt to Phrygia in Asia Minor. Papias was said to have known
the apostle John and learned from him a number of Jesus' sayings that
did not make it into the Gospels. Most notable was a description of an
Edenic world after the Parousia: Nature will become so bountiful that
each stalk of wheat will have ten thousand ears, and each ear, ten thousand grains, and each grain will produce ten pounds of the best flour.
Grapevines will yield the same superabundance; and when a saint takes

a bunch to eat, another bunch will say: "'I am a better bunch, take me. Bless the Lord through me." Animals will no longer fear each other and will become completely subject to mankind. A virtually identical passage appears in a Jewish work, the Syrian Apocalypse of Baruch, from the late first century.

Papias made the most striking of the Christian expressions about the earthly paradise into which many expected the world to be transformed at the Millennium, expressions also common in late Jewish apocalyptic literature. The miraculous fertility found in transformed nature would extend to the human race; according to several texts, each male saint would have a thousand sons. One of the Sibylline Oracles proclaimed that those who were alive at the end would not die but would propagate an infinite number of offspring throughout the Millennium. Although such views were found throughout the early Church, they were particularly associated with western Asia Minor. This was the region where, after the Bar Kokhba revolt, Christians and Jews had their most extensive contacts, and it was long noted for its ecstatic pagan cults. Papias's contemporary, Cerinthus, who allegedly proclaimed a return to a highly sensual Garden of Eden after the Parousia, came from the region. He was later denounced as a heretic for his view that Jesus was human only, and those who wished to exclude Revelation from the Bible argued that he, not St. John, had written the book.

Asia Minor is most associated with Montanism, the first movement within the early Church to become a millennial cult. Most of what we know about Montanism is secondhand from its opponents, a problem that we will encounter again and again for such groups. According to mostly hostile sources, Montanism arose in Phrygia about 165, when Montanus began prophesying in ecstasy and speaking in tongues, activities often associated with millennialism. It was a time of famine and earthquakes in the region. His opponents later said that Montanus had been a priest of the goddess Cybele, whose worship was strong in the region, and had castrated himself as that cult required. Montanus declared that his visions and prophecies, the "Third Testament," came from the Holy Spirit; more precisely, the Spirit spoke through him, using him like a lyre. He would fall into a trance, not moving or speaking for hours; suddenly the Spirit would bring him to a frenzy of admonition, exhortation, and prophecy. Closely associated with him were two female prophets, Priscilla and Maximilla. Their exact relationship to Montanus is not clear, but there is no reason to accept later accusations that they engaged in sexual relations. It is possible, however, that one or both had abandoned husbands to become prophets, as sources suggest, although Maximilla was called a virgin. The Spirit spoke through both women, and Priscilla in fact produced more of the prophecies associated with Montanism than did its eponym. Based on Galatians (3:28): "In Christ Jesus there is neither male nor female," women were given a major role in the movement, not only as visionaries but also as priests and bishops. The role of women was one of the complaints against Montanism made by orthodox Christians.

A key point on which Montanists broke with other Christians was the belief that the Spirit would give a new revelation to visionaries. By the mid-second century most Christians agreed that the time of revelation had ended with the death of the last apostle. Although Montanus's New Prophecy was not deemed heretical at first, it contained a chiliastic millennialism more urgent than that of other Christians of the era. Few Christians had yet abandoned the expectation of the Parousia soon to come, but for many it no longer dictated their daily behavior. The new prophets declared that the faithful must urgently prepare for the New Kingdom that was coming soon. Too little is known of the Montanists to say for certain that they were perfectionists, who believed that it was possible for humans to be without flaw and free of sin. Some Christian sects have taken literally the gospel command, "Be perfect, therefore, as your heavenly Father is perfect" (Matt. 5:48), and believed that it is within the reach of souls to become perfect. Many such groups hold that perfection can be achieved by following much the same lifestyle as the Montanists did: celibacy, fasting, no alcohol, and a special diet, which for the Montanists consisted of only cabbage and radishes. Sexual abstinence was greatly praised, and the Montanists approved of spouses leaving marriages in order to devote themselves to preparing for Christ's return. They strongly opposed remarriage upon the death of a spouse. Martyrdom was regarded as a good, and at least some Montanists courted death, as some other Christians did.

Despite later assertions that the Montanists predicted the Parousia would occur in 177, there is no evidence that they actually set a date, but they apparently did pick a place. A female prophet, either Priscilla or, from several decades later, Quintilla—Epiphanius, writing two centuries later, was not sure which—received a vision in her sleep in which Jesus appeared dressed as a woman in a bright white robe to impart wisdom. The vision's key point was that the new Jerusalem would descend to earth on a mountain near Pepuza, a place in Phrygia whose location remains uncertain, although it probably was close to Philadelphia. From the limited information, the new city would be a material place, not spiritual. Epiphanius does not indicate whether a date was set for this spectacular event, but he reports that in his time the faithful were still going to the place where Pepuza had been (for it had been destroyed) to wait for Christ and his reign.

Like many millennial groups, the Montanists developed an organized church while awaiting the end. They ordained both men and women as priests and bishops and held Eucharist services at which seven maidens dressed in white led the priests to the service. Montanus collected donations from the faithful for the support of proselytizing and appointed a treasurer, perhaps the first Christian group to do so. Like many other millennial leaders, Montanus and Maximilla died violently; the sources disagree on whether they were executed by the Romans or hanged themselves while in prison. Either death fits the millennial context; millennialists frequently seek martyrdom, but suicide is often acceptable as the only way to escape the power of the evil one.

Before she died, Maximilla reportedly pronounced that after her there would be no more prophets, only the end. Nonetheless, prophets continued to appear among the Montanists and the end did not come. Montanism flourished in western Asia Minor for some time despite the failure of the predictions of the end. Roman persecution sapped its numbers, but more devastating to Montanism was persecution by the Christian emperors. In mid-sixth century under Justinian, heresies of all sorts were proscribed with brutal vigor. The tomb of the three great Montanist prophets, which was still a shrine for many people, was broken open and the bones were destroyed. Many Montanists locked themselves in their churches and set them afire. For millennialists, persecution is nearly always taken as a sign of the coming endtime, and fire is the preferred mode to end the world and their own lives, should they resort to suicide. In a great number of biblical passages, fire is the instrument of divine cleansing. Christ said: "I came to bring fire to the earth and how I wish it were already kindled" (Luke 12:49); and Paul wrote: "When Jesus Christ is revealed from heaven with his angels in flaming fire, inflicting vengeance on those who do not know God" (2 Thess. 1:7–8). Revelation abounds with references to divine fire. The Montanists were the first of many millennial groups to perish in fire, either setting it themselves or manipulating their enemies into lighting it.

Before its destruction Montanism had spread beyond Asia Minor, especially to North Africa. North Africa, called the Bible Belt of early Christianity by one modern historian,[2] already had a reputation for strict morality and controversy within the early Church. Montanism had a solid foothold among North Arican Christians by 180 although it is impossible to get an idea of their actual numbers. It provided early Christianity with a brilliant theologian, Tertullian, and a famous martyr, Perpetua. Tertullian was a lawyer and theologian who died about 222, thirty years after he became a Christian and twenty years after he joined the Montanists, attracted by their strict morality. The endtime took on added urgency for him. Certain that the end was near, he eagerly cited reports that a city had been seen suspended in the morning sky above Judea. His major effort regarding the endtime was to refute a common belief that at the beginning of the Millennium the resurrected and perfected bodies of the dead saints would be taken to heaven. According to Tertullian, in the course of the Millennium the bodies of the saints will rise, remaining largely as they were in life, and live in the New Kingdom on earth. Afterward the world would be destroyed; the final judgment would take place; and the saved would enjoy life with God while the damned would suffer forever in hell. Since he was a Montanist, Tertullian's influence was less than it might have been; yet he helped to establish the doctrine of heaven for the Catholic Church, largely through his lost *About Paradise*.

Perpetua was a young married woman from a notable family of Carthage, who in converting to Christianity fell afoul of an imperial law issued in 201 prohibiting conversion. She was a new mother, and her servant Felicitas was pregnant when they were thrown into prison in 203. She kept a diary, which (as the *Passio Perpetuae*) became one of the major works of Christian martyrology. There is little in it that identifies her specifically as a Montanist except her visions and a strong sense of martyrdom and the approaching endtime, but Tertullian among others believed she was one. The two women feared that because they were new mothers, their execution would be delayed past that of fellow Christians, and they successfully prayed that it would not. In the nights before the appointed date, Perpetua had visions in which she was taken to heaven to be shown the reward that would be theirs. Prior to their executions both women had to abandon their babies, which they did willingly because they were entirely committed to their new family, the Christians. Here is a first powerful example of the importance of group coherence for millennial cults; even the bond between mother and infant can be broken for the group.

Around 200, Montanism was condemned as heresy for its belief that a new revelation was possible and that authority in the Church belonged to the prophets, not the bishops. Its chiliasm no longer agreed with the eschatology of most Christian leaders, who denounced its emphasis on setting a date for the Parousia and seeing the New Kingdom as a material realm of earthly delights as "Judaizing," because of the importance of both points in late Jewish apocalyptic literature (although rabbinical Judaism, which had become the dominant form of Judaism by the third century, had largely abandoned messianism). More telling for the accusations of Judaizing was that many of those who did expect the immediate return of Christ also mandated adherence to Mosaic law. Since Gentiles made up an ever increasing proportion of Christians, distinguishing themselves from the Jews was becoming ever more important.

Another factor in the growing opposition to chiliasm was the passage of time. Because two centuries had passed since Christ's promise to return, many Christians no longer expected it to occur soon. Tertullian reported with disapproval that some were actually praying for a delay of the Parousia. Christians were beginning to look to their own salvation as individuals rather than as part of the community. Furthermore, as a large portion of the Church now consisted of Roman citizens, antagonism toward Rome had far less appeal. Such Christians wanted to be Rome, not destroy it. Irenaeus in the late second century was the first major church figure to describe Antichrist as not Roman but Jewish, from the tribe of Dan. The passage of time had two major effects: It delayed the expected Second Coming and changed Rome from the beast of Revelation to Paul's restraining force that kept Antichrist from manifesting himself.

About 204 Hippolytus of Rome introduced the elaborate system for calculating the endtime that has remained so important a part of millennialism. He determined from the number of generations since Adam that Christ's first coming had occurred 5,500 years after the Creation. From the cosmic week found in Genesis, Daniel's seventy weeks of years before the end, and the statement in Psalm 89 that for God a day is like a thousand years, he determined the present world would last 6,000 years. After that comes the Sabbath of the saints, that is, the Millennium. Thus, the events forecast in Revelation would occur 500 years after Christ's birth or 300 years in the future, a point that Hippolytus emphasized against those who were expecting an imminent Parousia. Antichrist, who would mirror Christ in all respects except his divinity and descent from Dan, not Juda, would win over all nations to himself. The faithful remnant would suffer severe persecution, and at its worst the two messengers Enoch and Elijah would come to prepare for the Second Coming of Christ and the defeat of Antichrist. Christ would gather the faithful into the New Kingdom and reign for the millennial Sabbath before the final conflagration of the world and the Last Judgment.

Cyprian of Carthage, who lived in the midst of great disorders in the Roman empire of the mid-third century, adopted the chronology of the *Annus mundi* (year of the world) but calculated that Adam had lived 100 years farther in the past than Hippolytus had, placing the beginning of the end in the year 400 or barely a century in the future. He could thus emphasize that the current troubles were signs of the coming endtime, evidence of the decline of nature and the ruin of the human race by sin, which would occur before Antichrist appeared.

Dating the Parousia by the *Annus mundi* would become the dominant system for early millennialism, but for Christians living during the great Roman persecutions, it seemed impossible that the end was not at hand. The worst occurred under Diocletian, emperor from 284 to 305, and earlier efforts to delay the endtime quickly reverted to chiliasm. The most important millennial work to appear was Lactantius's *Divine Institutes.* A North African, Lactantius taught rhetoric at the imperial court until persecution of his fellow Christians convinced him to leave. One purpose of his work was to persuade the pagan elite of the truth of Christianity; he therefore avoided citing the Bible, favoring instead non-Christian eschatological sources such as Virgil and a Zoroastrian work from about 100 BC. Lactantius clearly used Revelation as his framework for the endtime but rarely cited it, adding details drawn from his other sources. The result was a millennial vision that combined much folklore and occult speculation with the Christian tradition. In particular, it provided far greater detail about the appearance and activities of antichrists, for Lactantius believed there would be two of them. The first would come from the far north and the second out of Syria. With the defeat of the Syrian Antichrist, the saints would enjoy a millennium of peace in an Eden with Christ: "The mountain rocks will drip with honey, the brooks will run with wine, and the rivers overflow with milk."[3]

Lactantius's native North Africa became the center of one of the early Church's greatest controversies during the persecution by Diocletian. Diocletian demanded that the Christians hand over their copies of the Scriptures to the authorities. Those who refused were subject to penalties, including execution. Many were added to Christianity's roll of martyrs, but others complied. Then, with what Christians could only see as divine intervention, the empire changed hands, and the Edict of Toleration of 313 was issued. Free from state repression, the Church faced the question of what to do about those who had handed over the Scriptures. In North Africa, the reaction against those in the clergy who had given up the sacred texts was especially harsh: They lost their right to administer the sacraments because they had "lost the Holy Spirit." During a disputed election of the bishop of Carthage, the rigorists' candidate, Donatus, gave his name to their movement. Donatists insisted on rebaptizing those baptized by lapsed clergy, and they became identified with the view that a priest had to be free of sin for the sacraments he administered to be valid. While this set up an impossible standard for both the clergy and the laity, who could never know whether their priests were worthy of performing the sacraments, Donatism would reappear frequently in church history, often in millennial movements.

The immediate result of the schism in North Africa was the intervention of Emperor Constantine, who even before his baptism felt obliged to enforce church unity. In 317 he sent Roman troops to arrest the Donatist leaders and seize their churches, but that only created martyrs for the Donatists, who were proud to be the party of martyrdom, and it raised their millennialism to a fever pitch. This was the first time that state authority was used to repress a dissenting movement within Christianity; previously dissenters were dealt with by shunning if persuasion failed to convince them they were wrong. Constantine's example set a dangerous precedent for future rulers in regard to millennial groups, and ironically the first Christian emperor became the first Christian ruler to be identified by some Christians as Antichrist.

The emperor's action against the Donatists made clear the danger to Christianity of the state allying itself with the mainstream element within the Church. Although this alliance had its benefits, one consequence was that opposition to government policy often became identified with opposition to the state-supported religion, or vice versa. The Donatists were strongest in rural areas where heavy taxes imposed by emperors created deep resentment toward the imperial government and where Latin was not spoken. Hostility to imperial policy also explains the appearance of a violent group called the Circumcellions, from the Latin for *excise*. They were the shock troops of the Donatists, willing to use violence against their opponents but also, according to one source, ready to demand that their opponents give them the crown of martyrdom. The Circumcellions carried heavy clubs but refused to use swords, probably following Jesus' command to put up the sword. They pillaged and destroyed Catholic churches, beat priests and killed some, and robbed travelers who could not prove that they were Donatists. The Circumcellions proclaimed that they were celibate and, to prove their commitment to celibacy, had virgins as companions. Their enemies alleged that their claims of celibacy were fraudulent and accused them of saying that they were not bound by society's laws. The Circumcellions became so serious a problem in the province of Numedia that the imperial government was forced to send an army to crush them in 372. Donatism survived their defeat and lasted as a quietist movement in the North African countryside until the coming of Islam.

Out of the fervor of fourth-century Donatism came one of the major figures of early millennialism. Tyconius was a Donatist layman who around 370 wrote a lost commentary on Revelation. We know much of its content because later authors referred to it extensively, until it disappeared in the ninth century. The tradition of the North African Church regarded the true Church as only the elect, namely, the martyrs, including those imprisoned, but Satan had established an antichurch consisting of sinners with most of the signs of the true Church. Only the members of the true Church would be admitted to the New Kingdom at the Parousia. The persecution of the elect (namely the Donatists) by antichristians taking Rome's side proved that the end was at hand: "Beneath the purple and scarlet robes of the apocalyptic whore they could still recognize Rome."[4] Tyconius rejected this view. For Tyconius, the Church contained both the holy and the wicked. The two groups were bound to remain mixed together until the judgment day, when Christ would separate the grain from the weeds. Only then would the Church become the pure Bride of Christ. Following St. Jerome, he argued that the martyrs were not the only Christians who would be gathered in the New Kingdom, as suggested in Revelation. Persecution in itself does not serve to identify the saints, nor does it necessarily prove the Parousia is imminent.

Excommunicated by the Donatists for his views, Tyconius argued that the apocalyptic texts of the Scriptures could not be taken literally, especially the numbers used to establish the time of the Parousia. They were all symbolic or, more correctly, mystical. Thus, the use of six in 6,000 years represents the lack of perfection found in human time, not a real length of time. Only the Father knows the hour and the day, although Tyconius believed that the persecution of the Donatists was the abomination of desolations marking the beginning of the time of trial. Antichrist was already in the world in the form of false priests in the Church and those who hated their brothers. Tyconius believed that the Second Coming had to be close but doubted that it would happen in the way that previous generations had interpreted the Biblical texts.

Tyconius's views have importance in the history of millennialism largely because of their impact on Augustine of Hippo. Augustine found them a godsend in his debates with the Donatists, but they also had a profound impact on his *City of God,* the major statement of his eschatology. As a North African, Augustine had been immersed in its rampant millennialism in his early years. He later reacted sharply against the belief of many in his time that feasting and sensuality would be the fortune of the elect in the next kingdom, as he also reacted against the unrelenting date setting for the Parousia. As a young man he was a Manichaean for a time, which deeply impacted his thinking, although he later bitterly denounced its teachings. It influenced his concept of original sin: Humans at birth have a corrupt nature thanks to Adam. It can be made good only through the grace of God. Infant baptism, common by his time and strongly defended by Augustine, proves that God freely gives grace without regard to a person's acts since a child has done nothing to merit such grace. Baptism makes the child capable of doing good, but it does not lead to sinlessness; no human can achieve perfection in this life. Augustine condemned perfectionism. These views not only have had a great impact on future Christian theology, they also helped to form his idea of the Church, which in turn molded his eschatology in *The City of God.* The Church on earth consists of those in both the city of man, the damned, and the city of God, the saints, according to Augustine; there is no distinction among them on earth. Taking the sacraments does not make one a member of the city of God, nor does the worst sin necessarily place one in the city of man. There is a fixed number of saints who have been predestined to share eternal glory with Christ, but that number is not 144,000, because it, like all the numbers in Revelation, is symbolic. Here the number is twelve (symbolizing completeness) times twelve, and so it symbolizes the fullness of the body of Christ.

Augustine applied the same type of analysis to the apocalyptic passages in the Bible but was willing to accept some literally; for example, he believed that the Gospel had to be preached to all the nations before the end. He denounced the belief in a paradisiacal millennium on earth as a fable. The Parousia, the end of the world, and the Last Judgment will occur, but trying to know how or when is useless speculation. Because only the Father knows the time, calculating the endtime is forbidden. The sack of Rome by the Goths in 410 was proof for many Christians that the endtime was at hand, but Augustine in *The City of God* was adamant that humans could not know the time of the Parousia. He accepted the idea of the six days of human history, with five ages of the world prior to the Incarnation, while the sixth age began with Christ's birth. The Millennium of Revelation refers to the period of Christianity's existence, however long that will be. One thousand, as the cube of ten, signifies the fullness of time, not a specific period. Christ's first coming has chained the beast in the abyss and he can no longer do as much evil to mankind as he had, but he has not been made entirely powerless. Antichrist is anyone who denies Christ by his deeds, whether a member of the Church or not. Beasts and horns do not refer to states and certainly not to Rome. Neither a persecuting pagan emperor nor a benevolent Christian one have anything to do with the endtime. There is a worldly history where empires rise and fall, and a divine one where Christ came and will return. Catastrophic disasters or major political changes are not signs the Parousia is at hand. One must not look for Antichrist in every hiccup in secular history. Augustine's amillennialism took the present out of millennialism.

Along with Jerome, who made his contribution to amillennialism by calling the idea of the earthly kingdom of a thousand years a fable, Augustine and Tyconius established what became the standard interpretation of the end of the world for the Middle Ages and the Catholic Church down to the present. It is an interpretation that looks for the conversion of the Jews, destruction of the present world, resurrection of the body, and reign of the saints with Christ in heaven at some indefinite time in the future. Meanwhile life in the world will go on, with individual humans obliged to seek salvation of their souls through the agency of the Church. As the Nicene Creed from 325 put it, "Christ will come in glory to judge the living and the dead, and his kingdom will have no end"; but there is no hint of how or when all this will happen. Most Christians replaced the urgency of the coming end of the world with concern for their personal endtime—their death and judgment. But the fires of millennialism were not extinguished in Christianity; they were only temporarily dampened.

IV

THE FIRST
MILLENNIUM

T HE SOLUTION TO MILLENNIAL ANXIETY offered by Augustine of
Hippo quickly became the accepted one for Latin Christianity,
while by 400, for the Greek Church, more concerned with disputes over
Christ's nature, the absence of Donatism reduced the sense of millennial
urgency. The relative calm in respect to millennialism has remained the
norm for the Eastern Church to the present, except for flare-ups during
the Muslim conquests, and in the Russian Orthodox Church. In the
Western Church several centuries passed during which the furor over
the endtime was muted.

One reason why millennialism in the West was never as quiescent
as in the East was the difference in their political situations. The eastern
Roman empire after such disasters as the defeat at Adrianople in 378
was able to recover its equilibrium, surviving to the end of the Middle
Ages as the Byzantine empire. The western empire, however, continued
to suffer from the barbarian onslaughts that led to its final demise. The
signs of the endtime continued to appear all around the western Christians. For example, a Donatist author found the number 666 in the name
of Gaiseric, the Vandal king who sacked Rome in 455. Who else could
Vandals, Goths, or Huns be but the hordes of Gog and Magog?

The invasion of the Roman empire by tribes from the east and north
helped verify a legend, first found in Josephus, that Alexander the Great
had erected an enormous gate of bronze somewhere on the northern

frontier of his empire to prevent the barbarian hordes he encountered there from entering the civilized world. At the end of time the barbarians would break through the gate, or in the Christian version, Antichrist would open it and lead them through, bringing about the end of the world. Any invasion of Europe from the east by Huns, Magyars, Mongols, or Turks was seen as the opening of Alexander's Gate and a clear signal of the endtime. Another component of the legend appeared later, according to which Alexander would return to give over his empire to Christ, who then would "hand over the kingdom to God the Father after he has destroyed every ruler and every authority" (1 Cor. 15:24). This formed the basis of the tradition of a last world emperor, not Alexander, whose appearance would signal the coming Parousia.

By the late 400s the time was rapidly approaching for the end of the sixth age and the coming Millennium according to Hippolytus's *Annus Mundi* system of dating the world, which placed the Parousia around 500. Despite Augustine's strictures against millennial calculating, some Christians remained convinced that the Parousia would occur according to Hippolytus's schedule. The decline in civilization in the West was obvious, and the proposition that this was proof of the rapid approach of the end was hard to refute: The earth grows old and it will end. Fearing a wave of millennial hysteria, church authorities opposed dating the endtime to a year so close at hand. In addition to emphasizing the Augustinian position, they promoted a second version of the *Annus Mundi*. The time between Adam and Christ was recalculated to yield a span of 5,200 years, thus pushing the endtime back by 300 years to about the year 800. When 800 approached, church authorities again discounted it as the time for the Second Coming. As part of the tactics for avoiding millennial hysteria in the near future, the next target date was set at 1000, a millennium after Christ's birth.

Predicting the Parousia for the year 1000 received a boost from the creation of a new dating system. About 525 a monk, Dionysius Exiguus, undertook the task of updating the table of the dates for Easter. Because Easter was celebrated on the first Sunday after the first full moon following the spring equinox, the date moved through a cycle of nearly a full month of possible days, requiring some astronomical knowledge to place it correctly. The Church made Easter tables available so that the feast could be celebrated on the same day everywhere. The table Dionysius was asked to update had as its starting point 284, the year when Diocletian took the imperial throne, and the monk felt it most inappropriate for such an enemy of Christianity to be so honored. Instead, he set the birth of Jesus as the year 1, the starting point for his table. He was not the first Christian to do so, but his decision proved the most influential. The Gospels do not provide a precise date for the Incarnation, and Dionysius chose one that is probably four years too late. Nonetheless, *Anno Domini* (In the Year of the Lord) or AD became the system of time for Western civilization and the modern world. The use of Anno Domini means that 2000 AD takes on greater significance than in the Roman calendar, where it is an ordinary 2753 AUC (from the founding of the city).

The new dating system was slow to catch on; for the next several centuries most scholars continued to use older systems. An Anglo-Saxon monk, the Venerable Bede, did much to establish AD and introduced the idea of dating before Christ, BC, in his *Ecclesiastical History of the English Nation,* written about 731. Earlier he had made a radical change in calculating the age of the world in his *Concerning Time.* Complaining about the ignorant rustics who expected the end to come during their lifetimes, he concluded that Christ had been born 3,952 years after the Creation, and thus the Second Coming was at least 1,300 years in the future. He emphasized that Christ would return like a thief in the night. A charge of heresy against Bede for his innovative calculations went nowhere in the Church hierarchy, which suggests that the higher clergy supported putting off the endtime.

Before 800 arrived, however, Christianity found itself facing its most dangerous threat since Diocletian. In less than a century a new religion from Arabia had gained control of half the Christian lands. Islam is not as apocalyptic as Christianity; it has no equivalent of Revelation but it has a messianic element. Mohammed, who began receiving visions about 610, was familiar with Judaism and Christianity. It can be assumed that he knew some apocryphal apocalypses since Islamic messianism has some similarities to them. He was convinced that the end was near because the world was growing old. The Qur'an itself has little on the endtime. There will be a Day of Doom when the trumpet is blown and terror descends, rocking the earth and crushing the mountains. Then the dead will rise and be judged, being divided into the companions of the right and those on the left. The former will be admitted to the Garden of Delight with spreading shade, running waters, and refreshing fruits; the latter will be chained in hell with burning winds, boiling waters, and smoking fire.

The Muslims soon began to add to that belief, through the sayings *(hadith)* attributed to Mohammed; these sayings seem more clearly than the Qur'an to draw on the traditions of the older religions of the Middle East. The most obvious similarity is the Muslim equivalent of Antichrist, the *Dajjāl,* described a one-eyed Jew from the east, riding a donkey and having the word "Unbeliever" written on his forehead. With vast power to perform evil, he will seduce people away from the truth, but his reign will last only forty days. Then Jesus, whom Mohammed accepted as a great prophet of Allah but not divine, will return to Palestine to kill *Dajjāl* with a spear. Jesus will then lead all Jews and Christians to Islam and will reign in peace for forty years, after which he will yield his power to the *Mahdi,* the Messiah from the family of Mohammed, who will return Islam to the original purity of Mohammed's time as the prelude to the Day of Judgment.

This scenario, with several variations, is common among the Sunnis, the large majority of Muslims. As in Christianity, Islam has had its schisms over the source of authority in the Muslim community. The Sunnis maintained that authority came from the community, which could choose the caliph; the other large group in Islam, the Shi'is (the Party of 'Ali, Mohammed's son-in-law, who was assassinated in 661), held that it rightfully belonged to Mohammed's descendants alone. Consigned to the margins of Islamic society and usually oppressed, the Shi'is developed a powerful messianism centered around the Mahdi. The Mahdi, a descendant of the Prophet, will rise at a time of the worst oppression of true Islam to create a world completely dedicated to the full truth of Islam, social justice, and peace. Although Jesus will return to signal the endtime, it is the Mahdi who kills the *Dajjāl* and judges mankind.

The Shi'is know who the Mahdi is: He is the twelfth *imam* (spiritual leader), who went into occultation (hiding) in 872 to avoid assassination, the fate of his predecessor and father. The return of the twelfth imam is the subject of the same sort of prognosticating as the Parousia. For example, it will occur in the month of Ramadan in which there is both a solar and a lunar eclipse. Belief in the Mahdi has created messianic groups within the Shi'is. Some claim to know when and where he will rise, others declare that he has already risen and is leading them against their oppressors. To a lesser degree than Christianity, the Shi'is have had cults, which believe it is necessary to prepare the way for the Mahdi with violence. Describing the Shi'is as millennialist, however, is a misnomer, because for the Muslims, it is the end of the century, not the millennium, that has eschatological overtones. The Mahdi will rise at the turn of a century, but which one remains Allah's secret. The Islamic calendar does not conform to the one used in the West: It begins with Mohammed's move to Medina in 622 AD, and it is lunar, not solar, with twelve months of thirty days each, or 360 days in a year. Thus, the end of the current century in the Gregorian calendar is 1420–1421 in the Islamic calendar, which does not coincide with the millennium's end in the former. At least there is nothing to fear from a double whammy of eschatological calendars in 2000 AD.

The eschatology found in Islam had limited direct influence on Christians, although an occasional well-informed millennialist has argued that even the Muslims believe in Antichrist and the Parousia. The rise of the Islamic empire, on the other hand, had a strong impact among both Jews and Christians. The seventh century saw the strongest surge of messianism in Judaism since the Bar Kokhba revolt. Rome was still the enemy in the form of the Byzantine empire, and when the Persians seized Jerusalem from the Byzantine emperor in 614, many Jews saw the fulfillment of numerous prophecies in Judaic apocalypses of a second Persian restoration of the Temple. Those hopes were dashed in 628 with the Byzantine reconquest of Palestine, only to be raised even higher with the Muslim occupation in 636. Not only was the Judaic influence on Islam strong, but the Arabs believed that they were fellow descendants of Abraham, through his son Ishmail. One Jewish apocalypse had predicted that the Messiah would come and the Temple be rebuilt in 648 AD, a thousand years after the Persians had permitted the first rebuilding.

Frustrated by the failure of the prophecies, some Jews followed self-proclaimed messiahs. The most noteworthy was Abu 'Isa who lived in Persia in the eighth century. Espousing a theology that called for Jews to study Christ and Mohammed along with the Hebrew prophets, he headed a revolt against Muslim rule that led to his death in 755 while marching on Baghdad. His followers were convinced that he, like many other messianic figures, had escaped and taken refuge in a mountain cave from which he would reappear.

Many Iberian Jews believed that the Muslim conquest was a sign of the coming of the Messiah. Around 720 a charismatic Jew named Serene persuaded many of them to sell their property and go to Jerusalem to wait for the New Kingdom, which he would establish by driving out the Muslims. The local Muslim ruler seized him and handed him over to the rabbis for punishment for violating rabbinical law. Shortly after 800 a Jewish traveler, Eldad Ha-Dani, claimed to have found in eastern Africa the Ten Lost Tribes, whose restoration to Palestine was an essential part of messianism. His report is said to be the source of the legend of Prester John, so important in medieval views of world geography

The Muslim capture of Jerusalem resonated deeply in millennialism. Early Christians had been obviously wrong when they designated Rome as the last empire: The rise of the Muslim kingdom signaled the imminent end, and Mohammed was Antichrist. This view was strongest among the Christians of the Middle East and the Iberian peninsula, lands overrun by the Muslims. The most important of the works promoting this belief is known as the *Revelations* of Pseudo-Methodius. Methodius was a fourth-century bishop-martyr known for his many writings. The book with his name appeared after 660 and reflects the Muslim conquest of the author's homeland, likely Mesopotamia. The author blamed the Christian defeat on the prevalence of homosexuality in his time. His vision of the endtime involves a great Christian emperor, a descendant of Alexander the Great. The emperor will defeat first the Muslims, imposing on them a yoke a hundred times heavier than that which they inflict on the Christians, and then will destroy the forces of Gog and Magog, soon to be released from Alexander's gate. According to the book, "The whole earth will be terrified at the sight of them; men will be afraid and flee in terror to hide themselves in mountains and caves and graves."[1] After his victories the emperor will go to Jerusalem to reign over his empire for ten and one-half years until Antichrist appears. In order to destroy him, the great emperor will climb up Golgotha and place his crown on a cross raised there. Both items will be taken to heaven, and the crown given to Christ, who then will return to earth, defeat Antichrist, and reign forever. The scenario found in Pseudo-Methodius had a powerful impact on millennial works into the early modern era. An *Apocalypse of St. Peter* rewritten about 920 predicted the downfall of the Muslim empire as the event leading to Christ's return. It traced Mohammed's ancestry to the tribe of Dan and, reinterpreting many apocalyptic symbols, applied them to Islam.

In Spain the Muslim conquest gave rise to even more fevered anticipation of the Parousia. The Muslim victory, occurring as it did in 711, gave added urgency to the revised Annus Mundi dating of the endtime as the year 800. The most notorious of the Spanish millennialists of that era was Beatus of Liébana, who wrote *Commentary on the Apocalypse* in 786. It is notable for its powerful illustrations of the end of the world. Beatus calculated that the time from Adam to his day was 5,986 years, and the end of the sixth millennial week would occur in fourteen years. At least in this work, he hoped to forestall undue anticipation of the Parousia by arguing that it was possible for God to shorten or lengthen the time because only he knows the day and the hour. Apparently, Beatus was far less restrained in his preaching, as he was reported as telling his flock that the world would end during Holy Week in 800 and the dead would rise on Easter Sunday. The people fasted until the ninth hour on that Easter waiting for the end.

There are scattered hints from the Carolingian period of similar episodes of millennial anxiety and charismatic leaders who took advantage of it. They describe the fear created by natural events such as comets, meteors, eclipses, earthquakes, and pseudo-events such as two suns in the sky, which were taken as signs of the endtime. Whether they were stimulated by the revised Annus Mundi system that placed the end in 800 is impossible to say because such phenomena always sparked that kind of reaction. Curiously, the great event of the era, the coronation of Charlemagne on Christmas 800, passed with little millennial

comment. What other event could have had as many millennial overtones as the coronation of a Christian emperor in Rome on the anniversary of Christ's birth at the end of the sixth millennial week?

The paucity of millennial commentary on Charlemagne's coronation probably reveals the overall lack of concern for the endtime in the
century after 800 on the continent. In the British Isles, however, the sudden onslaught of the ferocious seafaring Norse in 793 provided ample
reason to think the end was at hand. The Norse fit perfectly the prophecies of the evil from the north (Jer. 6:22) and the beast from the sea
(Rev. 13:1) that herald the last days. Hearing of the destruction of the
great abbey of Landisfarne, Alcuin of York declared that judgment had
begun and greater tribulation was to follow.

Thanks to the Icelandic sagas, we have a good knowledge of Norse
eschatology, which, most scholars agree, is nearly identical to that of
earlier Teutonic peoples. According to the Norse, the end of the cosmos,
like its creation, has little to do with the gods, who themselves are both
created and have an end. The end is called *Ragnarok,* the "fate of the
gods." The elements of decay have been present in the world nearly
from its beginning. As the end nears, the evidence of corruption both
among the gods and humans becomes more obvious. Perjury, seduction,
murder, and war become rampant in both groups. A great wolf swallows
the sun and blackens the sky; a terrible winter lasting as long as three
ordinary winters kills animals and humans; and the giants and demons
led by Loki slip the bonds placed on them by the gods and destroy them.
When the gods die, the earth, after having been burned by a raging fire,
slips back into the sea from which they had raised it. Yet all does not
end; the cycle will begin again, with gods and humans enjoying the
same golden age that existed at the beginning of the present cosmos.
The Germanic sense of time has been described as resembling a container of events, which, when filled at the time of Ragnarok, must overflow into a larger container.

Since nearly all of what we know of Germanic mythology is found
in sources written by Christians, there is the problem of the extent to
which Christian beliefs may have been slipped in. Parallels can be found
between the two eschatologies; Loki, for example, resembles Antichrist.
Both traditions probably reflect primal legends about the endtime rather

than any direct influence, but there are several works from German lands that seem to be a blend of both. The best known is the Bavarian epic *Muspilli,* written down about 850. The second part of the word comes from an old Germanic word for destruction. Three elements in it can be described as apocalyptic: the battle between Elijah and Antichrist, the signs preceding the endtime, and the Last Judgment. According to the poem, although Elijah will be victorious, he will be wounded in the battle, and when his blood drips down to the earth, "then the mountains will catch fire, no tree at all will be left standing, the waters will dry up, the marshland will swallow itself up, the sky will be aflame with fire, the moon will fall, and the earth will burn."[2] The word *muspilli* referred to the events at the end, but the Norse took it to signify a person, the chief of the fire demons who will destroy the world. Thus, he takes on the characteristics of Antichrist in several works that combined both eschatologies.

The most important tenth-century work on the endtime was written about 950 by a French monk, Adso. His *Letter on the Origin and Life of Antichrist* was written for Queen Gerberga of the West Franks. He wrote that Antichrist will be contrary to Christ in every way, and his every action will oppose Christ. Thus, he reasoned, it is wrong to say that Antichrist will be born of a virgin, an opinion that appears in a number of ancient texts; he will be conceived in sin at Babylon, and the devil will enter his mother's womb at the moment of conception and possess him entirely. Antichrist, "the devil's son," will not appear until the last emperor, who will serve as the consummation of the Christian Roman empire as its greatest ruler, places his scepter and crown on the Mount of Olives. Then the man of sin will appear, torment the world for three and a half years, kill Elijah and Enoch, and martyr many faithful. Adso is uncertain whether Christ or the Archangel Michael will kill Antichrist, but it will happen on the Mount of Olives, opposite of the place where Jesus ascended to heaven. Adso has nothing on the timing of these events except to say that the Last Judgment will not occur immediately after Antichrist's destruction. The length of time remains in the providence of the Father.

As long as the Norse successfully raided western Europe, thereby convincing Christians that they were Antichrist's minions, there was little chance that they would convert to Christianity since their gods obviously were bringing them good fortune. But with the cessation of raids after 950, the Norse began to turn to Christianity. In 1000 the settlers in distant Iceland agreed to accept a Christian law code for the island. With the Norse and the Magyars, the other pagan scourge of Europe, converting to Christianity around 1000, it appeared that the gospel had been preached to all the nations just in time for the millennial anniversary of the birth of Christ. There were also the usual signs of the coming end: displays in the heavens, extraordinary events in nature, and clear evidence of moral decay.

One of the standard slanders of nineteenth-century historians against the Dark Ages, often cited today in anticipation of the end of the second millennium, pronounced that Christians, in their ignorance and blind religious fanaticism, cowered in dread of the year 1000. They were said to have crowded the churches on December 31, 999, in hopes of being among those taken in the Rapture, which ignores the fact that for most of Europe the new year began on either the Feast of the Annunciation, March 25, or Easter Sunday. They allegedly rushed by the thousands to Jerusalem to be there for the Parousia, and there is some evidence of an upsurge in pilgrimages. For most of the twentieth century, historians have been busy debunking the supposed "terrors of the year 1000," arguing that there is no evidence that the masses of people even knew that the year 1000 was about to occur. Contracts, penances, and wills were written to take effect decades in the future, and buildings were designed to last for centuries. Recently the emphasis has changed again; a new generation of historians has found evidence to suggest a heightened millennial expectation approaching 1000, even if there was no widespread terror. Yet their search for evidence from the decades around the millennium has resulted in making too large a contrast between that era and any other in the Middle Ages. The Middle Ages were a period when everyone read or, more accurately, saw and heard about the endtime constantly; it constituted a major part of the medieval mental landscape. What one finds in regard to the year 1000 differs from any other medieval period only in that there was some heightened anticipation; in content, millennialism remained largely the same.

THE FIRST MILLENNIUM | 57

Certainly the educated churchmen were aware of the coming of the millennium. Even if they did not use AD dating, as few did in 1000, the fact that a thousand years had passed since Christ's birth was well known among them. Yet the only way that the laity would have known about it was through preaching. Surely some preachers gave hellfire-and-brimstone sermons on the imminent end of the world, causing the common people who heard them to feel the terror of the coming of the year 1000, but there is little evidence for such sermons, except for one unequivocal report. Abbo of Fleury reported in a work written about 995 that, in his youth, he had heard a preacher in Paris proclaiming that once the thousand years since Christ's birth were up, the Last Judgment would quickly follow. Abbo wrote that he refuted this erroneous opinion as vigorously as he could. He also cited a prediction that the Parousia would occur on the Easter Sunday after a Good Friday that fell on the Annunciation (March 25). Since that had happened in 970 for the first time in centuries, Abbo knew it was not true for his time.

One churchman who revealed a strong sense of the impending endtime was Ralph Glaber, a monk who was convinced that "Satan will be unleashed soon because the thousand years have been completed."[3] He regarded the increased number of heretics, especially some of the popular preachers, who were proclaiming a fevered chiliasm, as evidence of the false prophets of the endtime. Glaber's fear that Antichrist was active in the world was also evident in the passage where he relates the obscene behavior of a group of heretics accused of participating in a Satanic orgy and then sacrificing to Satan the babies born from the often incestuous unions. Of the fourteen persons accused of Satanism, thirteen refused to abjure their beliefs and were burned at the stake, the first of many executions for heresy to come. These are the usual accusations targeting dissenting groups and need not be accepted at face value; but when such charges appear, and when the authorities respond as they did, it suggests that millennialism is in the air.

Glaber describes the many portents, some natural such as the fire that destroyed the church on Mont-St-Michel, others more fanciful like the apparitions of the devil, that announce the coming of Antichrist. Yet Glaber knew that the world had not ended in 1000 because his *Histories* were written after 1033; he died about 1050. His solution to the failure of the prediction seems to have been "realized eschatology": Christ had indeed come but without the apocalyptic events expected. His return resulted in a renewal of Christendom and a religious revival. Glaber's statement on this is often cited in the context of the history of architecture: In the third year after the millennium of Christ's incarnation, the whole world appeared to be shaking off the burden of the past and robing itself in "a white mantle of churches." The Latin word Glaber used for white was not the common one but the one used in Revelation for the robes of the saints.[4]

Glaber's work extended past 1033, the millennium of Christ's death, and he detailed another surge of expectations centered around it. Although most of those answering the question of when the Parousia would occur looked to the Incarnation to begin counting, some used the Crucifixion and looked to 1033 when 1000 proved to be incorrect. Among the signs that the end was coming was a great famine in France during which the wild animals feasted on the bodies of those who had starved, suggestive of the battle against Gog and Magog. The sources emphasize the number of Christian pilgrims going to Jerusalem to be there when Christ came. When 1033 passed without any terrors of the endtime, the same sort of revival of optimism that occurred after 1000 took place. The "Peace of God" movement in southern France has been tied to that revival as an outpouring of relief that the world had not ended.

It was possible for the Christian pilgrims to go to the Holy Land in 1033, for the Arabs had rarely restricted their passage in peacetime. Two decades later, the takeover of the Middle East by the Seljuk Turks placed Jerusalem under the control of militant Muslims, who largely halted the pilgrimages. For Christians, this raised the stakes over control of the Holy Land and helped set the stage for the First Crusade. Pope Urban II's call for a crusade in 1095 in central France was the product of a large number of factors coming together—to note two of the most important, the Byzantine emperor's need for troops to recover Asia Minor, which had been lost to the Turks in 1071, and the pope's desire to assert his supremacy in Christendom. But millennialism also had a role in inspiring Urban. One account of his sermon of 1095 says that he referred to the necessity of a Christian reconquest of Jerusalem before the Second Coming, which was already near. The pope declared that with the end of the world at hand, how better could Christians make ready the way of the Lord than by retaking Jerusalem from the infidels. It is easy to see how the crusaders believed that the delay in the Parousia could be made good by a holy war against Christ's enemies who controlled the place where he would return to earth.

For most of the knights who made up the First Crusade, the belief that they were helping prepare for the Parousia probably took a back seat to the hope of gaining lands and glory in Palestine. Millennialism, however, had a powerful impact on what are known as the People's Crusades. Strange and awesome portents appeared, as related by Ekkehard of Aura, who died about 1125, in his *Jerusalem Journey*. One was a comet with a tail shaped like a sword; another was the appearance of two warring knights in the sky with the one welding a cross defeating the other; the most powerful was the apparition of a heavenly city with a multitude of people marching toward it from every direction. Popular preachers mesmerized their audiences with descriptions of Jerusalem as the new Garden of Eden, the paradise of delights. Jerusalem was now in the hands of the enemies of Christ, who was calling on them to free it for his return. One of the chronicles describing the capture of Jerusalem in July 1099 emphasized that it happened on Friday, the day that Christ redeemed the world; and another, that it was a "new day, the day of our exaltation."

With the People's Crusade, evidence of social antagonisms, often important in later millennial movements, appears for the first time, as does millennial violence, which was rarely seen in earlier centuries. In western Europe a famine in 1095 badly dislocated the peasants and the urban poor, who directed their anger at the nobles and urban magnates who demanded the rents and did little to relieve their suffering. An epidemic also raged through a population highly vulnerable to contagious disease because of malnutrition. The popular preachers such as Peter the Hermit played on the fears and suffering of the poor by emphasizing how they, Christ's chosen ones, would take Jerusalem from the infidels and be there to enjoy the New Kingdom when Christ returned. Thousands of the poor assembled, sometimes in association with the knightly crusaders but often separate from them, and began to march toward the east. Lacking resources for the long journey, they took what they needed from the lands through which they traveled. They easily justified such foraging as doing God's work. If they were the true heirs of the kingdom to come, then they had a right to take what they needed now, for the wealth of the world was really theirs. This concept, later called the dominion of grace, has a long history in millennial groups.

A more horrific aspect of millennialism that appeared first among the crusading poor was the belief that the success of their efforts to bring about the Second Coming required the deaths of the "enemies of Christ." Millennialist beliefs led the crusaders to seek to cleanse the world of Jews and Muslims. It is easy to see how, caught up in the bloodlust of battle, they could massacre God's enemies, as they did in Jerusalem when they took the city in 1099. But before going to fight in the Holy Land, they had felt the need to cleanse Christendom of "Christ's first enemies," the Jews, resulting in the deaths of Jews in several Rhineland cities. There is evidence to indicate that for many of the crusaders, popular and knightly alike, millennialism played a role in many atrocities that they committed. Antichrist would be a Jew from the tribe of Dan and his most devoted followers would be Jews. Since the Parousia would not take place until all the Jews had converted to Christianity, the event would be hastened by forcing them to convert and killing those who refused. It seems clear enough that religious belief was the primary reason behind the massacres of Jews in medieval Europe, because baptized Jews were assured of the safety of life and property.

The Jews responded to the violence against them with their own apocalypticism. A verse from Jeremiah, "Sing with joy for Jacob!" was found to have the numerical value in Hebrew of 1096; the year coincided with the first outbreak of killings of Jews in the Rhineland. It was argued that the violence was a sign of the coming of the Messiah. When 1096 came and went, many Jews set other dates for his appearance; for some, calculating the coming of the Messiah was an important aspect of medieval Judaism. For those in Muslim lands, the crusade suited their calculations by destroying Muslim rule over Palestine. Thus, an old prediction that the Messiah would come 500 years after the beginning of the Muslim conquests, placing his coming in the year 1130, nearly coincided with the First Crusade. Many Jews migrated to Palestine to await the Messiah's appearance, and several claimed that they were indeed he.[5] The great philosopher Maimonides described an intriguing case of messianism in Yemen, where in 1172 a Jew proclaimed himself the Messiah and provoked enough unrest that he was arrested. This self-proclaimed Messiah boldly announced his mission to the local king, and when asked for a sign, declared that if his head were cut off, he would return to life. He was quickly put to the test. Maimonides observed that years later some Jews were still expecting him to rise from the grave.[6]

The atrocities of the First Crusade that inspired the upsurge in messianism among the Jews were largely the work of a group called the *Tafurs,* probably meaning "vagabonds." It is hard to take as fact all of the stories about them, such as cannibalism, but many ring true if seen in a millennial context. The Tafurs were said to have exalted poverty and forced out of their company anyone carrying money, for God chose the poorest of the poor to win his city back. They had a charismatic leader, King Tafur, reputedly a noble who gave away his wealth and weapons to lead the poor. Some followers apparently identified him as the last emperor who would retake Jerusalem and hand it over to Christ on Mount Olivet. He allegedly demanded the extermination of the Muslims as enemies of Christ and agents of Satan. What happened to him, if he did exist, is unknown, but for centuries he was the subject of legends of miraculous reappearances to lead God's people.

The later crusades, made necessary by the Muslim resurgence after 1100, had far less participation by the poor. The popular crusading zeal and the special circumstances that led to so many poor people taking part in the First Crusade were largely lacking in the subsequent crusades, and their leaders took care to prevent a large mob of unruly and poorly armed men from participating. The belief, however, that the last emperor would lead a crusade was given a great boost in the later ones, because, except for the Fourth Crusade, their leaders were the great rulers of Catholic Europe. With France's Louis VII commanding the Second Crusade in 1147, the sense that he was the last emperor was raised substantially only to be cruelly dashed when he proved to be incompetent. The Third Crusade saw such millennial hopes raised again and even higher, for now it was a real emperor involved, Holy Roman

Emperor Frederick I Barbarossa. His disappearance in a river in Asia Minor in 1190 only added to his eschatological value, for prophecies quickly appeared predicting his return from a cave in the Hertz Mountains, where he was said to be waiting for the right moment to lead a great crusade to recapture Jerusalem and set the events of the endtime in motion.

With the crusades, violence became a common part of millennialism. To be sure, there is ample precedence and justification for religious violence in the Old Testament. Psalm 138 (19–22), for example, declares: "Do I not hate those who hate you, O Lord? . . . I hate them with perfect hatred; I count them my enemies." The crusaders made attacks on the enemies of God (whom they defined as Jews and Muslims) a necessary condition for the Second Coming. For many later millennialist movements, anyone, even churchmen, often especially churchmen, who did not accept their vision of the Parousia, was a proper target of violence. Violence was henceforth common in millennial belief.

V

THE AGE OF THE SPIRIT: THE HIGH MIDDLE AGES

W HEN RICHARD THE LIONHEART was traveling through Italy in early 1191 on his way to participate in the Third Crusade, he stopped at Messina for an interview with the great medieval prophet Joachim of Fiore. After Richard received an optimistic but largely inaccurate prediction of success for his expedition, the great knight and the aged monk spent time discussing Antichrist. Joachim told him that he believed Antichrist had already been born at Rome and was active in the world, which explained the manifest corruption present everywhere, especially in the Church, for Antichrist would be an antipope. The king objected that he had always heard that the final enemy would be born in Babylon, touching off a heated debate between Joachim and the clerics in Richard's party over the signs of Antichrist.

This episode underlines two key points about millennialism in the later Middle Ages. Everyone, including kings, regarded the endtime as a worthy topic for discussion, and Joachim of Fiore was a major figure in that discussion. Joachim ended his life as the confidant of popes and monarchs. Emperor Henry VI visited him while he served as confessor to Empress Constance. His early years, however, were similar to many other millennial prophets with far less political clout. He gave up his career as a notary after a pilgrimage to the Holy Land and became a hermit on Mount Etna, and then an itinerant preacher before entering the Cistercian order. He left the order about 1190 to found his own monastery at Fiore in southern Italy, which he led until his death in 1202. Since the Cistercians refused to sanction his departure, his standing as an abbot was dubious, but the use of the title gave his millennial works greater prestige. Joachim attributed his inspiration to visions he had on Easter of 1183 and at Pentecost a year later. These visions led to his *Exposition on the Apocalypse,* the major source for his views, but millennialism permeates all of his works, even those written before his visions.

Joachim's visions did not contain a new revelation but enabled him to see the truths of the Scriptures, especially those about the endtime. His view of history is complex, filled with a myriad of ages and divisions of time, yet the crucial periodization is a simple threefold division. The age of the Father was the age of the Old Testament, and law, marriage, and water were among its characteristics. The age of the Son, the present one but rapidly coming to an end, is the age of the New Testament and of faith, the clergy, and wine. The age of the Holy Spirit will be the age of perfection, love, monks, and oil. Just as there had been 42 generations of 30 years apiece between Adam and Christ in the age of the Father, so there will be the same number in the age of the Son. Joachim calculated that forty generations since Christ were completed in 1200, and the age of the Son would end in two more generations, presumably in 1260. God might foreshorten the length of the generations, however, because the trials of the endtime may prove to be too awful for even the saints to withstand. Thus, he avoided contradicting Christ's statement that only the Father knows the day and the hour of the endtime.

Joachim believed that the end events of the age of the Son as foretold in Revelation had begun. Antichrist, not a Jew but a false Christian, was already present in the world; his malignant power was already being felt, as shown by the Muslim victory in recapturing Jerusalem in 1187 but even more in the corruption that Joachim saw in the Church. His focus was on the false teachers warned of in 2 John and 2 Peter, who he said came from among the clergy. Antichrist will probably take the form of an antipope, not the Holy Roman Emperor, whom many authors had identified as Antichrist during the bitter feud between popes and emperors of the previous century. An angelic pope will carry the banner of Christ against Antichrist. He will succeed in winning Jews, Muslims, and pagans to Christ with the help of two monastic orders made up of spiritual men, one consisting of preachers, the other of contemplative hermits. The first order will appear to be new but in fact will not be; its members will be clad in black. Their task will be gathering in the elect through preaching, and their life "will be like rain watering the face of the earth in all perfection and in the justice of brotherly love." The new order of hermits will imitate the life of angels, and their endtime task will be "to consume and extinguish the wicked life of evil men so they do not abuse the patience of God any longer." They will become "a blazing fire . . . to gather in the harvest of evil."[1]

The description of these two apocalyptic orders would have a powerful impact on the future. Several religious orders would claim to be Joachim's new order of preachers. Of more significance is his order of hermits. It closely resembles a revolutionary elite who must use violence to bring about the new age. The use of violence to destroy the evildoers had been deemed necessary before, but this was the first time a specific group was identified as God's avenging angels. Many a millennial group applied that designation to itself in the centuries that followed.

Once the angelic pope and the two orders have done their work, Antichrist will be destroyed, and there will be peace and justice throughout the earth. War will disappear because the great dragon will be imprisoned in the abyss. Following John of Patmos, Joachim believed that after this age of peace, whose duration is known only to God, there will be a loss of virtue among humans, and the dragon will be released to persecute the saints for one last time before the end of the world and the Last Judgment. Joachim had little to say about those events; he was far more interested in describing the age of the Holy Spirit soon to begin. That age will see the triumph of the spirit over the flesh and the creation of the perfect human society on earth. The Church will be renewed, and the corruption that Joachim saw in the contemporary institution eliminated. The new people of God will be organized around the perfect monastery, modeled on the Heavenly City, in which the "spiritual father who governs all" will live. It will not consist only of the monks of the new order: These perfect monks will serve as an example to the six other levels of the new society—hermits, teachers, laborers, the aged, the clergy, and the married. The clergy and the laity will live outside of the monastery yet close enough to be supervised by the spiritual father. The married will have sex only for procreation, not pleasure. The people of God will live a common and simple life without idleness and want. But not all mankind will live in this manner; tribes at the ends of the earth will continue their evil lives and will serve Antichrist in the last battle.

Joachim of Fiore has great importance in the history of millennialism for several reasons. One is his tripartite theory of history, although he worked hard to fit the cosmic-week periodization into it so as to not reject its long tradition in Christianity. Another is his sense of progress—the steady improvement of the human race from one age to the next. While the progress is first of all spiritual, there is also a sense that the material conditions of human society are improving, most obviously but not exclusively in the third age. Although he saw moral decline around him and expected periods of tribulation in the near future at the end of the second age and again at the end of the third age, they would be brief. Finally, Joachim's description of human society in the third age was the first utopian community identified with Christian millennialism, and arguably the first one of any sort since Plato. Joachim was not a revolutionary in that he did not seek to overthrow either the existing society or the Church but predicted their perfecting; there was, however, much in his thought to attract future millennialists who were more truly revolutionary in their goals.

Joachim's thought reflected the increasingly bitter feud between pope and emperor that began in the late eleventh century. Both sides tossed about accusations that their opponents were the minions of Antichrist, if not the evil one himself. Joachim avoided taking sides, but the same cannot be said of numerous other millennialists who either were recruited for the fray or threw themselves into it. To accuse an opponent of being Antichrist or his minion was common inflammatory rhetoric in the era, and many of those who used it had no more than the usual vague sense of the Second Coming. There were those, however, for whom pope or emperor as Antichrist did play a major part in their visions of the coming endtime. The presence in the world of a particular papal or imperial nemesis was proof of its imminence.

One of the earliest to cite the emperor as antichristian was Hildegard von Bingen, the first woman to have a significant place in millennialism since the Montanist prophets. She was the abbess of a Benedictine convent at Bingen in the Rhine valley at the time of her death in 1179. Her major work, *Scivias,* was written in 1151. Hildegard believed that Emperor Henry IV's attack on Pope Gregory VII was one of the signs of the beginning of the endtime, although the apocalypse was still years away. Her major contribution to millennialism lay in her visions of the birth of Antichrist. In sharp contrast to Jesus' birth, usually described as painless for his mother, Antichrist's birth will be violent and bloody. The wicked woman who conceived him by the worst possible sin will suffer enormous pain and anguish at his birth. Hildegard describes at length his hideous appearance as he tears his way out of his mother's womb. Fully grown and already at the height of his powers, he tries to ascend to heaven only to fall back to earth when he is struck by lightning from on high. On earth Antichrist wages war against the Church, a battle that Hildegard described in terms of sexual assault on a beautiful maiden. She emphasizes also that the assaults of Antichrist will be directed especially against chastity and celibacy. She saw the inability of so many clerics to live chastely as one sign that Antichrist was close at hand.

The urgency of the papal-imperial feud is also evident in the works of Gerhoh of Reichersberg. Gerhoh ardently defended the papacy against the emperors, including Frederick Barbarossa who, despite his reputation as a crusader, was involved in the election of an antipope against Alexander III. Shortly before his death in 1169, Gerhoh wrote *On the Investigation of Antichrist.* He believed that the bitter antagonism between pope and emperor, who should have been the beacons of Christian faith and justice in the world, was a sign of the coming end. Emperor Henry IV was the first of several antichrists to precede the final Antichrist. Gerhoh was all too aware of the corruption in the papal curia as well. The cleansing of the curia and the papacy would occur at the time of tribulation, after which the pope would rule over all the nations. Thus, he anticipated Joachim's angelic pope.

No other emperor was as often identified as the final enemy as was Frederick II. This son of Joachim of Fiore's confidants had a most difficult time securing the imperial title and his thrones of Sicily and Germany after his father died in 1197, when Frederick was only three years of age. His successful struggle to survive and win his crowns against enormous odds was one element of the legends built around him that presented him as having a greater destiny than simply earthly rule. His millennial value received a great boost when he took as his second wife the widowed queen of Jerusalem and claimed the title of king for himself. Possessing an immensely curious and quick mind, he learned much about the occult, magic, and Jewish and Muslim traditions, while revealing a deep skepticism about Christianity, which branded him an atheist. Pope Innocent III, his guardian, had helped him claim his titles; once Innocent was gone, Frederick's relationship with the papacy deteriorated into bitter conflict. Excommunicated by Pope Gregory IX in 1227 for failing to fulfill his vow to lead a crusade, he nonetheless proceeded to go to Palestine. There he negotiated a treaty with the Muslim leader that allowed him to crown himself king of Jerusalem in the Church of the Holy Sepulcher. Upon his return to Italy the battle between emperor and pope raged on unabated. Frederick's unprecedented behavior and curiosity led to his being called *Stupor Mundi,* The Wonder of the World.

The papal party's rage at Frederick II was so fierce that it accused him of being Antichrist. In 1239 a papal letter identified him as Revelation's "beast rising from the sea." Papal invective reached its height in 1245. A papal proclamation declared that Frederick, the beast from the sea, the impious one, and the seed of Babylon, was deposed for his sins against the Church. The papal anathema encouraged rebellion against Frederick, but he retained control of his realms until his death in 1250. It did not put an end to the speculation about his true identity. Stories that he had not died or had risen from the dead abounded, especially in anticipation of the year 1260. The best known of these legends involves the story that he had been seen riding with 5,000 warriors on their way to Mount Etna, where they would stay until their return to the world.

The arrival of the Mongols in eastern Europe two decades earlier, who with good reason were identified as the forces of Gog and Magog, gave even more urgency to the approach of 1260. The appearance and behavior of those ferocious warriors could only make sense in the context of the endtime, and it was prophesied that Frederick would rise from the dead to lead them in the final battle.

Yet for many the expected return of Emperor Frederick II was not the coming of Antichrist. He had become a messianic figure, the last emperor, and it was the pope who was Antichrist. Frederick and his supporters gave back to the popes as good as they received. In a letter to Pope Innocent IV, the emperor denounced him as antipope, as the great dragon who leads the world astray, Antichrist himself. One of his supporters decoded Innocent IV as 666, the number of Antichrist. The idea of an evil pope as Antichrist had its appeal. Had not St. John warned about false teachers who would deceive the faithful? How better could Antichrist violate the bride of Christ, the Church, than by becoming pope himself?

Joachim of Fiore, who had provided support for identifying the emperor as Antichrist, also spoke of the evil pope of the last days. In the long term his remarks on the evil pope had more import because they became part of the beliefs of the Spiritual Franciscans, whose antipapal invective was unmatched until the Protestant Reformation. It is one of the ironies of history that the followers of gentle St. Francis became involved in such a vicious shouting match with church authorities, and some took it much further. Francis received papal approval for his new style of religious life in 1210. It emphasized apostolic poverty: Just as Jesus had no place to lay his head, so his followers ought to own nothing but live by begging. The mendicants (from the Latin for beg) included both the Franciscans and the Dominicans, founded about the same time by St. Dominic as the Order of Preachers. Many people, both members of the orders and nonmembers, identified the mendicants as Joachim's two orders of preachers and hermits. The Dominicans' similarity to one of them is obvious: Joachim described one order as being made up of preachers and wearing black (the Dominican garb was black and white). Although Francis had been a hermit for a time, equating the Franciscans with Joachim's order of hermits is less evident since the

Franciscans, mostly from the urban bourgeoisie, ministered to the urban poor. Nonetheless, for many in the thirteenth century, the two new orders made Joachim's predictions on the approach of the end appear irrefutable.

A crisis in the Franciscan order within a quarter-century of its founding gave Joachim's prophesies greater urgency and a more radical interpretation. The order's astounding growth created the need for more central organization and greater use of property. The many friars who felt this concern with property was totally alien to the spirit of their founder were called Spiritual Franciscans. They believed that Joachim had prophesied the coming of St. Francis as the angel of the sixth seal of Revelation. The appearance of the *Commentary on Jeremiah* shortly after 1240, probably written by a Franciscan, emphasized the Church's corruption and the role of Joachim's two new orders; it firmly designated the year 1260 as the end of the second age. When a Spiritual Franciscan, John of Parma, was elected minister general of the order in 1248, the urgency of the coming end seemed ever greater. He promoted Joachimism in the order and sent one of its most outspoken proponents, Gerardo of Borgo San Donnino, to the University of Paris to study theology. There Gerardo created a fire storm among the theologians in 1254 with his *Introduction to the Eternal Gospel.* The book declared that the Church as it existed would disappear entirely in 1260, to be replaced by the two orders, and that Joachim's writings would succeed the Gospels as the primary source of religious truth. Furthermore, he prophesied that a man guilty of the sin of buying a church office would become pope in 1260, thereby becoming the papal Antichrist foretold by Joachim. Loud complaints from theologians in Paris caused the pope to condemn Gerardo for heresy and imprison him for life, and John of Parma was forced to give up the leadership of the Franciscans in 1257.

Three years later, the date set for the end of the second age passed without any signs of change, and many Joachimites abandoned the movement. For the Spiritual Franciscans, however, the prophecy's failure hardly ended their commitment to Joachimism. They set about recalculating the date, finding that the correct starting point was Christ's death, not his birth. When the new date also passed without the end occurring, other changes were made in Joachim's numbers, such as increasing the length of a generation. Those who have done this sort of re-calculation usually come up with a date that is within their own proba-ble life-span, for what good will the Parousia be for those who crave vindication if it occurs when they are already dead? The Spiritual Fran-ciscans deeply desired vindication, for in their zeal to bring their order back to what they saw as its original ideals, they ran afoul not only of its leadership but also of the papacy. For them, apostolic poverty be-came not only a way of life for those who wished to live it but also a ne-cessity for all the clergy. Such a vision was incomprehensible to the high churchmen who controlled great wealth in the name of Christ.

The leading thinker for the Spiritual Franciscans in the last decades of the thirteenth century was Peter Olivi, a theologian at the University of Paris, who was more explicit in assigning major roles in millennial-ism to St. Francis and the papal Antichrist. His endtime scheme drew from Joachim in the use of the 42 generations, but he argued that the counting began in the year 40 when St. Peter became the bishop of Rome—a gentile city. Thus, the end of the second age would occur in 1300. Olivi, however, also used the idea of two sets of seven ages, the first for the Old Testament and the second beginning with Christ. St. Francis, the new Elijah, ushered in the sixth age, an age of renewal to be achieved by a new order (that is, the Spiritual Franciscans). The at-tacks on apostolic poverty were signs of the coming of Antichrist or, more correctly, two of them. The first one Olivi called the mystical An-tichrist, an antipope who would oppose the Spiritual Franciscans by at-tacking apostolic poverty. His successes would bring into existence the great Antichrist, who would combine in himself all the evils of the Mus-lims and bad Christians as well as the evil emperor and the antipope. His ultimate defeat would usher in the final kingdom.

Olivi defended his views with great vigor and much success during his lifetime, but after his death in 1298 church authorities acted against them. A series of judgments against his works culminated in the deci-sion by Pope John XXII that his major work, *Commentary on the Book of the Apocalypse,* was heretical. The Spiritual Franciscans' rage at that pope, however, came even more from his condemnation of apostolic poverty. Refusing to accept his judgment, several were executed, four of them at Marseilles in 1318; more were imprisoned; others went into hiding. The already strong tendency among them to view the pope as Antichrist increased, for what else could this persecution mean but the beginning of the endtime? After the papal condemnations the Spiritual Franciscans made clear both the dread with which they anticipated worse trials in the near future inflicted by the carnal church, the antipope, and Antichrist, and their joyful expectation of the subsequent coming of the age of the Holy Spirit and their vindication. They were largely correct in regard to the first but not to the second; by the late fourteenth century the group had petered out under constant persecution. By then they had provided a great deal of ammunition to those who later denounced the Roman Church as the whore of Babylon and the pope as Antichrist.

Until virtually the end of the movement, the Spiritual Franciscans stayed within the Church despite their bitter disagreements with its leaders. Other groups attracted to apostolic poverty, mostly laity, were far less willing to remain in Mother Church. Invariably such groups took on a fierce anticlericalism, for the contrast between their ideal of apostolic poverty and the wealth of the Catholic clergy was overwhelming. Lacking the lingering loyalty of the Spiritual Franciscans to the clerical state if not to the leaders of the clergy, they were far quicker to reject the Church and even to resort to arms against it. The first such group appeared at Parma in 1260, probably drawing on Joachim's date. Gerardo Segarelli, an illiterate would-be Franciscan, drew a large following, as many as 4,000 people, by preaching apostolic poverty and millennialism. He claimed for his followers, including some Franciscans, the designation as Joachim's new order of the third age. In 1275 the Church banned all groups without official recognition; when Segarelli ignored the ban, he was executed in 1300. Leadership passed to Fra Dolcino, probably a priest's son. His followers, known as the Apostolic Brethren, avoided all the trappings of a religious order. Dolcino declared that there were four ages of the world: the age before Christ, the age of the pure early church up to the time of Constantine when it began to own property, the current age of the carnal church, and a forthcoming age of the true church. The brethren would bring about the end of the current age not only by their life of apostolic poverty but also through violence. The pope and the clergy would be exterminated through the agency of the last emperor, identified as King Frederick III of Sicily. The angelic pope appointed by God directly and a new clergy living in apostolic poverty would restore the Church. The world would then live in peace until its end.

In 1303 Fra Dolcino, who identified himself as the angel of the Church of Thyatira (Rev, 2:18), proclaimed that these predicted events would take place in the next two years, with the slaughter of the evil pope and clergy to occur in 1305. As many as 1,400 disciples gathered in the mountains northwest of Milan in 1304 to await the moment to take over the Church. The passage of 1305 without the fulfillment of his predictions failed to discomfit the group, and the next year the pope ordered a crusade directed against them, largely because their foraging for food was terrorizing the region. Dolcino declared that his followers had the right to imprison or kill those who supported the established Church and to destroy their towns and villages. A bloody battle in 1307 resulted in the deaths of some 400 of the brethren and the capture of Fra Dolcino and his consort, Margaret of Trent, who were executed. The survivors scattered across Europe; mention of them occurs intermittently over the next century as far away as Poland. Dante immortalized Fra Dolcino in canto 28 of the *Inferno*. "Now then, you who will perhaps soon see the sun, tell Brother Dolcino, if he does not want to follow me down here soon, to provide himself with enough food."[2]

Millennial violence had already erupted in Europe before 1307. The Church in response became ever more willing to use violence to defend its wealth and its claim to know the truth, which included the proper interpretation of the Millennium. Shadowy groups had appeared and disappeared in a haze of blood since the First Crusade, although the lack of sources makes it difficult to determine how far millennialism motivated them. The most fascinating of these little-known sects was a group of movements collectively known as the Heresy of the Free Spirit. What we know about them comes largely from their enemies, especially from the theologian Albert the Great, who compiled a list of their errors around 1270. He defined their principal doctrine as the belief that through apostolic poverty and individual perfection, the soul could achieve union with God, thereby being deified itself, and enter sinlessness. There was little need for Christ, whose equal some said that they had become, and none at all for the Church and the clergy. The Free Spirits were decidedly antinomian: Virtue consisted of doing the opposite of what the Church and civil law demanded. What the clergy denounced as sin was to be openly and frequently practiced. Lies, thievery, and especially free love with members of both sexes helped unite the soul to God or were signs that such a union had been achieved.

These groups were more quietist than actively violent, and their eschatology consisted mostly of the idea that when enough people reached union with God, the present world with its corrupt Church and clergy would become a new Garden of Eden without sin. Perhaps it was the major role of women in the sects that explains their lack of violence despite the Church's active persecution. Many urban women, especially the unmarried and the widowed, were pushed to the margins of society. They formed an eager audience for radical preachers who gave them attention, a community, a sense of belonging and love, and, often, sexual pleasure. One source for their beliefs is *The Mirror of Simple Souls* by Margaret of Porète from Belgium, written prior to her execution for heresy in 1310. Margaret was a disciple of Olivi, whom she identified as the angel of the Church of Philadelphia. Her book describes the seven stages that the soul passes through on its way to union with God. When the soul reaches the final stage, it returns to the innocence of Adam before the Fall and becomes sinless. There is, however, no hint that the soul ought to engage in those acts previously denounced as sinful. She proclaimed that each soul among the spiritual elite who achieve union with God has its own millennium. A German treatise penned by a Sister Katherine had much the same point of view, but it defined sexual freedom as one of the signs of union with God.

Radical millennialists received a boost with the onslaught of the Black Death in 1347. Plague is one of the woes of Revelation, and any catastrophe with the impact of the Black Death would lead almost every Christian to conclude that the endtime was at hand. Considering the enormity of the death rate, about a third of the people across Europe, the response to the Black Death was less intensely chiliastic than might be expected. Most of the survivors took the passive yet optimistic view that there was nothing that could be done, but the Parousia, certain to come soon, would end such disasters once and for all.

Some people, however, felt that a more activist response was demanded. Among the activists were the Flagellants, who traveled from place to place whipping themselves as public penitence in the hope that this would allay God's anger and persuade him to shorten this time of trial. While the public whipping was extreme, the Flagellants demonstrate the most common Catholic response to evidence that the endtime might be at hand: Repent and pray that God's anger at humanity's sins might be assuaged so that either the tribulation might be deferred or its duration drastically reduced.

The tremendous disruption of society caused by the plague, besides serving as clear evidence of the coming endtime, provided an opportunity for the radical groups to gain members. Prophets among the Free Spirits announced that Antichrist now held the world in his sway, and that they were the new Adam whose coming would free it. There had been Adamites in the early Church about whom Epiphanius, the major source of knowledge about Montanism, provided some (mostly negative) information. As with similar shadowy medieval groups, it is difficult to get a good sense of their beliefs and strength, but it appears that their key doctrine was that some humans could replicate Adam's condition in Eden before the fall. Marriage was a consequence of original sin, which was sexual in nature, and those who would return to Eden had to be celibate and live in a state of Edenic innocence. They imitated Adam and Eve in Eden by assembling nude. Of course, most outsiders were convinced that their secret assemblies were scenes of wanton sexual orgies.

Medieval Adamites added a Joachimite element with their belief that they would begin the third age during which people would live in an earthly paradise. Christianity would disappear because its purpose was to control the imperfect souls that dominate the present age. Sin and all evils would not exist. The Adamites' most notorious trait was nudity, but some were accused of saying that Edenic innocence meant that they were incapable of committing sin, especially in regard to sex. Conrad Kannler, a German interrogated for heresy in 1381, proclaimed that in the new age not only could a man have sex with his mother or sister without sin, but that it would restore her virginity as well. He further declared that he had the right to kill all those who might try to impede the coming of the new age. The idea that the new Adam could kill to inaugurate the new age was not unique to Kannler, but it appears that few Free Spirits took up the call to violence. They suffered violence from the Church, however, as many were executed for heresy.

There is no question that the most important of the late medieval millennial movements, the Taborite wing of the Hussites, perpetrated violence. The Hussites, who appeared in Bohemia in the early fifteenth century, are noteworthy as the first popular movement influenced by university scholars. Jan Hus, for whom the movement is named, was a theologian at the University of Prague during the early fifteenth century. He was heavily influenced by John Wyclif, an Oxford scholar posthumously condemned for heresy in 1415. Wyclif was well known for his attacks on the papacy; he branded the institution itself and those who supported it as Antichrist. His millennialism did not extend to setting a date for the endtime, and he was sharply critical of those who did. Yet he did argue that papal behavior since the time of Innocent III was evidence that the final days were approaching. In particular the Great Schism with its two rival popes was proof enough. He also espoused the dominion of grace that became important for many later millennialists who regarded themselves as the saints of the last days. Authority and property belonged only to those in the state of grace, just as Adam and Eve had dominion over the world until they sinned and lost it. For Wyclif it meant rejecting the corrupt clergy's right to own property, hold authority, and perform the sacraments. Donatism was a major element of his theology, which also included renunciation of clerical property before the Church could be purified. Both were key doctrines of his followers, the Lollards, who endured despite active repression until the sixteenth century.

The marriage of Princess Anne of Bohemia to England's Richard II brought many Czech students to Oxford, and Wyclif's attacks on the papacy and the clergy resonated deeply among them. The higher clergy in the Bohemian Church, mostly Germans, controlled much of the property in the realm, and the papacy was imposing a heavy financial burden on the Czechs. A tradition of criticism of the papacy already existed among the Czechs. The leading Czech critic of the Church, Jan Hus, had not been to England, but he picked up Wyclif's thought from those who had returned. Ethnic antagonisms between the Germans in the University of Prague who opposed the call for reform and the Czech scholars who adamantly supported Hus joined with doctrinal disputes to create a volatile situation.

The situation ignited with Hus's excommunication in 1412 and the execution of several supporters in Prague. Hussite preachers issued calls to arms, declaring that violence was necessary to purge the Church of its German heretics and restore the true Church. In 1414 the Hussites significantly changed the ritual: They made the Eucharist available to the laity in both the bread and the wine, a practice that had disappeared in the twelfth century. They became known as Utraquists, from the Latin word for *both*. Hus was summoned to the Council of Constance in early 1415 to answer charges of heresy. He agreed to go under a pledge of safety offered by Emperor Sigismund. The council quickly found him guilty of heresy and had him burned at the stake despite Sigismund's pledge, which was ignored on the grounds that it was not permissible to keep faith with a heretic.

Hus's execution in July 1415 detonated violent outrage at the papal Antichrist and the emperor, his henchman. With the support of most of the Czech nobles, the Hussites proceeded to establish a national church free from the authority of the papacy and to implement the reforms proclaimed by Hus. For four years the reform of the Bohemian Church went ahead, little hindered by the growing divisions between the moderates and radicals within and the Catholic opposition. Then, Bohemian King Wenceslaus, under great pressure from the pope and his brother Sigismund, began to crack down on the Hussites. Their response was rebellion. Urged on by preachers, the more radical artisans and day laborers in Prague seized control of the city government, killing a number of royal officials. In the countryside peasants assembled in large groups on hilltops, following Jesus's admonition to flee to the mountains (Mark 13:14). One site south of Prague became identified as Mount Tabor, which an old tradition said was the place of Christ's transfiguration and the site where he would return to the world. Mount Tabor was the central focus of the radicals, who became known as Taborites. They believed in Utraquism, Donatism, apostolic poverty for the clergy, and the imminent Second Coming.

The Taborite meeting places became virtual cities as thousands of peasants flocked to them, abandoning their crops and obligations in their villages. This sparked a violent reaction from the nobles, who were losing their labor force. A pitched battle occurred in November 1419 with heavy losses for the Taborites. Meanwhile, the royalist Catholic forces, mostly German, retook Prague, and great numbers of radicals were expelled. The stage was set for an explosion of radical millennialism. The Taborites were convinced that the persecution proved that the tribulations of the last days had begun. Their leaders issued a summons for all the faithful who wished to be counted among the saints to flee from Babylon and assemble at Mount Tabor and four other places; in 1420 God would destroy the world and all those in it except for those in the five holy cities. The people in these cities were to share all things in common, and they handed over to their priests the goods that they brought with them. All persons were equal in the Taborite communities except for the difference between the laity and the priests, who preached and celebrated the Eucharist but had no other special rights or privileges. Wives were told to abandon their husbands if they refused to take refuge in the holy cities; that the admonition was phrased this way suggests that the Taborites had greater strength among women.

What made the Taborites different from nearly all prior millennial groups was their use of violence as an appropriate response to persecution, unlike most Spiritual Franciscans and Free Spirits who were committed to pacifism and quietism. John Capek, a Taborite priest, provided the theoretical support for chiliastic violence with tracts described as "more full of blood than a fish pond is of water."[3] The Taborites fiercely debated whether violence was permitted in their circumstances; some abandoned the movement when the decision was affirmative, but most accepted it without reluctance, perhaps even with relish. What could be sweeter than vengeance in the name of the Lord on those who had been repressing and persecuting the saints? In a practical sense violence was necessary because the thousands of people in the holy cities were running out of food, and they were forced to forage for it in their regions. More seriously, the Taborites faced the royal army as it moved through the Bohemian countryside in the spring of 1420. They found a captain of unusual brilliance in Jan Zizka, who has been called the only military genius of the Middle Ages. Using war wagons and the martial discipline created by religious zeal as the means for his infantry forces to fend off charges by the German knights, Zizka defeated the royalists repeatedly until his death in 1424.

While Zizka's army engaged in warfare, other Taborites followed the commands of their priests to wipe the sinners off the earth, as God himself demanded, with "the sword that punishes the ungodly with destruction" (Sirach 39:30). The failure of Christ to appear in 1420 led to the idea that he had indeed come but remained hidden, full of rage and retribution. According to the Taborites, he willed that the saints prepare the earth for his public return by cleansing the world of all sin and sinners, who were defined as all those who had not joined the Taborites. After a few years Christ would openly appear to take up his kingdom in glory. The living elect would then join with the resurrected saints in Paradise, where the saints would have children without pain or sin. The extent to which Taborites who were not in Zizka's army engaged in the murder of nonbelievers is difficult to determine, but there is sufficient evidence that those who were in the army slaughtered their defeated foes out of religious zeal as much as the bloodlust of battle.

The Taborite apocalypse, however, had not yet reached its furthest extreme. Word that the millennium was coming to Bohemia brought zealots from across Europe to the realm. A group of 40 Free Spirits mostly from Picardy in France arrived in 1418. These "Pikarti" brought their antinomianism with them; about 300 Taborites adopted it enthusiastically and became so radical that they were expelled from Mount Tabor. They became known as Adamites, accepted a blacksmith as their leader, and proclaimed him as the new Adam-Moses with the new Mary as his consort. According to sources for their beliefs and acts written by hostile authors, they apparently announced that they had returned to the innocence of Adam and Eve in Eden and spent much of their time naked. Free love was important to them, and monogamous marriage was deemed a sin. Not only was sex to be entirely communal, so was all property; no one was to own anything separately from the community. Because they were the elect, they had a right to everything in the world and freely robbed those not in their sect. Their attitude toward outsiders, however, went well beyond the dominion of grace; they deemed themselves God's agents to cleanse the world of sinners and slaughtered them. Adam-Moses supposedly gave them an injunction to kill sinners until blood filled the earth to the height of a horse's head. Christ would then return and set them up as the rulers of the world and encourage them to be fruitful and multiply.

Even the Taborites could not tolerate this violent chiliasm that was leading to massacres in Czech villages. In 1421 Zizka led a hand-picked band of soldiers against the Adamite stronghold on an island in a river. Although Adam-Moses claimed that God would blind their enemies, the Adamites were slaughtered. In the Taborite revolution, this event served as what later theorists of revolution call the Thermidorian reaction; that is, when most of those supporting change decide that the fringe elements have gone too far in attacking the established society. Supporters of change seek to consolidate the new status quo, but that proves difficult because the excesses of radicals (in this case, the Adamites) have galvanized the conservative elements of the society against moderate change. In fifteenth-century Bohemia, Zizka's death in 1424 cost the Taborites their best captain, and the moderate Hussites badly defeated them in 1434. The victorious Hussites then reached an accommodation with the emperor and the pope that allowed for Utraquism in the Bohemian Church while it remained officially in union with Rome. This situation prevailed until the Reformation began in the next century. There is ample evidence, however, that Taborite and Adamite beliefs continued to circulate throughout central Europe, providing a powerful stimulus to similar millennial movements in the Reformation era a century later.

VI

THE REFORMATION ERA: DON'T LET YOUR SWORD GET COLD!

T HE LEARNED HUMANISTS OF FIFTEENTH-CENTURY Italy knew little of the bloody events transpiring in Bohemia, but they too were influenced by eschatology although not to the point of violence. The humanist tripartite scheme of history involved the belief in a past golden age during the early Roman empire; an age of corruption in the Middle Ages; and a return to the golden age, which they were bringing about through their restoration of classical learning. While this idea of history owed more to ancient Roman authors than Christianity, the book of Revelation was never far from the minds of most Renaissance humanists. The cultural movement known as the Renaissance, while hardly a hotbed of millennialism, had its millennialists, who influenced the Protestant Reformers in their understanding of the endtime.

During the Renaissance, astrology became a respectable science of prognostication. The scholastic theologians had been quite dubious of its claims to foretell the future, but the belief that astrology came from ancient Egypt and Babylon gave it great cachet in the Renaissance. Astrological predictions of the end of the world became common by the late fifteenth century. Astronomical events such as the great conjunctions of Jupiter and Saturn were regarded as having special significance, and many expected a great conjunction of 1484 would mark the beginning of the endtime. When the year passed uneventfully, astrologers sought a new meaning for it. Since it nearly coincided with Charles VIII's succession to the French throne in 1483, astrologers declared that the conjunction had marked the coming of the new Charlemagne, who would defeat the Muslims as the first had done and establish the kingdom of God at Jerusalem. Charles himself seemed convinced of this destiny, as it became a factor in his decision to lead his army into Italy in 1494 to capture Naples as a staging place for his crusade.

One consequence of the First French Invasion of Italy of 1494 was the ouster of the Medici family from power in Florence as the French army marched past. This provided the opportunity for Girolamo Savonarola to rise to power in the city. A Dominican from Ferrara, he believed that 1484 marked a significant apocalyptic date, and he began a career as a millennial preacher. He came to Florence four years before Charles VIII arrived, preaching fiery sermons about the need for repentance before the endtime. He gained a large following in what then was surely the most sophisticated urban center of Europe. One of his themes involved the destruction of Florence before Christ's return, and the arrival of the French in 1494 seemed to fulfill the prophecy. That they left the city untouched hardly damaged Savonarola's reputation, and his prestige grew even greater. Upon the removal of the Medici, he controlled the government. Savonarola's millennial message then began to take the optimistic view that the city, once reformed and with Antichrist defeated, would become the new Jerusalem, the spiritual and temporal center of the world. Although some early Christians had identified the Roman empire as the New Kingdom, this was the first time that a specific state had been so designated. It began a powerful tradition of infusing millennialism with a political agenda and patriotism.

Although Savonarola had established himself as the dominant authority in Florence, he did not abandon his call for repentance. If anything, his cry became more insistent as he contemplated the role of his city in the Millennium. His strong puritanical streak became fiercer as he denounced gambling, sodomy, prostitution, and drunkenness. He focused on the clergy since he saw the need for reform was most urgent in the Church and the papacy. He did not repudiate papal authority but regarded the incumbent, the infamous Pope Alexander VI, as incorrigibly corrupt. His denunciations of Alexander caught the pope's attention, as did his alliance with the French against Alexander's anti-French league. In mid-1497 Alexander excommunicated Savonarola and imposed penalties on the Florentines for following him. Food shortages, riots, and an attack by the Medici made 1497 a dismal year in Florence. Savonarola responded by denouncing Alexander as neither pope nor Christian and stepped up his message of millennial urgency. By early 1498 most of Florence had turned against him. A botched trial by ordeal involving two followers led to his arrest, torture, and burning at the stake as a heretic. For his followers, his death only confirmed the wickedness of their time and the coming of Antichrist. Savonarolist predictions of the endtime continued for twenty years after his execution.

By the time the last of Savonarola's supporters grew silent, a new reform movement appeared in Germany. Its denunciations of the ills of the Catholic clergy were hardly more bitter than his but far more effective. When Martin Luther and early Protestants used the term Antichrist to refer to the pope, as he did in one of his earliest printed works, *Against the Execrable Bull of Antichrist* (1520), it meant they were convinced that they were living in the last days because the papacy was responsible for the great apostasy before the Parousia. For them, the signs of the coming endtime included the papacy's nonbiblical authority in the Church, proof of the manifest corruption of their era. Another sign was the success of the Ottoman Turks, obviously the hordes of Gog and Magog, in taking Constantinople in 1453 and most of the Balkans over the next decades. Important too was a prediction by many astrologers that the 1524 conjunction of all the major planets in the zodiac sign of Pisces, a water sign, meant that the world would end in a great flood despite God's promise to Noah.

Early on, Luther followed Erasmus in questioning Revelation's canonicity. The Dutch humanist argued in his Greek New Testament of 1516 that language analysis, content, and the testimony of early church fathers called into question whether John the Apostle wrote the book, but he accepted the consensus of the Church on keeping it in the canon. In 1522 Luther stated that he found nothing apostolic in Revelation and seemed ready to agree with Huldrich Zwingli of Zurich in arguing that it was not a book of the Bible. He later backed off his criticism and accepted it, although his opinion of it never rose very high. Luther's attitude toward Revelation says much about his eschatology, in which he was largely an Augustinian. Following Augustine, he noted that the Church had existed for over a millennium, and it was well past the time for Satan's unbinding, already evident in the corrupt state of affairs in Christendom. He perceived Antichrist as collective evil clearly manifested in the papacy. Luther was impressed by fifteenth-century prophecies that early in the sixteenth century a man would appear to reform the Church and overthrow the papacy. Because such a reformation was now underway and the true Gospel was being preached, the founding of the new Jerusalem had to occur soon. It was God's decision alone as to the time and place, and attempts to learn the date were blasphemous and dangerous. Yet the intractable refusal of the pope to accept reform, the decline into corruption of the Christian world, and the Turkish advances all helped to convince Luther that the end was close, certainly by 1600, a belief that became stronger as he aged.

Luther had reason to view apocalyptic date setting with alarm; not only did he know the history of the Hussites, but he also found millennial radicals in his own camp. It took little time for millennialists to appear in Wittenberg, partly because any loosening of control by the Roman Church immediately led to an outpouring of radical millennial beliefs, as it frequently had in the late Middle Ages. Radicalism was also a consequence of one of Luther's key principles, that the Bible should be available to the people in their own language, contrary to the Catholic position of keeping it in Latin and accessible only to the priest. Making the Bible available to the people, however, was a two-edged sword. While it sparked the enthusiasm of a vast number of people and committed them to Protestantism, it also opened the way to an infinity of interpretations of the Bible. Even the village idiot, not just the priest, was now free to form an opinion on such things as the meaning of the symbols in Revelation. Reading the Bible on their own or listening to a preacher who quoted it liberally brought the laity into real contact with Revelation for the first time. Catholic liturgy made little use of it except for All Saints' Day. Reading its striking imagery, denunciation of evil-doers, and predictions of the imminent endtime with its attendant terrors both thrilled and terrified those already convinced that the signs of the end, as given in popular lore, were all around them. The Gospels also contained much, especially in respect to justice for the poor, that the established Church had not made a prominent part of its message. Issues of justice attracted those prepared to go beyond Luther's stance on social and political change. The development of the printing press sixty years earlier provided not only Luther but any apocalyptic prophet the means to spread their ideas through thousands of cheap copies of their writings.

Thomas Müntzer emerged as the most outspoken of the radicals who immediately became associated with Luther, who just as quickly disowned them. Müntzer, well educated for someone with his modest background, knew Greek and Hebrew. He was a parish priest near Wittenberg when word of Luther's 95 Theses arrived. He responded by going to Wittenberg to earn a degree in theology. He soon disagreed with Luther, arguing that divine revelation had not ended in apostolic times and the Holy Spirit could reveal new truth to individuals such as himself. In the new Church, the Holy Spirit would instruct the elect directly. In 1520 Müntzer went to Zwickau, where he associated with a group of lower-class radical preachers called the Zwickau Prophets. Their attacks on the established order forced him out of the city in a year's time, and he traveled to Prague, where he made contact with the Hussites. His emerging doctrine of social revolution, recalling that of the Taborites, again forced him to leave. After a year traveling about eastern Germany, he settled in as preacher in the small Saxon town of Allstedt in March 1523. There his insistence on preaching without permission of the local authorities landed him in trouble, and Duke John of Saxony moved to silence him. Müntzer lost hope that the secular authorities would institute real reform, and he denounced their power and demanded its transfer to the common people who would do God's will. In August 1524, he escaped Allstedt by climbing over the wall at midnight and traveled to Mülhausen in Thuringia, where he gained political control.

By 1524 Müntzer had completed his transformation into the archetypal violent millennialist. His starting point was the parable of the wheat and the weeds (Matt. 13:24). Weeds (that is, evildoers) had sprung up in the Church once the apostolic era had ended. Now was the Holy Spirit's harvest time, and those in the Spirit had the task of separating the weeds from the wheat and restoring the Apostolic Church in preparation for the Parousia. Müntzer proclaimed that Hus and Luther were the early prophets for the Second Coming, but he was the final one. Early on he viewed the Turks as having a major role as the agent of destruction and predicted a catastrophic defeat at their hands for 1522. When that did not happen, Müntzer decided that God had chosen the princes to wield the sword against the godless. Quickly disappointed in them, he concluded that he had to take a direct role in bringing about the endtime: He would be God's scythe for his harvest.

Müntzer also preached another idea commonly found in radical millennialism: ownership of goods in common, which would be the state of the godly in the New Kingdom. He declared that the people's attraction to material goods kept them from possessing the Holy Spirit. Therefore, they had to follow the example of the first Christians and pool all of their goods in order to give to each according to need. On the other hand, Müntzer did not advocate free sex. The only purpose of sex among true Christians was procreating an elect child, and then only when a couple had received a revelation that such a child would be conceived. Any other use of sex turned women into whores. Those who gave free rein to sexual appetites were weeds in God's field.

When Müntzer arrived in Mülhausen, the German Peasants' Revolt was already under way. There are hints that some peasants elsewhere regarded themselves as acting to bring about the endtime, but only Müntzer and the band of rebels associated with him provide explicit evidence of that belief. Even before his arrival in Mülhausen, he had given ample proof of his conviction that the saints had to exterminate the godless in order to prepare the world for the New Kingdom. Now he had an audience ready to respond to such calls to violence. His followers organized the League of the Elect and adopted the rainbow on a white background as its banner. They installed a new "eternal" city council in March 1525, which instituted the community of goods and other elements of Müntzer's program. By then peasant violence appeared in the region. Müntzer, aware that the princes were organizing their forces, was driven to a frenzy. He wrote a letter to followers in Allstedt that is one of the most often cited examples of millennial rage: "At them, at them, while the fire is hot! Don't let your sword get cold! Hammer, cling, clang on Nimrod's anvil! Throw their tower to the ground! So long as they are alive you will never shake off the fear of men. . . . At them, at them, while you have daylight. God goes ahead of you, so follow, follow!"[1] He henceforth signed his letters, "with the sword of Gideon." In one letter he declared that only three men in the Holy Spirit would withstand 100,000, but whether he meant literally that three such men could defeat a huge force or that their presence in an army would be enough to lead it to victory is not clear.

Meanwhile, the men of Mülhausen and neighboring villages were busy pillaging castles and monasteries in the region. The local princes assembled their forces and marched to Frankenhausen where the peasants were gathered. For three days there was a standoff. Müntzer rallied his followers, many of whom were wavering at the sight of the enemy, with fiery sermons. God, he proclaimed, was about to cleanse the world of the weeds. At the end of his sermon on the third day, a rainbow appeared, and this apparition of Müntzer's symbol was taken as proof that God was on their side. Müntzer promised that God would protect them from the weapons of their enemies; he himself would catch the cannonballs in his sleeves. On May 26, 1525, battle was joined. The peasants marched into battle singing "Come Holy Spirit." When the first round from the princely forces fell short, Müntzer reportedly shouted: "Didn't I tell you God would protect us from harm?" Unfortunately for the peasants, their enemies soon found their range and the slaughter began. Müntzer was captured and beheaded three days later at Mülhausen. He left no sect to carry on his cause because he had not organized one and, more importantly, because so many peasants had been massacred.

There were, however, some survivors of Frankenhausen who carried on the message of violent millennialism. One was accused in 1528 of planning a popular rebellion in Erfurt in order to make it the new Jerusalem. Even more notorious was Hans Hut, a bookbinder, who proclaimed that the Second Coming would occur on Pentecost 1528, three and one-half years after the beginning of the Peasants Revolt. Hut preached that, with the peasants defeated, the sword should remain sheathed. He traveled about central Germany baptizing with the sign of the cross to identify the 144,000 elect. When Christ returned, he would put the sword in the hands of these saints who would cleanse the world of evildoers, killing all who refused to be rebaptized. He would then establish his kingdom, where there would be free love and a community of goods. Hut died in prison in 1527, but his followers in Esslingen were accused of seeking to bring about the Millennium by violence in 1528.

Müntzer's vast correspondence contains an exchange of letters with a group of Swiss radicals from Zurich. Conrad Grebel, the first leader of the Swiss Anabaptists, briefly regarded him as a kindred spirit, but Müntzer was not concerned about the issue of rebaptizing adults who had been baptized as infants, the defining doctrine of Anabaptism. Rebaptism rose out of the concept of the church as a community of true believers who make an adult decision to join. Had not the first Christians made such a decision and been baptized as adults? Grebel rejected the idea accepted by Catholics and most Protestants that a child at birth was automatically a member of a church coextensive with the state. A number of major consequences followed from requiring adult baptism. First, the Church consisted only of the elect, who were few in number; the traditional view that it included saints and sinners whom Christ would separate at the end of time was rejected. The saints must separate themselves from the children of darkness. Second, it required the separation of church and state. If the Church consisted of only a few true believers, then it was not synonymous with the state, whose purpose was to keep the sinners from destroying each other. It followed that true believers were not obliged to pay taxes, swear oaths, and perform military service. Third, Constantine had condemned rebaptizing as a practice of the Donatists and made death the punishment for it under Roman law. The radicals insisted that what they did was not rebaptizing because infant baptism was not valid; they usually called themselves simply the Brethren. Both Catholic and Protestant authorities called them Anabaptists to bring them under legal liability.

Although some previous groups had elements of Anabaptist views, Grebel and other leaders provided a more coherent theology for the concept of the gathered church of the saints, a concept of far greater appeal in the sixteenth century. The model for a community of true believers was the Apostolic Church, and the Anabaptists sought to emulate it.

Their practices included community of goods, a greater role for women, shunning of nonbelievers, a rigid moral code, and nonresistance to persecution. An adamant refusal to use violence was characteristic of most early Anabaptists, and in September 1524, Grebel and others wrote to Müntzer rebuking him for his call to violence. Anabaptists tried desperately to disassociate themselves from Müntzer but failed. Being identified with him gave the authorities added reason to administer a "third baptism," death by drowning.

Persecution enhanced the deeply held view of most Anabaptists that they were living in the last days. In itself the concept of the gathered church need not be millennial, but it almost always has taken that direction. The concept arises out of a literal interpretation of the Bible and its eschatological verses. Revelation provides much of the sanction for a gathered church, and Anabaptists were convinced that they were living in the last days, watching Antichrist gather his forces for the final assault on the truth. By separating themselves from the sinners, they could avoid the time of tribulation to be inflicted on evildoers. Predictions of the end appeared among the earliest Anabaptists. At St. Gall, where Grebel fled after his expulsion from Zurich in 1525, his preaching won many converts. Some began acting in ways that confirmed the worst fears of the authorities: speaking in tongues, engaging in free sex, seizing property, and predicting Christ's return. A prediction that the Parousia would occur on a Sunday in February 1526 reportedly persuaded 1,200 people to take to the mountains to wait for Christ. Soon Swiss authorities imposed the death penalty on the most outspoken of the Anabaptists, although Grebel died a natural death in 1526. Other Anabaptists scattered across central Europe, carrying their ideas to a wide audience, although many radical groups sprang up without Swiss influence.

As is obvious from the example of St. Gall, not everyone attracted to Anabaptism accepted all of Grebel's beliefs. Hans Denck, for example, proclaimed that faith and love permitted anything. Such antinomianism helped to discredit Anabaptism in the eyes of most people. Jakob Hutter, however, came close to establishing Anabaptism as a viable way of life. Influenced by the Swiss, Hutter worked to establish Anabaptist communes in Austria. Persecution forced him to flee to Moravia by

1533, where much of the local nobility was tolerant of the pacifist radicals. He took over leadership of a group of Moravian Brethren plagued by dissension and imposed discipline on it. His concept of the apostolic community required that both production and consumption of goods be done in common. Since child rearing was communal, the communities involved most adult women in producing nonhousehold goods, adding to their economic success. The hard work, discipline, and dedication of the Brethren allowed the communities to flourish. As many as 120 of them, with 200 to 400 members each, existed in Moravia around 1560. Although many factors went into an individual's decision to belong to such a community, the belief that members were the saints of the New Kingdom, already separated from the sinners before the Parousia, motivated many. There was little date setting among the Moravian Brethren, but like the first generation of Christians, they were convinced that the Parousia would be soon. The passages of years failed to dampen the enthusiasm of most Brethren, and their communities survived, despite frequent persecution, through migration first to Ukraine and then to North America. The Moravian Brethren are the most enduring of all apostolic communities.

The most influential of first-generation Anabaptists was Melchior Hoffman, a furrier about whose early life little is known. In 1523 he was preaching Lutheranism in Estonia but broke with Luther when he became convinced that he had received the Holy Spirit and the power of prophecy. An episode of image-smashing led to his expulsion in 1526 and he wandered about Germany until he arrived in Strasbourg in 1529. There he fell under the influence of Anabaptists such as Ursula Jost, a visionary who proclaimed the immediate Parousia. Hoffman declared himself the new Elijah, the first prophet of the endtime, and said Strasbourg would become the new Jerusalem in 1533. When the Holy Spirit was poured out on 144,000 saints, they would go about the world rebaptizing true believers. While the Anabaptists had to be pacifist and not take the sword themselves, Strasbourg and other German cities would come under the control of the saints and lead the final struggle against the emperor and the pope, agents of Antichrist. Hoffman's attacks on the emperor led to his expulsion from Strasbourg, and he spent three years spreading his views through the lower Rhine valley. In 1533 he returned to Strasbourg to await the Second Coming but was thrown into prison, where he died ten years later.

Hoffman had great success in gaining followers among the urban poor of the Rhenish and Dutch cities, where economic recession and bad harvests had created enormous stress. In such troubled times the promise of being among those who would receive eternal reward (described in highly materialistic terms), while the nobles, merchants, and prelates would be vanquished, was too powerful to give up easily, even when the year 1533 ended without the Parousia. Hoffman never did visit Münster, the German city just east of the modern Dutch border that would always be associated with his apocalyptic vision. It was one of many cities in Germany where the bishop served as both spiritual and temporal lord. During the late Middle Ages tensions between the town and the bishop had been severe and worsened with the arrival of Protestantism. Bernhard Rothmann, an ex-priest, served as the leader of the Lutherans in the city, but by 1532 he was advocating rebaptism. In preparation for a public debate with Lutheran theologians in August 1533, he invited several Dutch Anabaptist preachers to the city to bolster his cause. The result was a stalemated city council that refused to take action against the Anabaptists, and the city quickly became a refuge for radicals.

One such radical was Jan Bokelson, who arrived in Münster in January 1534. He proclaimed himself one of the twelve apostles of Jan Matthys, the new Enoch, who would be the second prophet of the endtime. A tailor by trade and self taught, Bokelson had traveled widely in western Europe. His forceful personality and political skill gave him a major role in the events that led to an Anabaptist takeover of Münster in February 1534. Word that the bishop was coming to retake control created an alliance between Lutherans and Anabaptists, who jointly issued a declaration of religious freedom for evangelicals and the expulsion of remaining Catholics. Rothmann sent a letter to all the cities and villages of the region announcing that Münster was the new Jerusalem where the temple of Solomon would be rebuilt. He invited the true believers to come there and avoid the vengeance of the Lord, since only Münster would be spared the coming destruction of the world. About 2,500 people accepted the invitation.

Matthys, a tall thin man with a long black beard, soon arrived at Münster, declaring that the coming Easter would mark the beginning of the end. He was a baker from Holland whom Hoffman may have converted to Anabaptism. He had left his wife for an ex-nun named Divara. On February 25 he declared to the Anabaptists that in order to build the realm of God, the godless must be purged from the city. Matthys advocated death for anyone who refused to be rebaptized with the mark of the *tau,* citing Ezekiel (9:1–10), in which God orders the death of all those in Jerusalem left unmarked. Opposition from several prominent Anabaptists persuaded him to accept instead the expulsion of the "godless." Two days later, armed men drove them out, forcing them to leave behind all they owned. All who remained were rebaptized in the city square. They now addressed each other as brother and sister, and the city was declared free of sin and united in love.

The expulsion of both Lutherans and Catholics persuaded the local Lutheran nobles to ally with the bishop against Münster. This new threat to the city led Matthys to appear in a church with two stone tablets on which he had written a message from God: Their city was the new Jerusalem, and the elect had a right to take the sword to defend it. Anabaptists in Münster quickly approved of violence since for the first time they had their own city to defend. Frenzied efforts were undertaken to strengthen the city for the attack of the enemy. When the siege began in earnest in March 1534, Matthys appointed seven deacons to gather up and distribute to the faithful all the goods, especially food, from the houses of those who had fled or been expelled. He soon instituted a complete community of goods. Because all in Münster must be one people, it was necessary to bring all their money together so that one person would have as much as another. Those who refused to hand over their money or deeds were locked in a church under armed guard for most of a day. When Matthys entered the church brandishing a weapon, they begged him to implore God for mercy. He responded that if they complied with God's will, they could return to the community. Nearly all did as he demanded.

On March 15, Matthys ordered the burning of all books except Bibles in a bonfire since the Bible was all that saints needed. He came close to clearing the city of all other books. He insisted sex be restricted to married Anabaptists. Adultery and fornication, defined as applying also to married people who were not Anabaptists, were capital offenses. An outspoken blacksmith declared that Matthys was inspired by the devil, not God. He was seized and taken before the community, and Matthys denounced him for defiling the pure city. The man was condemned to death with Matthys inflicting the fatal blow.

As the siege lines around Münster tightened in late March 1534, Matthys announced that he had received a command from God to drive the enemy away from the walls. On Easter Sunday, April 4, the appointed day of the Parousia, he led a band of men on a sortie, promising them that God would protect them from the enemies. He did not. Matthys was killed; his body was hacked to pieces; and his head hoisted on a pike. Jan Bokelson, Matthys's lieutenant, now took control of Münster. He had been an actor in street theater in his youth and his rule took on a highly theatrical content. His first act involved running naked through the city in ecstasy on May 3, then falling silent for three days. When he recovered his speech, he declared that God demanded the establishment of a new government based on that of the ancient Israelites, to consist of a council of twelve elders from the twelve tribes with complete authority over everything, including life and death. He also drew up a set of rules for the common life of the city based entirely on the Bible. Most notoriously, polygamy as practiced by the Hebrew patriarchs was mandated. There was a very serious imbalance of women in the city by April 1534, perhaps as high as three to one. Many former-nuns-turned-Anabaptists had migrated to the city, providing much of the zeal behind the radical leadership, and many of the Catholic and Lutheran men had either fled the city or had been killed, leaving their wives to fend for themselves. Bokelson felt the need to regularize this explosive situation. Yet it is clear that his own sexual appetite played a role. He took fifteen wives, none over age twenty, including Divara, Matthys's widow. Bokelson declared as absolute law the divine command in Genesis to be fruitful and multiply; no one of marriageable age in the city could remain single. Resistance to the new sexual code led to more executions, often of women who refused to be unfaithful to their absent husbands.

While Bokelson was busy turning Münster into the new Israel, and demonstrating thereby that religious zeal can turn a motley band of men and women into a competent fighting force, the bishop's forces besieging the city proved to be inept. A botched assault on the walls in August convinced Bokelson that the third age had truly begun. He declared himself king of the entire world with Münster as his new Jerusalem until Christ would come to accept David's scepter from him. The cathedral square was renamed the new Mount Zion while all the streets and gates were given biblical names. A new set of names was established for the newborn, with Bokelson choosing the name for each child. Coins were minted with the slogan "One King over all, One God, One Faith, One Baptism." Bokelson, now King Jan of Leiden, was the absolute lord of the new realm of the entire world. Complaints, many directed against the new king's luxurious court, were punished with death. In October 1534 it was announced that over the next several weeks there would be three blasts of the trumpet; at the sound of the third, everyone had to assemble on Mount Zion. They would then burst out of the city and wreak God's vengeance on the sinners outside, each ten of them would be capable of killing a thousand sinners. Once victorious, they would march to the Holy Land without hunger, cold, or want. When the third trumpet sounded and the people assembled, Bokelson, dressed in fine armor, rode up and chose officers to lead the army of saints. When all was ready, however, he announced that he was only testing the loyalty of his subjects. Since they had proven it, he invited them to a banquet.

Bokelson did not rely exclusively on divine aid. Apostles were sent throughout northwest Germany and the Netherlands urging Anabaptists to come to Münster or take over their own towns and villages. Several such attempts were brutally crushed, and princes throughout the empire became convinced of the need to cooperate with the bishop of Münster in destroying the threat. By early 1535 an effective siege was in place, cutting off the flow of food and reducing the city's population to starvation. A reign of terror, conducted mostly by immigrants fanatically loyal to Bokelson, kept the starving people from overthrowing their king. Two men escaped and revealed weak points in the city's defenses to the besiegers. On June 24 they broke through the walls, massacred the defenders, and captured Bokelson and Divara. The victors quickly beheaded her; they put him in a cage and exhibited him around north Germany until January 1535, when he was returned to Münster and tortured to death. The cage with his corpse was hung in the cathedral tower, where it remained for centuries.

The Münster Anabaptists provide the most extreme example of millennial violence in history. Their vision of the endtime led to several thousand deaths. The Münster Anabaptists exhibit nearly every feature in the life-span of a millennial cult, and they provide the first and perhaps best example of two of them. One is the role of a dictatorial cult leader with the power of life and death over his people, who does not have to follow the same rules as they did and enjoys the bounty of the earth while they live in apostolic poverty. Another is the idea that the saints of the Millennium will be the new Israelites living by the Mosaic law and under a Davidic king. The Münsterites, however, did not dress like the ancient Hebrews or follow their dietary laws as some later cults did.

The events in Münster inflicted a black eye on Anabaptism and seemed to justify the already harsh persecution of Anabaptists, encouraging the authorities to take stronger measures. Anabaptism was saved from possible extinction by the work of several theologians who returned to the quietist beliefs of its first adherents. The most important was Menno Simons, a priest who became an Anabaptist through the influence of Melchior Hoffman about 1531. Menno's brother had died in an attack on a monastery in Friesland inspired by Bokelson's apostles. This led Menno to condemn the call to violence although he would be identified as a Münsterite throughout his life and would never live in one place for long. He died in 1561. He rejected the idea that there would be a millennial king on earth before the coming of Christ, the one true king. His belief was similar to Hutter's in that a few saints made up the true church, which had to suffer persecution until the Parousia. Then they would be lifted up to enjoy life in the New Kingdom while the wicked would suffer the worst imaginable torments. By convincing most Anabaptists that suffering persecution by the wicked was a sign of their election, Menno was able to turn them away from violent resistance to the authorities. As a biblical literalist, he emphasized the statement that only God knows the day and the hour of the Parousia; the saints must wait patiently for it to occur. Thus, for over four centuries, Mennonites and the later Amish have lived as hard-working, productive, but nonconforming people within a society they reject.

The episode at Münster had another consequence besides forcing Anabaptists to return to quietist millennialism; it helped shape the thought of John Calvin, one of the most influential Christian theologians. His exile from France in 1534 was caused in large part by an episode in which a Zwinglian-inspired denunciation of the Catholic doctrine of the Eucharist was posted in King Francis I's château of Amboise. The king's violent reaction to this act, which occurred as the Münsterite revolution was unfolding, was motivated largely by the belief that the doctrine found on the placard was Anabaptist. Although Calvin had no known role in the affair, he fled France for Switzerland. Eager to show that he was not an Anabaptist, he dedicated the *Institutes of the Christian Religion,* the major statement of his beliefs, to the king. Calvin, one of the most consistent of Christian theologians, certainly would have given millennialism a limited place in his thought even without such a motive for downplaying it, but there can be no doubt he sought to reduce apocalyptic frenzy among his followers.

Calvin knew that the canonicity of Revelation had been disputed in the early Church and regarded it as having less authority than the Gospels. He cited it very little. There were, however, many texts with millennial views elsewhere in the Bible. Calvin agreed with Luther that the papal Antichrist exhibited the marks of the great apostasy to occur before the endtime, and that the reform of the Church was bringing about the final age of the world. He was less inclined to see current events as proof that the endtime would happen within a specific time frame. He avoided using the numbers in Daniel or Revelation to set a date for the Parousia, emphasizing its hiddenness, but he was convinced it would be soon. He deemed it blasphemous to suppose there was anything that humans could do to help bring it about, a clear refutation of the Münsterite position, except to repent and wait for God's mysterious will to bring about the events foretold in the Bible. Nor was there any sense of a gathered church in Calvin's thought. The weeds and the wheat will be in the Church together until the harvest time; only God knows who is which. Calvin was certain about one thing, however: The pope was Antichrist. Both Luther and Calvin conformed largely to Augustine's views on the endtime, but they made one major change. For them the events of the present, namely the ongoing reform of the Church, would bring about the Parousia. They put history back into millennialism.

Calvin's caution about millennialism had a restraining influence on his followers, but it was impossible to keep it under complete control, especially since he had jettisoned amillennialism. Millennialism was too much a part of both Scripture and Christian tradition to keep Calvinists from seeing persecution as evidence of the coming endtime and themselves as the martyrs of Revelation. In France the monarchy's repression of the Huguenots, as French Calvinists came to be called, caused an upsurge in millennialism among them that led to a wave of iconoclastic attacks on Catholic churches by 1560. The Huguenots concluded that the presence of the Catholic clergy and graven images in the churches provided evidence of Antichrist's pollution at work in the world. They could prepare the way for Christ's return by cleansing the world of that pollution. Huguenot millennial violence had a limited scope directed largely at images and priests.

The French Catholics had their own eschatological response to the presence of the Protestants. They saw the Huguenots as the pollution spread by Antichrist in the form of Luther and Calvin, which had to be cleansed before the Second Coming could occur. Thus, their response was more violent than that of the Huguenots and directed against the persons of the heretics who defiled society. The notorious St. Bartholomew's Massacre of August 1572 in Paris was so bloody—perhaps 3,000 Huguenots killed—in part because Parisian Catholics believed that they were acting to eliminate Antichrist's hordes and thereby would bring about the endtime. Paris would then be the place where the heavenly Jerusalem would come down to earth.

Millennialism was strong among Catholics in the late sixteenth century, even if there were no specifically Catholic millennialist groups. Many Jesuits, as sober and rational a group as found in the era, believed that their order was the new order of monks foretold by Joachim of Fiore. The Council of Trent reaffirmed the authenticity of Revelation and other books under challenge from the humanists and Protestants. The great nova that appeared in November 1572 agitated Catholics and Protestants alike, and it was followed by the great comet of 1577. Such extraordinary celestial events were always taken as signs of the impending end of time, and the anxiety that they created was compounded by the great conjunction of 1584. Conjunctions of Jupiter and Saturn occur every twenty years, but over a period of just under 800 years they follow a cycle through the twelve zodiac signs until one reoccurs in exactly the same spot in the same sign. The conjunction of 1584 occurred in Aries at the point astrologers calculated was the location of the two planets when the world was created. Extraordinary events such as the birth of Christ and Charlemagne's reign had occurred at previous such conjunctions. Considering other celestial signs, the miserable conditions in the world, and the belief that the world could not possibly last for another 800 years, this conjunction surely signaled the end of the world. Pope Gregory XIII's proclamation of a revised calendar in 1583 proved to Protestants that he was Antichrist, for Daniel (8:25) declared that the fourth beast would be guilty of "changing the times and the law." A Lutheran author took the pope to task for calling the new calendar perpetual and thereby denying the doctrine of the end of the world.

Among the Catholic peasants of north France, anxiety over the coming endtime led to an outpouring of devotion known as the "white processions." Thousands dressed in white shifts, singing, praying, and doing penance, took to the roads in pilgrimages to shrines and cathedrals in late 1583. Even King Henry III marched in one such procession in Paris. Millennial fear played a significant part in the events that unfolded in Paris over the next ten years. It had an important role in the Catholic League, organized in 1584 to oppose the succession of the Huguenot prince Henry of Navarre, who became the royal successor when Henry III's younger brother died that year, childless. The Leaguers denounced Navarre as Antichrist, and when the king arranged the assassination of the leader of the League in 1588, he also was denounced. The next year a zealous Leaguer in turn assassinated Henry III. Navarre, now Henry IV, laid siege to Paris over the summer of 1590, raising the millennial zeal to a fever pitch. The Leaguers declared Paris the new Jerusalem under attack by King Antiochus. The belief that they were fighting the hordes of Antichrist and that Christ would soon arrive to save them helped the Parisians hold off what was perhaps the worst siege in the city's history. Relief did come but in the form of Spanish troops sent by Philip II. The Spanish army stalemated the situation in France until Henry IV converted to Catholicism in 1593 and took control of the realm. Five years later he issued the Edict of Nantes granting toleration to the Huguenots. With the return of peace and stability, the monarchy restored its authority and set the foundations for royal absolutism. Millennialism had no place among the subjects of an absolute king ruling by divine right, and the Huguenots, looking to the monarch to protect their rights in the Edict of Nantes, muted their belief until Louis XIV revoked the Edict in 1685.

VII

THE PURITAN
REVOLUTION:
THE SICKLE OF
DIVINE JUSTICE

WHILE MILLENNIALISM AMONG THE FRENCH Calvinists was muted during their persecution, their English coreligionists demonstrated that Calvinism was not immune to exaggerated outbursts. It was once again a period of political instability—in this case, the Puritan Revolution—that allowed millennial fever to come to the fore. Although such major figures in English religious history as John Wyclif and John Foxe had made the endtime a major part of their theology, England had not seen much millennialism previously.

Foxe fled England during Mary Tudor's reign and spent time in Swiss Protestant cities. His beliefs about the endtime were common among mainstream Protestants of his era, who believed the two antichrists were the Turks and the pope. The use among the English of the pejorative term "the beast of Rome" became so widespread that to designate living creatures the word *animal* supposedly replaced the more commonly used *beast* because of the latter's evil connotation. According to Foxe, Satan had been allowed to persecute the early Church until the time of Constantine when he had been bound for 1,000 years. His unbinding coincided with the persecution of Wyclif and Hus by the Roman Church and continued to Foxe's day. Foxe's *Book of Martyrs* (1559) was intended to number the Protestant martyrs, particularly those executed under Queen Mary, among the 144,000 sealed of Revelation. He made no precise predictions about the duration of the persecution, but he believed that it would last about as long as the Romans persecuted the first Christians or until around 1600, although God could shorten the time.

The *Book of Martyrs* quickly became one of the most popular books in England. It provided a divine sanction for England's war with Spain's Philip II, Antichrist's tool, and promised that the Protestant cause would be victorious with God's help. England, land of the elect, would have a special place in the final victory over Antichrist, and it was easy to believe that the final battle would take place in England. Foxe's millennialism, moderately activist and compatible with Calvinism, appealed to the Puritans, those dedicated Calvinists determined to purify the Church of England of its corrupt Catholic practices. Doing God's work on earth to build the New Kingdom was a major part of the Calvinist worldview, and the Protestant view that Biblical prophecy was being fulfilled in the present encouraged the sense that the believers could play a role in bringing it about.

The Church of England under Elizabeth I was largely as it had been under Henry VIII, keeping much of its medieval tradition. The Puritans annoyed Elizabeth with demands that she create a truly Protestant church, but she handled them adroitly and kept them from becoming a political threat. The Puritans caused greater problems for her successors James I and Charles I, embroiling them in controversy over church policy. By 1629 they were a near-majority of the House of Commons. Faced with their demands, Charles dissolved Parliament and might have succeeded in removing Parliament as a check on royal authority had he not tried to force Anglicanism on the Church of Scotland in 1637. The Scots revolted, and Charles, lacking funds to crush the revolt, summoned the English Parliament in 1640.

The Puritans now controlled the Commons and refused new revenues for the king until he conceded on church policy. He did so and used the money granted him to put down the Scots' rebellion in 1641.

He then ordered the arrest of the Puritan leaders in Parliament, who took arms to defend the true religion. Millennialism surged among the Puritans, who identified themselves as God's elect facing the hordes of the papal Antichrist and his ally, the king. Once serious fighting began in 1642, the belief that this was the final showdown between the armies of Christ and Antichrist pervaded the parliamentary forces and helped to raise their morale and instill discipline. Led by Oliver Cromwell, Parliament's New Model Army defeated the royalists and captured the king in 1646. Put on trial in Parliament for treason against the English people, Charles was found guilty and executed in January 1649.

The fight against the king kept the Puritans united in their common cause, but once Charles was no longer a threat, divisions among them shattered that unity. The major division was between those who favored an official Church of England that was Presbyterian and those who wanted to disestablish the church and create independent churches of the saints, that is, gathered churches. Cromwell and most of his army were Independents, and the Puritans of Parliament were largely Presbyterians. Cromwell's success in taking control of the government in 1649 and four years later gaining the title Lord Protector of the Commonwealth put the Independents in power, but typical of revolutionary scenarios, the Puritan movement split into moderate and radical elements. The Independents' belief that each congregation had the authority to decide doctrine opened the way for radical interpretations of the Bible; and the stress and anarchy of the civil war meant that extreme millennialism could take root in England. The king's execution through legal proceedings, the first such event, signaled that a momentous change was taking place on earth. The end of the human monarchy demonstrated that the time was near when King Jesus, a favorite Puritan phrase, would come to take back his throne, if he had not already done so at the moment "the sickle of divine justice" had cut the king down.[1]

Over the previous half-century a vast range of prophets had predicted that the end of the world would occur soon after 1650. The year 1666 became a favorite choice, because it contained the number of the beast. It seems to have been first proposed by Heinrich Bullinger, Zwingli's successor at Zurich, who arrived at it by adding 666 to 1,000. John Archer, writing in 1642, found that the pope had gained power over the Church in 406, and that power was to last for 1,260 days. Since a day is a year for God, the papacy would be destroyed in 1666, but Christ's Second Coming would be delayed for a period of a jubilee of 49 years. Mary Cary, declaring that in the new age both men and women would prophesy, proclaimed that the Jews would be converted in 1656 and Christ would return in 1701. The noted mathematician John Napier, inventor of logarithms, used his skills to calculate that the seventh trumpet had sounded in 1541 and the events of the endtime would play out over the next 147 years (three jubilees) until Christ returned in 1688. His *Plaine Discovery of the whole Revelation of Saint John* was published in 1593 and was reprinted three times during the 1640s alone.

The most influential millennialist in England during the seventeenth century was Joseph Mede, a member of the faculty at Cambridge. His *Clavis Apocalyptica* (1627) calculated the beginning of the Millennium as the year 1736, based on the idea that it would happen 1,260 years after the end of the Roman empire in 476. Mede's work involved a thorough systemization of the symbolism and numerology in Revelation. He found that they applied to specific events of history; for example, the fifth of the seven trumpets represented the rise of the Muslims, and the sixth, the Turks. The seventh trumpet had not yet sounded. When it did, it would signal Armageddon, when the forces of God would destroy the papal Antichrist. Most millennialists, concerned about where Antichrist would find the forces of Gog and Magog to battle Christ, had looked to Asia, but Mede found them in America. Most descriptions of the Amerindians then circulating in England painted them as satanic savages, and it seemed logical for Antichrist to enlist them. Mede's view became standard in seventeenth-century England.

Mede also revived the old tradition, largely ignored since Augustine, that there will be a resurrection of the martyrs after Armageddon. They will reign with Christ over the New Kingdom for a millennium before the final resurrection and judgment. Then the wicked will be cast into hell for all eternity and the saints taken to heaven, while the world will come to an end. Mede's millennialism had the advantage of returning to the proper Biblical texts at a time when a literate laity was reading and debating Scripture. The English translation of his major works

in 1642 placed his ideas before a broad readership as the struggle between the Puritans and the monarch heated up.

Since that struggle involved political as well as religious issues,
such as questions concerning the nature of authority and who held it,
many of the radicals had a heavily political agenda. That was true of the
Levelers led by John Lilbourne, Cromwell's friend, who objected to his
policies after the king's execution. Lilbourne, an Independent, believed
that the Second Coming would happen soon, but until then, it was necessary to establish a just government in England. As the name Leveler
suggests, he proposed that all men twenty-one years or older with a
modest amount of property have equal rights, including the right of
electing members of the House of Commons, the only institution to
have authority, and the right to be elected themselves.

More radical than the Levelers were the Diggers. Gerard Winstanley, their leader, inspired by visions from the Holy Spirit, published *The
New Law of Righteousness* in 1649. He called his followers the True
Levelers because he wanted to extend the political franchise to universal adult male suffrage. Their better-known name came from his attempt
to create a community of goods in Surrey in 1651, in which its members
set to work tilling the soil in common. The same year, Winstanley, who
declared that he came from the Hebrew race, argued that humanity lost
its innocence when men began to buy and sell property, and thereby create distinctions among men based on wealth. If the land was free for use
by all and the world was restored to its "virgin state" by returning to the
communalism and equality of the early Church, it would set the stage
for the Parousia.

Even more millennially focused were the Fifth Monarchy Men.
More numerous than the first two groups and stronger in the New
Model Army, they caused more controversy and were deemed a greater
threat to proper order. Their name comes from the Book of Daniel,
where the destruction of the four beasts representing the four great empires of the world was foretold. The description of the last of the ten
kings of the fourth evil kingdom seemed to fit Charles I and his end
perfectly: "He shall speak words against the Most High, shall wear out
the holy ones of the Most High, and shall attempt to change the sacred
seasons and the law." At the appointed time, "The court shall sit in

judgment and his dominion shall be taken away, to be consumed and totally destroyed." After his fall, "kingship and dominion and the greatness of the kingdoms under the whole heaven shall be given to the people of the holy ones of the Most High" (Daniel 7:25–27). This everlasting kingdom was the Fifth Monarchy, where the saints would govern until King Jesus returned. In February 1649, a petition from high-ranking army officers demanded that Parliament and Cromwell act to establish the dominion of the saints in England and throughout the world.

Since Cromwell drew much of his rhetoric from apocalyptic texts, he was sympathetic to that idea, but he was also a practical man who had to deal with governing a realm. The Fifth Monarchy Men were influential enough to persuade him to hold an assembly in 1653 to consider the question of how the dominion of the saints could be instituted. Their proposals for reform were broad and far sighted. They wanted reform of the extensive abuses in the legal system, provisions for civil marriages, reductions in taxes and tolls, and elimination of the tithes the government collected from everyone for the church. This last proposal was favored by all the Independents since the tithes were the major link in the establishment of a state church. The Fifth Monarchy Men sought a Parliament elected from among the saints with an executive council of twelve men whose credentials as saints would be unimpeachable, while "mere worldly men" would have no rights. The saints would govern until King Jesus came to take his throne.

Cromwell and the more moderate Independents rejected these excessive demands, and he proceeded to establish the Protectorate. Soon the Fifth Monarchy Men denounced him as the beast of Daniel and called for his overthrow by the sword of the saints for usurping the place of King Jesus. In early 1657 the most militant Fifth Monarchy Men were involved in a conspiracy to create the rule of the saints through rebellion. Government informers made it easy to break up the conspiracy, and its leaders were imprisoned. After Cromwell's death in 1658 and the restoration of the monarchy in 1660, several Fifth Monarchy Men were hanged for their role in Charles I's execution; 400 others revolted in London in early 1661. Again the government easily quashed them, yet the Fifth Monarchy Men did not disappear from history. They took up the prediction that the Millennium would begin in 1666. One after another the most militant among them were arrested and executed for treason. When 1666 passed without the predicted end, the Fifth Monarchy Men gradually abandoned their militancy and turned into a quietist group patiently waiting for the Second Coming. Some migrated to America. As late as 1710 a small remnant could be found in Buckinghamshire.

The Fifth Monarchy Men hold a rare place in the history of millennialism, since they included men of great power and high status—two generals, several lords, and many members of Parliament, although artisans made up the largest group among the some 10,000 members. They pursued a millennial agenda at the highest levels of government and came the closest of any such group to implementing their ideas of how to bring about the New Kingdom. Their proposed reforms at the 1653 assembly contained numerous ideas eventually instituted in England and elsewhere.

While the Fifth Monarchy Men were mostly respectable in status and quite moderate in belief, the chaos of the Puritan Revolution also threw up the Ranters, their opposites in nearly every respect. They gained their name, a term of insult, from their practice of shouting outrageous comments about religion in the streets and public places. For example, one allegedly said the words of consecration over a cup of ale in a tavern: "Take and drink, for this is my blood." Because the name was used by their enemies and most of what we know about them comes from hostile sources, it is difficult to describe their beliefs and activities with any certainty; the problem of identifying those who can be considered Ranters is no less difficult. The lack of any sort of organization or clear leadership further compounds the problem. The most that can be said is that there were individuals who held similar views and gathered in small groups whose behavior outraged those who came into contact with them, including that gentle soul George Fox, leader of the Quakers. There were some Ranters in the New Model Army who were cashiered for ranting, and some had been Puritan ministers. Most came from below the midlevel of English society, which injected an element of class antagonism into their attacks on established society.

The starting point for what is a mostly incoherent set of beliefs attributed to the Ranters is the Second Coming of Christ and the new age of the spirit. For the Ranters, the new age has already been established; as believers, they are living in the spirit and have been freed from law and traditional religion. Their denunciation of religion was particularly scandalous to their contemporaries, who regarded it as atheism. One Ranter was indicted for saying that he would trade all religion for a jug of ale; another, for affirming that there was no God ruling above the heavens except the sun that shines on all. They combined antinomianism with a vague pantheism—nature is divine—to argue that not only were they above the law but also they were uniting themselves directly to God by doing what the law forbade. God inspired all the acts of those in grace, and to declare an act sinful for them was to attribute sinfulness to God himself. There was neither good nor evil in anything the true believer did. To be free from sin, one had to do the act deemed sinful until the belief that it was wrong disappeared. Such views led to all sorts of unsociable behavior, but the Ranters were accused of transgressing social norms most blatantly in regard to sex. They were accused of proclaiming that adultery, fornication, and incest were not sins and of practicing what they preached by participating in the nude in their assemblies that ended up as orgies. To what extent all those who were called Ranters actually believed these ideas and acted accordingly is impossible to say, but there is adequate evidence to show that some did.

Similar to the Ranters in a number of key respects and beliefs were the Quakers. The Quakers came from about the same level of society but were more rural in origin. Many had been involved in protests against the tithes early in the Puritan Revolution, and a good number served in the New Model Army. The Quakers believed salvation came through the presence of the Inner Light of the Spirit in the soul. The ecstasy of the Spirit's presence moved them to quake and tremble rather than shout and rant. They also had little respect for traditional Christianity and regarded themselves equal to the Bible as sources of truth. All the radical sects gave greater opportunity to women since the concept of an adult commitment to a gathered church required that women as well as men make that decision for themselves. (One of the major issues for such sects was the presence of many married women whose husbands had not joined.) They also believed that God could inspire prophetic visions in a woman as well as a man. Among the sects the Quakers provided the

greatest role for women, an equal one, as preachers, prophets, and proselytizers: Paul's dictum that women be silent in church had passed away
for those in the Spirit. Certainly, the Quakers were regarded as odd and
even dangerous by their neighbors, but they were not antinomian. They
made a strong effort during the 1650s to distinguish themselves from
the Ranters but were not always successful in the minds of the larger
population. Some occupied the fringes between Ranter and Quaker;
going naked as a sign of conversion, for example, was common among
the first Quakers. Their morality largely coincided with that of the Puritans, but they did have peculiar traits that marked them as Quakers, especially their insistence on plain dress and speech and their refusal to
take oaths.

George Fox and his followers, perhaps 40,000 strong by 1660, were
as convinced as the Ranters that the new age had already been established. Christ had returned in the Spirit to those of the first Christian
generation, was returning to the true believers of their own era, and
would come in the future to some of those who had not yet received
him. Christ comes to wage war with Satan, but it is largely a spiritual
war fought within each person because Antichrist is present in everyone,
although Satan's minions use physical violence against the saints. Although many early Quakers had fought against the king, Fox denounced
the Fifth Monarchy Men for their violent rebellions and after 1660 introduced the principle of nonresistance. The Quakers believed that at
some point in the future the world would be transformed and the Resurrection and Last Judgment would take place, but they had little to say
about it. They emphasized what was presently in the heart of the individual. Such an approach had the advantage of avoiding date setting,
and that, along with their nonviolence, helps to explain their survival to
the present.

The millennial fever of the era of the Puritan Revolution had a long
lasting impact on the national consciousness of the English people and
on America through the many Independents who migrated to the English colonies. The great literary men of the time also reflected the per-
vasive interest in millennialism. Greatest among them was, of course,
John Milton. Mede had taught him at Cambridge, and he also drew
heavily on the ideas of John Foxe. He believed fully in the idea that

England would lead the fight against the papal Antichrist and that the prophecies applied especially to England, which after Christ's victory would become the seat of the New Kingdom. Although his great poems *Paradise Lost* and *Paradise Regained* have limited millennial content, his descriptions of Christ, Satan, the Resurrection, the Last Judgment, heaven, and hell have had perhaps as much impact on the popular imagination of the English-speaking world as the Bible itself.

After the Stuart Restoration in 1660, millennial fever declined significantly in England, although there were still so many millennialists in the realm that works dedicated to setting the date for the Second Coming continued to come off the presses through the rest of the century. An intriguing example involved the prophecies of Mother Shopton, an obscure Yorkshire visionary, which were reprinted over twenty times prior to 1700. Her prediction for the endtime appeared in a couplet:

> The world to an end will come,
> In sixteen hundred and eighty-one.

When that failed to come true, the couplet was "discovered" to have originally read:

> The world's end we'll view,
> In sixteen hundred and eighty-two.[2]

English millennialism shifted considerably under the influence of a German visionary, Jakob Boehme, who used the term *theosophy,* divine wisdom, for his views. A self-taught shoemaker who died in 1624, he experienced an ecstatic vision of God in 1600. The vision revealed God as penetrating all existence, even the abyss of nonbeing. The human soul, composed of the fire of divine essence, was imprisoned in darkness. Nonetheless, it was possible to gain mystical union with the divine light and understand the wisdom of God; Christ's role was showing how that could be done. Having Christ in oneself eliminated the need for churches, although attending their services was permissible. Thus, true Christians did not have to separate themselves out from others. While it has always been attractive to many to distinguish themselves openly as the saints, others prefer to remain discreet in their belief. Boehme designated seven stages of time, and the last, the age of Enoch, will see the eternal victory of good over evil, peace over war, love over wrath, happiness over sorrow, and a return to Adam's lost perfection.

In 1644 several of Boehme's works were translated into English, in time to influence the more mystical and perfectionist sects during the Puritan Revolution, in particular the Quakers. His impact, however, was greater after 1660, when quietist millennialism returned to vogue. Among those influenced by his writings was Jane Leade, a widow with four children, who published *The Heavenly Cloud now Breaking* in 1681. She believed that the Parousia and the establishment of the glorified Church on earth was close at hand. One disciple placed the date in 1697; another claimed that the new Jesus had just been born in Germany. Leade organized her followers into the Philadelphia Society, after the perfect church in Revelation. The word *society* is important because she did not regard herself as forming a church; most members remained in the Church of England. At their meetings, similar to those of the Quakers, the members sat silently until the Spirit moved them to speak but without the ecstasy of the Quakers. When Leade died in 1703, her movement had more disciples in Germany than in England, and German Philadelphians migrating to the colonies brought her thought to America.

If it is true that the English Civil War created the conditions for an outpouring of millennialism, then it should have also permeated Germany during the Thirty Years' War, a far longer and more destructive war. Surprisingly, there was little. Despite the anarchy and chaos of the war, the Lutheran and Catholic Churches remained the established churches, which have always worked diligently to subdue millennialism. Certainly, there were comments from those caught up in the destruction of the war that these events had to be the trials before the Second Coming, but few Germans attempted a systematic exploration of millennial ideas, and no sects appeared with obvious millennial inspiration. The German Calvinist Johann Alsted published a book in 1627 that calculated the Parousia for 1694, but it was probably more influential among English Puritans than the Germans. The most noteworthy German millennialist in the seventeenth century after Boehme was not born until after the war ended. Quirinus Kuhlmann, born in 1651, believed that Germany had been chosen as the place for the Fifth Monarchy and the focus of the universal renewal that would take place after the Second Coming. Like Boehme, he spoke of returning to Adam's forgotten life in paradise on earth. Because corruption had existed in the Christian churches since apostolic time, they must be destroyed before the New Kingdom could be established. He spent most of his adult life traveling about Europe seeking to convince the princes to prepare for Christ's return by handing over power to the Lord's prophets. He made his way to Moscow to persuade the czar and paid for his audacity with his life in 1689.

Although he had some influence on the Russian sects, Kuhlmann found a hostile reception for his millennial teachings from the Russian government because the Russian Orthodox Church was then beset with its own millennial crisis. Millennialism was relatively uncommon in the Eastern Church. To be sure, Russian monks in the late Middle Ages often regarded their monasteries as places of transition toward the new world of the Parousia, and the Turkish conquest of Constantinople in 1453 was so catastrophic an event that it had to be given an apocalyptic interpretation. Since most Orthodox Christians set the creation in 5508 BC and expected a span of 7,000 years until the end of the world, the fall of Constantinople occurred very close to the endtime, namely 1492. When that year passed uneventfully, the Russians developed a new millennial theory. The first holy city, Rome, and the second, Constantinople, had fallen because their people had been unfaithful. Now Moscow had become the third Rome, the repository of true religion. The millennial content of the idea was perfectly expressed in 1511 by a Russian monk in a letter to the grand duke of Moscow: "Two Romes have fallen, but the third will last, and there will not be a fourth one."[3] Its task would be to keep Antichrist in check until the Parousia. This idea made millennial date setting more common in Russia.

The year 1666 loomed close enough in the future to be chosen as the endtime by some sixteenth-century authors, and in the mid-1600s it received greater meaning because of events in the Russian Church. In 1647 the *Seven Words on the Second Coming of Christ* by Ephrem the Syrian, a fourth-century theologian, was printed in Moscow in

Russian. It had a powerful impact with its pictorial representations of the endtime. Then in 1653, Nikon, the new patriarch of Moscow, introduced a number of changes in the liturgy and prayers to put the Russian church in conformity with the Greek church. The most visible change required that the sign of the cross be made with three fingers instead of the traditional two. Although the outcry against the changes was widespread, by 1666 ecclesiastical penalties had reduced the opponents to a small group of diehard clerics. The supporters of the old belief, called *Raskolniki* from the word for schism, became convinced that the Russian Church's falling away from the truth was the sign of the coming of Antichrist, who for some was Patriarch Nikon. He was accused of seeking to become the pope of Russia, a charge that carried as clearly an antichristian connotation for the Russians as it did for the Puritans; there was a long Russian tradition of denouncing the Roman Church as antichristian. The new sign of the cross was denounced as the mark of the beast, and other changes in the liturgy were found to be the abomination of desolations. When in 1666 Czar Alexis sided with Nikon and used his power to enforce the changes, the dissidents took it as clear proof that the time of tribulation had begun, especially since the numerology of the names of Alexis, Nikon, and a third prominent supporter of the changes added up to 666. The czar's involvement also brought into the dissident movement many peasants who deeply resented the government, which taxed them heavily and had reduced them to serfdom. The ousting of Nikon from power in 1667 failed to halt the growth of the Old Believers.

The stronghold of the Old Believers was the Solovetskii monastery on an island in the White Sea. Opposition to the new liturgy led its monks to rebel in 1667, and government forces put it under siege. As usual during a siege, the fervor of those besieged was raised to a fever pitch. They designated 1669 as the date of the Parousia, and monks escaping from the island carried the idea across Russia. Many Raskolniki, convinced that the end was at hand, gave up their daily activities to prepare for it. The failure of that prediction did not end the movement, of course; it continued to spread. After a siege of eight years, Solovetskii monastery was taken and its defenders massacred, but that only provided martyrs for the cause. As time passed, the issue of Raskolniki leadership became a problem. No bishop joined and many of its priests were dead. Although the sect divided into a myriad of groups demonstrating the whole range of possible interpretations of the endtime, there were two main groups: the Priestly, who were willing to accept priests ordained by bishops in the established church provided they underwent a purification rite, and the Priestless, who rejected such a compromise and thus wound up without clergy. With laymen, usually peasants, taking over the functions of the priests, the Priestless became ever more radical in their beliefs. They took a Donatist position in regard to the Orthodox clergy and their sacraments, and without priests, they could not administer the sacraments and had to insist that their members not marry. Since many Priestless could not remain celibate, they accepted concubinage, which gave rise to accusations of sexual license. The matter of sexual relations was the only point on which they approached antinomianism. They rebaptized those who joined their movement from the Orthodox Church. The Priestless also began to form communal villages, mostly in the region bordering Finland. Without any sort of clerical authority they began to split, over the issue of marriage in particular, into a vast number of sects by the end of the eighteenth century.

The most severe persecution of the Old Believers took place during the regency of Princess Sophia, Peter the Great's older sister. In 1682 she attended a church synod where Old Believer leaders denounced Nikon's reforms. She realized that they were calling her father and grandfather agents of Antichrist and responded with fury. She issued an edict in 1685 denouncing all Old Believers as heretics and rebels, and ordered a severe repression of them. Numerous Raskolniki leaders were tortured and burned. Their followers became convinced that the endtime was rapidly approaching since there were again martyrs for the true faith, just as in Revelation. Certain of the rapid approach of the Second Coming, many Old Believers began to search for martyrdom so that they would be numbered among the saints of the Lamb: When the number of the sealed reached 144,000, then Christ would return. They openly confronted the government, often by occupying monasteries, making it impossible for authorities to ignore them.

Not all of the Raskolniki, however, won the crown of martyrdom; some apostatized under the threat of death, and the government simply failed to execute others. The solution to these problems was suicide: "Let us baffle Antichrist." To die by one's own hand in defense of the true faith was deemed to be true martyrdom worthy of the Lamb. In 1688–89 there were incidents in which Old Believers under attack set themselves on fire as the troops closed in on them. The most notorious episode involved a monastery north of present-day St. Petersburg, where some 1,500 persons committed suicide as troops assaulted the walls in November 1688. Popular legend attributed even larger numbers of suicides to two more episodes. In 1689 Peter I took power from his sister and largely ended the persecution of the Raskolniki. He saw no value in killing his subjects for matters of so little importance. This did not earn him the gratitude of the Old Believers, for whom any czar was surely Antichrist. His irreligious attitude and extensive reforms also led many in the Orthodox Church to denounce him in the same fashion. He weathered their rage with no ill effects.

The late seventeenth century also saw a surge in messianism within Judaism. It was the most substantial one between the fall of Masada in 73 and the creation of the state of Israel in 1948. A long tradition among the Jews had set the coming of the Messiah for 1648, that is, the year 408 (from the numerical value of the Hebrew letters for "this year") of the sixth millennium since the creation. Coincidentally, the Cossack revolts in Ukraine in 1648 saw the worst outbreak of violence against Jews since the Black Death. For many Jews the massacres confirmed the approach of the Messiah, for they were the messianic woes that heralded his coming. A report by Antonio da Montezinos, a Portuguese who had returned to Judaism, that he had found the lost tribes while exploring the region of modern Colombia led Manuel Dias Soeiro, a Dutch rabbi of Portuguese background, to publish *The Hope of Israel* in 1650. Soeiro argued that the uncovering of the hidden Jews was clear evidence that the Messiah's coming was close at hand.

The major claimant to messiahship came from Greece. He was Sabbatai Sevi, a rabbinical student who at about age 22 fell into a deep depression when he heard about the 1648 massacres. In that condition he received a vision in which God told him he was the savior of Israel, who would gather his people from the corners of the world in Jerusalem. Filled with the spirit of God he made strange utterances and behaved so oddly that he was deemed mad. Banished from his native Izmir in 1651, he spent the next years wandering about the eastern Mediterranean region, reaching Palestine in 1665. There he quickly won the allegiance of many Jews but was expelled from Jerusalem at the end of the year by its council of rabbis.

By then Sevi had accumulated a following and a set of perfectionist doctrines. Most notably he proclaimed a new code of law and set of rituals through which the world would reach perfection. Not only was his attitude toward traditional Jewish law antinomian, he also proclaimed himself freed from sexual restraint: "Blessed is he who is permitted things forbidden." Sevi dispensed new names and noble titles to his followers, who, in the cities where they were strong, took over the synagogues, often by force. Some of his followers advocated violence in order to establish the new messiah's authority. Although the movement never became revolutionary, it came close to matching Christian millennial cults by abandoning traditional sexual morals and relinquishing property and positions in expectation of the end of the world.

Sevi's expulsion from Jerusalem had been a serious blow to his frail psyche, and he began to falter in providing leadership to his followers. Had not Nathan of Gaza, a prominent rabbi, supported him at this point, his movement would have certainly sputtered out after a few years, with no more impact than many similar self-proclaimed messiahs in earlier Jewish history. Nathan accepted Sevi as the Messiah in 1665 and immediately provided both intellectual and organizational leadership to the movement. He has been called Sevi's Apostle Paul, and the tag is appropriate enough, since his writings provided cohesiveness and purpose to Sevi's teachings. He also played a major role in spreading the movement across Europe and North Africa. Nathan, however, had to deal with a crisis of the sort that Paul never faced: Sevi, imprisoned in Constantinople in 1666, announced that he had converted to Islam! Nathan responded to this unprecedented apostasy by a cult leader by declaring that Sevi had joined the enemies of God to bring them into his people. Perhaps unintentionally, Sevi seemed to confirm that proposition by appearing in public with both the Qur'an and the scrolls of the Mosaic law. He also continued to practice many of the Jewish rituals and feasts and, as a result, fell in and out of trouble with the Turkish authorities. His behavior became ever more strange, and his antinomianism in regard to sex became more obvious. He fathered a child with the bride of a rabbinical student and claimed that he could have intercourse with virgins without deflowering them.

In 1676 Sevi led a group of followers in taking over the minaret of a mosque in Adrianople at midnight and from there delivered an address proclaiming it was time for him to lead the Jews to Jerusalem to reestablish divine order. Muslim fury at this act only subsided when he died later that year. Nathan of Gaza, who died four years later, declared that the Messiah had not died but had gone into hiding to return at the right moment. This satisfied most of the Sabbatians, who continued to believe in Sevi as the Messiah. The movement was similar to early Christianity in that it demonstrated much the same range of responses, from those who practiced traditional Judaism but believed in Sevi as the Messiah to those who followed his new law fully. The latter remained few in number. Nonetheless, Sabbatianism had its appeal across the Jewish world and especially in eastern Europe where Jews were facing violence. It lingered there long after it disappeared from the eastern Mediterranean. In 1699, for example, two Sabbatian leaders from Germany and Poland coincidentally led Jews to Palestine to await the Messiah.

News about Sabbatai Sevi and his claim to be the Messiah reached Christian millennialists as well. Some argued that his appearance confirmed the approach of the Parousia because he was one of the false prophets preceding Antichrist. Others were indignant that Jews would put their faith in a Jewish Messiah, thereby delaying Christ's return, since they had to convert to Christianity first. The conversion of the Jewish people was never far from the minds of Christian millennialists, and some, like the Puritan Increase Mather in the early seventeenth century, eagerly sought out news of Jewish conversions. Mather was born in America, where many millennialists discovered the Ten Lost Tribes of Israel. The discovery of the New World provided both new challenges and opportunities for millennialists.

VIII

MILLENNIALISM IN
THE NEW WORLD

B Y 1700 EUROPEANS HAD GAINED CONTROL over most of the Americas, thereby providing millennialism with new images and symbols and another theater of operation. Taking the discovery in stride, millennialists easily incorporated the existence of unknown lands and peoples into their explanations for the flow of time. It was highly fitting that in his voyages to the Indies, Christopher Columbus was inspired by the belief that he was acting out a scenario for the endtime. The New World served as the focus of millennial visions and would become the site of the largest number of millennialist groups in the centuries since 1492.

Columbus was immersed in fifteenth-century millennial expectations. As an Italian who spent most of his life on the Iberian peninsula, he was well aware of the advances of the Ottoman Turks in the Mediterranean and believed, as did others, that their victories made sense only as the work of Antichrist. Like the Portuguese explorers before him, he was eager to gain the wealth of the Orient and make alliances with non-Muslim peoples to defeat the Turks. He collected millennial predictions and claimed that Joachim of Fiore inspired him to work for the Spanish rulers through a prophecy (actually from the pseudo-Joachimite *Book of Prophecies*) that the Christian reconquest of Palestine would happen through Spain. In his own *Book of Prophecies* (1501), dedicated to Ferdinand and Isabella, he argued that his successful voyages revealed the Lord's hand in support of the goal of restoring Mount Zion to Christian control. The monarchs' conquest of Granada and their expulsion of the Jews, which would soon lead to their conversion, were also necessary before Christ would return. Columbus provided money in his will for a fund to finance the liberation of Jerusalem and called for using the wealth of the lands he explored for rebuilding the Temple. He predicted that his life's work would lead to the restoration of the world and the new age. In a letter from 1500, he acclaimed himself "the messenger of the new heaven and the new earth of which [God] spoke in the Apocalypse of St. John . . . and he showed me the spot where to find it."[1] He declared that the endtime would occur 7,000 years after the Creation, or 155 years after he wrote because now the gospel could be preached to all the nations and in all tongues.

Columbus and other early explorers opened up to the Europeans an unknown world that had to be assimilated into millennial theory. The first response of some Europeans proposed that it fulfilled the prophecy, "And there was a great multitude that no one could count, from every nation, from all tribes and peoples and languages, standing before the throne" (Rev. 7:9). Its clearest expression came from the superior-general of the Franciscans in 1524 when he dispatched 12 friars, the first group of missionaries in Mexico, to convert the newly conquered Aztecs. He admonished them that they were preparing for the Parousia by bringing the gospel to the ends of the world. For others, however, the existence of unknown peoples created a major problem; Augustine and most medieval theologians, citing numerous biblical texts, had denied the possibility of human habitation outside of the known lands. Perhaps they were from Antichrist, the hordes of Gog and Magog.

Once it became clear that the peoples whom Columbus called Indians were both human and an unknown race, it became crucial to Europeans to account for them within the traditional framework. The common solution was to identify the natives with the Ten Lost Tribes of Israel that had not returned to Palestine after the Babylonian captivity. The old explanation was that they had disappeared into Asia, but they had not been found there despite trips by many Christians across Asia in the previous 300 years. Great effort went into identifying the characteristics that the ancient Hebrews and Amerindians had in common and explaining away their vast differences. (Some scholars worked just as hard to refute the theory.) The idea had the appeal of not only explaining what had happened to the lost tribes but also providing evidence that the Parousia was approaching. Since John of Patmos included the lost tribes among the 144,000 sealed, the endtime could not occur until they became Christian. Converting the Amerindians would result in the fulfillment of the millennial prophecies.

The legend of Quetzalcoatl was one piece of evidence for the belief that the Aztecs were the lost Hebrews. Quetzalcoatl was the Aztec god of the arts and morality, but he was not originally Aztec. He was an important figure in the pantheon of the Toltecs, the people whose land the Aztecs had occupied several centuries earlier. According to Toltec legend, he had been a saintly king/god who provided all good things to his subjects in great abundance. Evil spirits conspired against him and tempted him with worldly things. Quetzalcoatl succumbed to these temptations and, ashamed at his failure, went into self-imposed exile. He promised that he would one day return to reclaim his homeland and, boarding a raft, sailed eastward across the sea. After his departure his city fell into ruin, and the Aztecs descended from the north to conquer the Toltecs and central Mexico. The Aztecs dreaded his return, for he would end Aztec society by reclaiming his throne. Comets, floods, and famines would herald the coming catastrophe. Aztec history was cyclical, and one common calculation for the end of the cycle placed it in 1519.

Quetzalcoatl was usually described as white in appearance. Rumors about white beings in houses floating on the sea began to reach the Aztecs at about the same time as omens foretelling their destruction appeared in increasing numbers. For example, voices were heard in the night lamenting, "Oh my children, your destruction is at hand." Only constant warfare and human sacrifice would help to preserve their world. The Aztecs captured males from surrounding tribes for the needed sacrifices; other victims were obtained by tribute levied on subject tribes. When the Spaniards under Cortes landed in 1519, most of the subject peoples were alienated from Aztec rule and eager to aid the newcomers. Their support was a major factor in the easy Spanish conquest of the Aztec empire. As important, however, was the Aztec belief in Quetzalcoatl, especially on the part of their last emperor, Moctezuma II.

He refused to use his forces to prevent Cortes from marching toward Tenochtitlán but prayed and sacrificed to keep away the returning god. When that failed, he welcomed Cortes into the city. In short order Moctezuma was dead and the Spanish controlled his empire. Its fall is an intriguing example of how an eschatological myth can lead to its own fulfillment.

For many Spaniards, this legend proved that the Aztecs were the lost Hebrews. The Dominican friar Diego Duran's valuable source on Aztec society, *History of the Indies of New Spain,* was written to prove it. He argued that the Aztec legends about their arduous journey to central Mexico, a tower that the gods threw down, and the coming of a promised savior from the east really came from the Old Testament. The legends had been distorted over the centuries as the Hebrews/Aztecs fell into paganism and sorcery. Because of their sins, for which they lost the right to their lands (thereby justifying the Spanish conquest), they turned the coming of the messiah into something to be dreaded. Once the Aztecs converted to Christianity, the return of the messiah would soon occur.

There is no question that the Aztecs and all the natives of Mexico endured a time of tribulation after the Spanish conquest. Newly introduced European diseases ravaged them and drastically reduced their population; slavery and servitude were the lot of most who survived. Most Spanish missionaries, while they believed the spread of disease was punishment for paganism, opposed enslaving the Indians. They saw the Spanish conquistadors bringing their vices into a land that they wanted to turn into a Christian commonwealth free of the evils of their native Spain. Franciscans in particular regarded themselves as the new apostles recreating the primitive church among the Indians, whose simple ways and innocence they contrasted sharply with the wicked sophistication of the Spaniards. The ideal of apostolic poverty had not disappeared entirely from the Franciscan order, and there was hope that it could be implemented in Mexico, provided the friars were given a free hand to convert the natives and direct their lives. Mexico City would become the new Jerusalem, the focus of the Joachimite third age. When conversion of the Indians was complete—and the friars could only regard it as a miracle that it was happening as fast as it was among the Aztecs—the end would come.

The most outspoken defender of the Indians against Spanish exploitation was the Dominican Bartolemé Las Casas, who prophesied that the end was coming because God would punish the Spaniards for their cruelty and degradation of the natives. The most ardent millennialist among the missionaries was another Dominican, Francisco de La Cruz, who was burned for heresy in Lima in 1578. He had visions that Spain, the Babylon of Revelation, would be destroyed for its crimes against the Indians, the Ten Lost Tribes. Only a few European Christians would escape to the New World, which would become the new paradise on earth. The clergy would be allowed to marry and polygamy would be accepted for the laity. The surviving Spanish in the New World and the Indians together would become the new chosen people, living in perfect harmony and great prosperity.

Two decades after La Cruz's execution, the millennial vision of the early missionaries faded. Continuing outbreaks of epidemics and the negative impact of the Spanish occupation had reduced the natives to a fraction of their original numbers, but the Spanish conquest and the introduction of European vices had not resulted in the expected end of the world. The new generation of missionaries was willing to accommodate the ecclesiastical and political bureaucracies created to govern the Indies, an attitude deadly to millennialism. While it reappeared only rarely among the Spanish in America for the next 200 years, there were several native uprisings that millennial prophets either inspired or played an important role in. The Campas revolt in the Amazon jungles of Peru was both typical and the most significant among them. In 1742 the Campas tribe, recently converted by the Franciscans, took in a Quechua refugee from Spanish justice, Santos Atahualla. He claimed to be descended from the last Inca emperor and called himself Apu Inca. As the son of God (whether Christian or Inca is not clear), he would deliver his people from servitude. Those who did not believe in him would be destroyed; those who did would receive a share not only of Spanish but also of Inca wealth, since he knew where the Inca treasure was hidden. He proclaimed a new church similar to the Catholic but with an entirely native clergy. Gathering a potent force for that region, he succeeded in driving out the Spanish, who did not return until after 1800. Santos reportedly died when a follower, testing his claim to be immortal, killed him with a slingshot.

A half-century later, as revolution against Spanish rule broke out, one premise of the early millennialists became prominent again among those who led the revolts. For many after 1750, the New World was the place where the human race would attain perfection in a secular paradise rather than the millennial kingdom. The Old World was too corrupt to be perfected, and America would become the site for the new age of perfection. The English colonists in North America reacted to the new lands and their natives in a similar manner, although they largely lacked the sense that the natives would be the residents of the New Kingdom. The English were more convinced that they themselves had that role, and that they had to destroy the Satanic hordes of natives, the forces of Gog and Magog, to achieve their goal. While the idea that the New World would become the New Kingdom was not absent from other English colonists (for example, Sir Walter Raleigh), the Puritans in New England believed it the most ardently. Many were already strongly millennialist when they arrived in America, fleeing from the royal government because of their radical Puritanism prior to 1644 and again after the Restoration in 1660. A significant portion of those who came after the Restoration were members of the millennial sects of the Puritan Revolution. Most arrived in the New World with a deeply embedded belief that they were in exile for their faith, an idea that always raises the fever pitch of millennialism.

From the first, Puritans showed that they thought of America as the place where they would serve as God's chosen instruments to establish the New Kingdom. It was the wilderness to which the godly were required to flee to escape the dragon. In 1629 John White proposed that God had chosen the English to settle New England and prosper there as a counterweight to Antichrist's empire created by Spain elsewhere in the Americas. In the same year, John Winthrop, the governor of the Massachusetts Bay Colony, said that he and his followers were carrying the gospel into those lands "to raise a bulwark against the kingdom of antichrist." In 1630 Winthrop made his famous remark, "For we must consider that we shall be as a City on a Hill, the eyes of all people are upon us." While the main inspiration for his statement (Matt. 5:14) lacks clear millennial overtones, the phrase "shining city on the hill" does draw on the description of the new Jerusalem in Revelation (21:10). It has become a common metaphor in American religion for the new age of the Millennium.

Millennialism pervaded Puritan life. The best-known literary work from the colonial period was Michael Wigglesworth's poem *The Day of Doom* (1662). Born in England in 1631, he migrated with his Puritan family to New England, where at the age of 22, he had a powerful dream of the Last Judgment. It led to his writing millennial poetry that was unusually pessimistic even for the Puritans; he paid special attention to the terrors of the last days while neglecting the promise of the Millennium. *The Day of Doom* relates with terrifying detail the events of the final day of human history:

> For at midnight breaks forth a light,
> which turns the night to day
> And speedily an hideous cry
> doth all the World dismay.[2]

Puritan theologians and preachers, men who had great influence on the development of American culture, were highly millennial. Any list of them would begin with the Mathers, father, son, and grandson, who thundered from the pulpits of Massachusetts from 1635 to 1728 and serve as exemplars of the changes in the understanding of the Millennium over the first century of settlement. Richard Mather arrived in the colony as an exile, forced out of his church in England for his ardent Puritanism. He believed that God had chosen to reveal the existence of the New World and to encourage the settlement of New England in order to create a place for his pure church to flourish while Antichrist ravaged the saints in the homeland. The English Civil War was the final struggle between the forces of Antichrist and true Christians. Proof that the Millennium was close came from the first conversions among the natives in New England, who had been highly resistant to Christianity until 1650. Mather argued that the spread of the true faith among Satan's children in America foretold the conversion of the Jews, the last step before the Parousia.

Increase Mather, born in America in 1639, followed his father in the pulpit. Realizing that his father's generation had been disappointed about the Second Coming, and that Antichrist seemed entrenched in control of England after 1660, he downplayed the Parousia's imminence during his first decades in the pulpit. He cautioned against trying to determine God's will and timeline. For example, he refused to see the Great Fire of London in 1666 as an eschatological sign. By 1700, however, his patience was wearing thin. Mather began to see such events as the Austrian defeat of the Turks in 1697 and the conversion of hundreds of Jews in Hamburg as signs that the Parousia was close at hand. He began to teach that belief in the impending Second Coming was a sign of faith: Those who believed it would have assurance of being among the elect.

Mather died in 1723, only five years before his son Cotton, who was born in 1663; Increase Mather's cautious millennialism was quite different from his son's more activist version. Cotton was faced with a society widely transformed from the small colony of saints that had founded Massachusetts. The hope that they would rebuild the Apostolic Church had largely given way to problems of schisms, heresies, and immorality. The third Mather was not as convinced that the Protestant church in New England would be the foundation for the New Kingdom. Perhaps to assure himself that the goal was in sight, Mather devoted great effort to date setting. At first he settled on 1697 because the Turkish Antichrist was to have power for 397 years after rising in 1300. Word of the Ottoman defeat that year and severe earthquakes around the world raised Mather's expectations, but he was disappointed. Shortly after, books by the English millennialist William Whiston came into his hands. Whiston, a friend of Isaac Newton, was as interested as Newton in dating the events of the Bible, but he argued that the veil of secrecy over the prophecies and the inaccuracies of the Julian calendar, still used in England, rendered predictions imprecise. Nonetheless, Whiston determined that the corruption of the early Church began in 456 and the allotted span of 1,260 years would end in 1716, but he set no date for Antichrist's final defeat. Mather, heartened by this opinion, adopted Whiston's prediction for the beginning of Antichrist's downfall.

In discussing these dates, Mather faced the problem of where Antichrist would recruit his forces to battle Christ. Mede had found them in America, but Mather refused to consign his homeland to the forces of

Satan, even if he had no high regard for the moral quality of the natives. It seemed clear to Mather, hearing of events in places such as France, where Antichrist in the person of Louis XIV was persecuting the saints, that the forces of Gog and Magog would come from Europe. His insistence on freeing America from being Antichrist's recruiting grounds lifted a burden from many New Englanders, who otherwise found Mede their favorite millennial author. It played into their tendency to see Europe as old and morally corrupt, and America as new and innocent. In rejecting Mede's interpretation, Mather helped to remove an important check on the tendency among English colonists to see America as the New Kingdom.

When 1716 arrived, Mather eagerly sought news of events revealing Antichrist's downfall. He had his moments of high hope during the year, but eventually he admitted disappointment, which resulted in a change in attitude for him. No longer was the role of good Christians simply to accept God's will and wait patiently for the endtime to unfold; instead they must actively involve themselves in bringing it about. Mather did not advocate millennial violence but emphasized the need for the believer to work to convert the world and make good Christians out of the multitudes. The Lord would come only when there were enough godly men infused with the Holy Spirit. Mather published extensively in the last years of his life and had broad impact on changing the direction of millennialism among the Puritans toward the idea that the faithful had a role, albeit minor, in creating the conditions for Christ's return.

A decade after Mather's death, all of the English colonies saw the outpouring of piety and religious fervor known as the Great Awakening. Sporadic revivals in New England towns suddenly became widespread up and down the Atlantic seaboard. Thousands of the unchurched began to attend sermons, while committed Protestants strove to transform themselves and live according to true religious principles. The principal revivalist in New England was the Puritan minister Jonathan Edwards (d. 1758), whose *Some Thoughts Concerning the Present Revival of Religion* of 1742 helped to define the movement. His success and that of other preachers convinced them that the Church was about to enter its day of glory, and that they had a role in bringing it about. Instead of seeing the human race progressively wors-ening, as had previous generations of preachers, those of the Great Awakening believed that all evidence indicated that the Church was be-coming stronger and purer and that the New Kingdom was close at hand. Unlike the Mathers, for example, who looked to catastrophic events to reveal the approach of the Lord's day, Edwards maintained that the outpouring of the Holy Spirit on human hearts would produce a change in society that would foretell it. Great fires or earthquakes, renting nature and causing suffering for mankind, were not needed to prepare the world for Christ, although Edwards did not deny that there would be great suffering for the saints at the end. Humans could serve as instruments through which the world would be purified and the Parousia made possible. This was a more optimistic view of God's grand design. It put less emphasis on God's decision to punish and more on what the individual could do by strong faith and love of God to prepare for the end. It also reduced the terror of the last days, not that Edwards was incapable of sermons brimming with hellfire and brim-stone, as in his famous "Sinners in the hands of an angry God."

Edwards's understanding of church history, to be sure, was little different from that of most other Protestant thinkers. Their basic premise was that God's hand in safeguarding the Church was obvious in history. The Jews had persecuted the first Christians, but they suffered a swift and overwhelming catastrophe in 71 AD. The pagan Romans, in a longer and more severe attack on the Church, sought to destroy it, but Constantine purged the evil of paganism from the Roman empire, and for a time the Church existed in a pure state. Satan healed the wound Constantine inflicted on him by introducing the power of the papacy into the Church. The rise of the papal Antichrist was gradual, and it was impossible to pinpoint the date precisely. Edwards thought 606, the date he assigned to the pope's gaining universal authority, was a likely pos-sibility. The end of Antichrist's power would come 1,260 years after that. Although Antichrist's destruction was at least a century in the fu-ture, there were signs of his coming demise. The Reformation and the discovery of America had opened up the way for a great renovation of the world, but more immediate was the revival of religion that Edwards saw all around him.

Edwards's endtime was quite different from that of his predecessors. It would not be a sudden, catastrophic event but a period of trial for the true Christians. In maintaining that those before him had misinterpreted Revelation by emphasizing its great calamities, he argued that in their scenario few would pray for the Lord's coming (a necessary condition for it to happen) because of the pain and tribulation that the saints would have to suffer. He understood the trial to be not physical agony but rather spiritual anguish in the souls of Christians caused by their knowledge of the sins and the unbelief of those bound by Antichrist. In the fullness of time, the beast of Rome will be destroyed; all Christians will accept the true Church; the Jews and the heathen will be converted to Christianity. Divine grace will spread across the world; all will live in peace as one community in the full knowledge of the gospel. It will be a period of great material prosperity and human progress, in things spiritual and temporal. For example, new means of communicating across the oceans and continents will be found so that all regions of the world will be able to communicate safe and easily. After this period of glory, the Millennium, which Edwards sees as more symbolic than a precise period of time, Satan will return to lead a brief but widespread rebellion against Christ. Christ himself will return to defeat Satan, raise the dead, hold the Last Judgment, thrust Satan and all the reprobate down into the pit, and take the saints to heaven for eternity. There will be a final conflagration of the world, which Edwards passes over without describing.

One key innovation in Edwards's millennialism involved the concept that Christ will return only once, in his physical body, after the period of the Millennium, and only at that point will there be the resurrection of the dead saints and final judgment. Without Christ's return to inaugurate the Millennium, it will begin without earthquakes, blasts of trumpets, destroyer angels, and the carnage of great battles against Antichrist. The first resurrection spoken of in Revelation will be the regeneration of the Church, which will lead to the first defeat of Antichrist. This is a more progressive view of the future, allowing for the gradual improvement of humanity. It has become known as postmillennialism. The view expounded by the Mathers, that Christ will bodily descend to begin the Millennium, usually with wrath and destruction, is called premillennialism. Full of hellfire and brimstone, it stays close to a literal interpretation of Revelation and the other apocalyptic texts. Because of its literalism, premillennialism has changed very little over the ages, and its exponents today often sound amazingly like Puritan preachers. Postmillennialism, on the other hand, has been more open to change and reinterpretation and has moved quite far from its origins with Edwards and others of his era.

Edwards believed that the number of saints would always be small. In that sense he remained loyal to his Puritan predecessors. Others later argued for a vast expansion of the saved. His student Joseph Bellemy argued that the vast majority of people who will have lived by the time of the end of the world will be saved, calculating the ratio of saints to damned at 17,000 to one. He reached that conclusion from two premises: There will be vast numbers of conversions to Christianity at the beginning of the Millennium, and the regenerated world will support a huge increase in population, doubling every fifty years. With less precision but greater foresight, Samuel Hopkins argued that the great learning and peace found during the Millennium will result in dramatic improvements in agriculture and industry, which will allow the earth to support a great population of true Christians. Enlarging the number of saints had an important consequence, occurring as it did a decade before the American Revolution. Most millennialists have a sense of the dominion of grace, some stating more explicitly than others that the world and its goods properly belong to the saints, and that after Christ's return they would take ownership. If the number of saints was small, then there would be an oligarchy of the elect ruling with Jesus. By making vast numbers eligible for membership in the New Kingdom, Bellemy, Hopkins, and others democratized it. It would be stretching the point to argue either that they were democrats at heart or that they preached democracy, but they helped to remove what could have been a serious barrier to it. Since 1960 many historians studying early American religion have found a causal link between this postmillennialism and the American Revolution. Recently the inevitable revisionism has appeared, but the case for a relationship remains persuasive, even if a little overstated by its advocates.

The Puritans took the great Lisbon earthquake of 1755 that shook the New England coastline as strong evidence of the imminent Parousia. It was certainly taken that way in Portugal. The principal millennial myth in early modern Portugal and its colonies involved King Sebastian, who in 1578 disappeared in Morocco on a crusade. His return would be a sign of the endtime, and a Portuguese nun predicted that it would occur on All Saints' Day in 1752. High expectations for that date and the following two years were disappointed, but the biggest earthquake in European history devastated Lisbon on November 1, 1755. The belief that this was the end seemed confirmed by the wild ringing of church bells set off by the jolt until the bell towers collapsed. The number of people killed is estimated at 30,000. Many survivors expected to see King Sebastian ride into the destroyed city leading his ghostly army followed by Christ himself. Although that did not happen, Lisbon's destruction, with its collapsed buildings, raging fires, and dead lying in heaps in the streets for days afterward served as the model for the image of the final days for decades to come.

For the Puritans, the French and Indian War in North America also served as a millennial event, even if the destruction was not at the level of the Lisbon earthquake. Their rhetoric changed very little from earlier periods of war. The French and their native allies served Antichrist by waging war on the people of God, and their early victories were signs that the great tribulation was beginning. The British victory in turn confirmed the deeply held belief among the English colonists that they were a chosen people building the New Kingdom in America. With the French driven out of Canada, however, the colonists no longer had reason to fear that Antichrist's hordes were just over the next hill, ready to pillage and murder God's people. Their new-found security combined with their sense of being God's chosen encouraged them to resist the British government's efforts to impose higher taxes. When violence broke out in 1774, it took little time for many preachers, who in New England were decidedly prorebellion, to use millennial rhetoric to explain what was happening. They had little difficulty identifying King George III as Antichrist, as Christians throughout history have easily changed the face of the beast to that of their current enemy. When France allied itself with the rebellion in 1777, Antichrist's right hand now was fighting on the side of the Lamb. The final victory against great odds was explained as God's favor to his people. It was a short step to finding that he had given his saints the right to rule the continent from sea to shining sea. Manifest destiny had in it a large dose of millennialism, even as it also drew from other sources.

As Americans began to build their new republic, they began to reveal a new faith alongside of Reformed Christianity: the belief in progress. Thomas Paine, a secular advocate of independence, proclaimed in 1776: "We have it in our power to begin the world over again."[3] Postmillennialists adopted this idea with little hesitation, and they helped to fuel it. The millennial vision of men like Edwards, Bellemy, and Hopkins described a time when a world truly Christian would be a paradise of peace and prosperity. They found support in John Calvin, who had spoken of the ever-increasing splendor by which God would display his light and truth. In a sermon in 1762 Bellemy laid out what the New Kingdom would be like. Kings will give up war, pledging to live in peace, and will no longer waste the lives of thousands of men. Merchants will not cheat their customers because they will have all the wealth they could want. Even the poor will be so much better off that they will not envy others. In 1776 Edwards's grandson, Timothy Dwight, proclaimed that the foundations of the coming glory were being laid. When the Millennium would be fully attained around the year 2000 (he was one of the few before 1800 who looked to 2000), the lives of people would surpass a hundred years in length because of new medicines and the end of starvation and malnutrition. He spoke of how human affairs were "constantly progressing toward what may be termed natural perfection. In this progress, they are preparing for the commencement of moral perfection."[4] This is a gradual process; there will be no astounding or terrifying events to announce it.

Dwight's progress was still a religious process: God is responsible for it and decides when it will take place. Nonetheless, other than its source, there is little to distinguish this Christian utopia of the Millennium from the utopias imagined by secular thinkers whom the Enlightenment inspired. By the end of the eighteenth century, the utopian notions had begun to merge together to create the modern idea of progress.

IX

THE MILLENNIUM
OF PURE REASON

Jonathan Edwards and his fellow Puritans introduced the idea that with divine aid the human race would progressively improve during the Millennium. At the same time, a group of mostly French thinkers was proposing that human progress without any divine intervention would lead to the perfection of the race. This new interpretation of history rejected traditional millennialism but reached the same conclusion: At the end of time humans will be in a state of perfection. The intellectuals of the French Enlightenment, the *philosophes,* would have rebuffed any suggestion that they drew on the old religious tradition of millennialism for their thought, but it did influence them even if they avoided explicitly using it.

The Enlightenment developed out of the scientific revolution, which in its first century largely involved Nicolaus Copernicus's heliocentric challenge to the traditional universe and the use of mathematics as the language of the new science. Both had an impact on traditional millennialism, but especially important was Johannes Kepler's discovery of the three laws of planetary motions in the early 1600s, which provided a rational, regularizing explanation for the movements of the planets. Kepler undermined astrology more than Copernicus had because astrology had grown out of the apparent capriciousness of the planetary motions that seemed to mirror the capriciousness of human life. Although astrology hardly disappeared from popular use, it was largely discredited among the European intellectual elite, and efforts to determine the endtime from astrology, which had marked much of the millennialism of the previous two centuries, declined rapidly.

The use of mathematics placed a greater emphasis on precision, and precision penetrated millennialism as well as other areas of thought. The best example was the work of James Ussher, Anglican archbishop of Ireland, who in 1650 established the creation of the world at dusk on October 23, 4004 BC. Persuaded by mathematical work in science that God would be exact in his timing, Ussher declared that six days of creation matched 6,000 years of human history, while God's day of rest prefigured the Millennium. There was little new about this calculation, but Ussher accepted the evidence that King Herod died in 4 BC and an error had been made placing Christ's birth in 1 AD. God in his divine precision will start the Millennium after exactly 6,000 years, or on October 23, 1996. Ussher made 4004 BC the date of creation for most English-speaking people for the next 200 years, and many Christians still use it today.

In the hands of Isaac Newton, mathematics seemed to his contemporaries to be the tool to unlock the secrets of the universe. Newton, however, was better regarded in his own era for his work in dating the Bible than for his scientific work. He devoted much time and effort to using astronomy to verify Ussher's dating of events in the Scriptures. He argued that Revelation was completely accurate in predicting the history of the great kingdoms since Christ, but he stopped short of setting a date for the endtime. That would impinge on the will of God, who alone sets the time. Nonetheless, his work verified Ussher's work in dating the events of the Bible and provided unintentional confirmation of the timing for the Parousia. Newton's great prestige thus helped to maintain key elements of traditional millennialism.

Newton also has a very different place in the history of religion. His work in establishing the scientific laws of physics in the universe was a major boost to deism, the term used for the Enlightenment view that the deity was the great watchmaker, who created the universe and set it into motion according to unalterable laws of nature. Deism owed a great deal to English scientists such as Newton, William Boyle, and Edmund Halley. (Halley's work showing that a great comet reappeared regularly undermined the view that comets predicted terrible events.) Deism, however, reached its most extreme positions among the French *philosophes* in the eighteenth century. Voltaire, Denis Diderot, and their fellow *philosophes* were far more hostile to traditional religion than were the English deists. The deists were willing to use the word God, even if their intended meaning was the great watchmaker. The *philosophes* preferred to indicate God's place in the universe by the terms *Providence* and *Nature* to designate the benevolent power that created the universe and sees to its working. Through the discovery of scientific laws, human reason is capable of understanding the workings of Nature, which intends only the best for humanity.

What does Nature intend for humanity? Nothing less than its perfection, according to the most optimistic *philosophes,* but not according to Voltaire. He was too well aware of such natural disasters as the 1755 Lisbon earthquake to regard Nature's intentions as entirely benevolent, but Diderot, one of the few avowed atheists in the eighteenth century, believed that Nature endowed humans with the ability to live in perfect harmony and happiness. He wrote a commentary on the reports written by a French sailor about his voyages to South Pacific islands to make the case that the people of Tahiti lived in this perfect state of nature. Diderot's utopia was the first one set in a real place.

The word utopia comes from Thomas More's 1516 book describing an ideal society, but More's understanding of the nonreality of the place he detailed is made clear in that utopia comes from the Greek words for *no place.* (It may also be a pun on the Greek for *good place.*) More and other pre-Enlightenment authors who wrote about utopias intended to provide a mirror for contemporary society in which they contrasted the virtues of the non-Christian inhabitants of their utopias with the vices of Christians, who ought to be better than non-Christians. Diderot, however, believed that the non-Christian Tahitians were superior to European Christians, whose priests and superstitions had not yet corrupted the Tahitians' harmony with Nature. For him the past had no value except to show that Europe had declined from the greatness of the classical age to the darkness of the Middle Ages, something so baffling to him he could not find a good reason for it except to use the same sort of deus ex machina that Antichrist provides for human ills among Christian authors. Diderot regarded any discussion of millennialism as the sort of religious superstition that was the true cause of evil in the world. Yet his description of a society living in harmony with Nature could have been written by Jonathan Edwards about the Millennium.

Few *philosophes* embraced Diderot's utopia of the present. The Baron de Turgot published a work in 1766 that reintroduced the Joachimite threefold division of history, but he assigned the moving force to progress, by which he meant change and innovation. Progress came about through the human intellect, not from the deity. The first period of history was the time of anthropomorphism, when humans knew little about the universe and attributed divine power to forces of nature described as humanlike figures. The second was the time of metaphysics, when humans began to understand more about nature and developed philosophy. The third and final period was the time of scientific and mathematical reason, when humans developed the scientific method that would eventually reveal all the secrets of nature. As humanity moves further into the time of science, conflict and violence will decline and disappear, and mankind will inevitably reach a state of perfection, namely, a perfect knowledge of nature that leads to the elimination of all problems, vices, and woes. The scientific millennium (not that Turgot would have used the term) thus begins. Turgot's was the clearest statement of an idea more vaguely expressed by other *philosophes,* and it would have a potent future.

Turgot's friend Louis-Sébastien Mercier fully adopted his idea of scientific progress and eventual perfection of the human race and placed the latter at a specific time in the future. In 1770 he published *The Year 2440,* the first futuristic utopia. By placing the perfect society in the future, Mercier made clear his faith that through progress the human race would eventually achieve that perfect condition. Turgot's greatest disciple was the Marquis de Condorcet, whose *Sketch for a Historical Picture of the Progress of the Human Mind* was written while he was in hiding during the French Revolution. He argued that history has ten stages—eight past ones, the present, and the tenth and final one close at hand. Each stage has shown human improvement, but natural human reason has been frustrated by the ill effects of superstition, religion, and ignorance, so progress has been very slow. Yet the efforts of those who have sought to prevent progress have contributed to it, in a way suggestive of how Antichrist's machinations hasten the Parousia. Finally, through the development of science and mathematics, humanity has arrived at the point where the final stage of history is in sight. It has the same certitude, proclaimed Condorcet, as any theorem of geometry.

Condorcet described at length the nature of society in that final stage. Progress and innovation will continue to build on each other to provide constant improvement of the humanity, although human nature itself will not change. Improved medicine and diet will create an indefinite lengthening of human life-spans, and the proper education in science and mathematics will allow for great accomplishments in art, literature, and all the activities of the intellect. Condorcet was convinced that the French Revolution was the final step to his tenth stage (the tribulation before the Millennium?), and despite being a nobleman he joined the Jacobins, the most radical of the revolutionaries. His noble status led the Jacobins to suspect his true motives and imprison him; because of his belief in the coming of the perfect society, he accepted imprisonment and died in prison in 1794.

Turgot as royal finance minister provided much of the incentive for the French Revolution, the first major effort to create a perfect society by force. Appointed in 1774, he was ousted two years later because of the opposition of the privileged classes to his proposed reforms. Not only did the rescinding of his reform edicts derail a possible aversion of the royal fiscal bankruptcy that sparked the revolution, it also proved to many French intellectuals that the monarchy was morally and intellectually bankrupt as well. Many became convinced that in order to achieve the perfect society they knew could be established, they had to take action to destroy the evil state that stood in the way. Like radical millennialists, they came to believe that only by using violence against the beast could that perfect future happen. Far more than the American Revolution, which also had millennial and utopian overtones, the French Revolution was the focus of both types of expectations. Leaving the millennial views of the French Revolution for later, here we will examine the utopians and their visions of humanity's future.

As the first events of the revolution unfolded in 1789, Thomas Rousseau, who became a Jacobin, published a French translation of

More's *Utopia*. A surprisingly large number of the revolutionaries, including Condorcet, Mercier, and Louis-Antoine de Saint-Just, one of the most violent of the Jacobins, wrote utopian works. Utopian thought, which had a strong impact on the leaders of the revolution, did not advocate violence until 1791. Before then the possibility of creating the perfect society described in the utopian literature appeared incredibly remote, and those who were optimistic that it eventually would happen agreed that it would be an excruciatingly slow process. By 1791, with enormous change already taking place, establishing the perfect society suddenly appeared not only possible but likely to occur in the near future. Violence had produced changes inconceivable two years earlier; violence could bring about a still greater transformation of society. It was the obligation of the men of reason to make it happen.

Men who had been appalled at the limited violence perpetrated by the monarchy now found themselves advocating it with vehemence: "Crush the Infamous thing!" To their surprise, such monumental changes as the fall of the monarchy, the founding of the republic, and the Declaration of the Rights of Man failed to create the new man as they had expected. The roots of ignorance and injustice truly ran deep, and harsh methods had to be employed to dig them out to achieve the triumph of reason and liberty. Like the argument regarding heresy that said heretics must be killed to keep them from infecting the entire body of the faithful, so the Jacobins declared that the Terror had to be used against supporters of the old regime, whom they defined as anyone not sufficiently supportive of the revolution. Only a few of the poor, the *sans-Culottes,* and their Jacobin mentors, the intellectual elite, would be worthy of residing in the new world.

If all of this seems amazingly familiar—for example, similar to Münster in 1534—there is good reason, since the same goal of creating a new people motivated the behavior of both groups. For the Jacobins it was the coming of the Age of Reason, not the Parousia, that drove them on, but their methods and ultimate goals were nearly the same. A new earth in which all true patriots lived according to reason and in liberty was not a great deal different from the new Jerusalem in which the saints live in bliss with Christ. Lacking a belief in God who will begin the Millennium in his own good time, the Jacobins had to take a more direct role than did most millennialists.

The similarities between the French Revolution and the violent millennial movements extend to the presence of similar types of leaders. Few millennial leaders have been as certain that they have been specially chosen for their mission as was Maximilien Robespierre, the Apostle of Virtue as the Jacobins named him; none have caused as much bloodshed. His climb to the top of the idealistic yet cutthroat Jacobins is as true an example of a successful charismatic leader as any cult leader. A provincial lawyer at the beginning of the revolution, he came to dominate the Jacobins because of his audacity and commitment to revolutionary ideals. The unchallenged leader of the Committee of Public Safety from September 1793 to July 1794, Robespierre was convinced that he was best suited to lead France and the whole world into the Republic of Reason and out of the darkness in which kings, priests, and nobles had held mankind in bondage. He declared that everything had to be changed, so that there would be a complete regeneration of the world and creation of a new people who followed only reason. Robespierre repeatedly justified the Reign of Terror, which was sending thousands to the guillotine, on the grounds that those who did not favor the Republic of Reason or were lukewarm in their support were traitors to the sovereign people and deserved death for their treason: "Who is not with me is against me."

"Incorruptible" Robespierre's zeal for revolutionary purity led him to denounce even those who shortly before had stood beside him in the same heat of revolutionary fervor. Some of his erstwhile allies succeeded in turning the tables on him and saw to his execution in July 1794. Robespierre's downfall occurred in the month of Thermidor in the new calendar created by the Jacobins to demonstrate that the founding of the French Republic in 1792 marked a new age for humanity. Since his execution also marked the beginning of the end of the Terror and the worst excesses of the revolution, this turning point is called the Thermidorian reaction.

Robespierre's death did not discomfit the expectations of all who believed the new age was about to begin, even as France slowly drew back from Jacobin radicalism under the government called the Directory. Only then did Gracchus Babeuf propose his radical theory of society. As a symbol of his commitment to the cause of human equality in the French Republic, François Babeuf had changed his name to Gracchus in honor of the great champion of the common people in the Roman republic. Babeuf drew heavily from Gabriel de Mably and the Abbé de Morelly, the Enlightenment's most radical thinkers, both of whom had advocated communism at mid-eighteenth century. They argued that, in the natural state, people had shared all goods in common, and that the use of private property was the root of all evil. Morelly demanded a return to communal property to reestablish the natural virtue of people. In his *Code of Nature* (1755), he set out in vast detail the structures and regulations of his utopian society.

Babeuf, from a peasant family, never received any formal education, but he educated himself enough to be employed as a local noble's clerk enforcing feudal claims and dues. This distasteful job convinced him of the evils of private property. He went on to serve as a minor functionary in the revolutionary government, although he also spent time in prison under it. Outraged by the direction of the government after Thermidor, Babeuf in 1795 became the editor of a radical journal, *Tribune of the People*. He argued that the objective pattern of human history and the future, found in what he called the "Book of Time and Destiny," foresaw the French Revolution. The French people, he declared, suddenly realized in 1789 that they had been deprived of their rights under the mutual contract that had created human society, especially in regard to property. The ordained flow of events, despite setbacks like Robespierre's execution, would lead eventually to a society of perfect equality and virtue.

In his *Manifesto of the Equals*, referring to the name Babeuf's disciples used for themselves, Sylvain Maréchal declared: "The French Revolution is but the forerunner of another revolution, far more grand, far more solemn, which will be the last . . . The moment for great measures has arrived. Evil is at its height; it has reached its maximum, and covers the face of the earth. . . . The days of general restitution are come."[1] The Equals watched with growing anxiety as the Directory drew back further and further from the Jacobin program. In May 1796 Babeuf organized a conspiracy to overthrow the Directory and put the revolution back on its path toward a perfect society, one without private property. Informers betrayed him, and Babeuf was executed.

Babeuf made a number of major contributions to the theory of revolution as it developed over the next century. One was the role of the revolutionary elite whose task it was to overthrow the tyrannical old regime and establish a true democracy; only then would the ordinary people share power. A second was the idea of continuous revolution until the final goal of the perfect society would be reached; reforming a corrupt society only strengthened it. A third contribution was the certainty of final victory; it was ordained by nature and was as certain as any law of science. Shortly before he died, Babeuf used the phrase "happy catastrophe" to refer to revolution. For him a revolution was like the disasters that herald the Parousia, a terrible time involving pain, anguish, and bloodshed; yet its final result will be glorious. He went on to describe that glorious future: "No more of the ever gnawing tooth of the general restlessness, of the personal perpetual anxiety of every one of us, about our lot of tomorrow, next month, next year, in our old age, the fate of our children and their children. . . . Guarantee to every one of its members a state of stable felicity, the satisfaction of the needs of all."[2] Babeuf's new earth is much like the new Jerusalem, where God himself "will wipe away every tear from their eyes" (Rev. 21:4).

Ironically, one of those who carried Babeuf's legacy forward was a man who had made a fortune as a war profiteer. The Comte de Saint-Simon, from petty nobility, had fought at Yorktown, then joined the Jacobins, thereby surviving the French Revolution, and recouped his family's losses by speculating in properties confiscated from the clergy and nobility. Although he lost his money in schemes for economic development such as canal building, he managed to maintain a cadre of disciples to whom he imparted his wisdom. His fits of frenetic activity followed by periods of passivity suggest a manic-depressive personality, and in 1823 he attempted suicide. He lived two more years.

The starting point of Saint-Simon's theory of society was human progress through the application of science and technology to human problems. He favored industrialization, which he thought would greatly improve the lives of common people if the industrialists recognized their obligation to the poor. He deeply respected scientists and engineers, whom he regarded as a third social category along with the propertied and the propertyless. They hold the balance of power between the other two groups, and they must assume the responsibility of directing society and solving social problems. In his last work, *The New Christianity* (1825), Saint-Simon added priests of a new Christianity to scientists and engineers, those who would direct society. Saint-Simon was not entirely hostile to Christianity, unlike most intellectuals associated with the French Revolution. He argued that it had introduced the key principle for human society, brotherly love, into the Roman empire, which had been founded on a master-slave relationship. The original purity of Christianity had been corrupted not in the early Middle Ages, as Protestants argued, but in the past four centuries, when the papacy and clergy became foes of brotherly love instead of its champions. He even used the term Antichrist about them. The new Christianity would need a new clergy, educated in science and technology, to preach to the people the principle of working collectively for the betterment of humanity.

In the final and perpetual era, scientists, industrialists, and priests would direct society for the benefit of the common people, who Saint-Simon believed would never understand enough to rule themselves. He was not opposed to the rich as long as they understood their obligation to advance the well-being of all. Thus, he was not a true socialist, since he allowed a place for an economic elite. He predicted that when industrialization was complete, advances in eradicating poverty and ignorance would eliminate the need for the state, which existed to control the public disorder those ills created. Rulers, intoxicated by power, in the past had diverted the state from its proper purpose to accumulating power and creating injustice and war. Once society was organized according to proper principles, the state would have less and less to do; declining in size and power, it would wither away. Not that Saint-Simon used Karl Marx's phrase, but their visions of the state in the new age were similar. Saint-Simon spoke not only for all socialists but also for most millennialists when he declared that he wanted to "shift the Earthly Paradise and transport it from the past into the future."[3]

Saint-Simon occasionally compared himself with Christ, and the comparison is apt enough when one looks at their movements in the first years after their deaths. Both had a small group of apostles who proselytized extensively and changed the movement's direction, although the Saint-Simonians lasted only for a generation as an organized group.

They came largely from the students at the Ecole Polytechnique in Paris, founded in 1794 to educate scientists and engineers whom Saint-Simon now expected to govern his new society. In a short time the Saint-Simonians changed from a philosophical movement to being almost a religion with a set of doctrines and rituals and a strong sense of eschatology. They believed that their master's life marked the turning point of history away from antagonism toward love. The world was being transformed, and human perfection was inevitable, although they set no timetable. When perfection was achieved, there would be no aggression or war. The Saint-Simonians formed a utopian community with common ownership of goods, as they changed Saint-Simon's limited endorsement of private property into a prohibition. They gave strong support to female emancipation, and some, to free love, because equality meant precisely that, for everyone, in everything. The influence of Saint-Simon and his followers was extensive, even if they had faded away as an organized movement by 1850. Like every religion, they quickly were rent with schisms, and the public ridiculed them for their exotic rituals and sexual practices.

Charles Fourier was a contemporary of Saint-Simon, both having published their first works in 1808, and his rival for influence among the intellectuals of their time. Both also had problems with mental stability, but Fourier was less successful in building a following during his life despite having been a salesman when young. With one major exception, little in his thought differs from Saint-Simon's, which is not to suggest that one borrowed from the other. The exception was that Fourier laid down exhaustively detailed plans for socialist communities that would prove the truth of his theory of human society. He called his community the *phalanstery* (from phalanx), which would be more agricultural than industrial since he distrusted industrialization. He intended that it would consist of 1,600 men and women, as equally divided as possible among the twelve personality types that he identified in humanity. The tasks of running the community would also be equally divided among the members. They would be paid according to a complex formula that considered the amount of capital they brought to the phalanstery and the kind and amount of work they did. Work and profit were to be communal matters, but personal property was not outlawed. Fourier banned marriage because he believed that most people, at least most men, could not be satisfied with one sexual partner for life. His view that all should frequently enjoy sexual pleasure resulted not in promiscuous sex but in a highly regulated system in which members made love with partners of different personality types and age groups. He also advocated freedom to engage in what he called "amorous manias," including homosexuality and sadomasochism. There is no evidence that the never-married Fourier, unlike so many cult leaders, ever lost his virginity.

Fourier believed that only a single phalanstery had to be built to begin the process of transforming the world. The almost supernatural influence of just one, properly designed, would lead to the building of more, until all of humanity would be organized into them. When that happened, war would disappear because the old political systems with their aggression and greedy rulers would no longer exist. The world would enter the golden age. Fourier argued that thousands of years ago mankind had all the knowledge that it needed to organize phalansteries but lacked a man of his vision to build them. Yet there had been men in the past, such as Christ and Newton, who contributed to bringing humanity closer to this great transformation. In all there had been fifteen previous epochs of human history before the coming age of harmony. In each era the relationship between the rich and the poor had become less exploitive until the time of Fourier, the "messiah of reason," when the world was poised to enter the final age of equality and harmony.

Fourier's place in the history of utopianism rests largely on the many attempts to create his phalansteries. He sought patronage from the rulers of Europe, lamenting bitterly that if only a tiny fraction of the money devoted to war went to him to build phalansteries, world peace would follow. The first appeared in Romania, where a Romanian noble who met Fourier in Paris decided to build one. It seems to have been quite successful until the local nobles, terrified of its impact on their peasants, destroyed it. While France itself was nearly immune to Fourierism, Saint-Simonism being far more influential there, phalansteries were organized across Europe, especially in Russia, but they were most common in the United States. The belief that new visions would flourish in the New World, unlike old corrupt Europe, combined with the availability of cheap land to encourage the founding of utopian communities. The most famous phalanstery, Brook Farm in Massachusetts, was organized in 1841. Its fame rests largely on the fact that Nathaniel Hawthorne was briefly one of its directors and wrote about it in his *Blithedale Romance.* No phalanstery came close to being organized as Fourier had proposed, and one can assume that he would have argued that this caused their quick demise.

A third leader of those Marx would call utopian socialists was Robert Owen, who probably coined the word socialism. A self-made man who rose from child laborer to textile magnate, he was determined to improve the lot of British workers, as the growth of industrialization in Britain had laid a crushing burden on them. About 1800 Owen transformed his factory at New Lanark in Scotland into a model for improving working conditions while increasing his profits. By 1817 he turned his attention to improving the lot of all society and invested his fortune in socialist communities in Britain and America. The most famous was at New Harmony, Indiana, where Owen spent two years and most of his fortune before it collapsed in 1828. A philosophical view of history motivated Owen less than it did other utopians, but he did lay out a social theory in his *Book of the New Moral World.* Dedicating it to the British king, Owen proposed a new natural religion that, he claimed, would give humanity endless physical, intellectual, and moral improvement and the attainment of permanent happiness. The Napoleonic Wars showed the time was right for creating the new society, to be accomplished through the proper education since human nature was malleable. Owen's social missionaries would educate young children in the sciences and virtue. He founded schools for young children in his factories to show that education could perfect human society, and his school for young children at New Harmony predated the first kindergarten by fifty years. Owen challenged the king to support his program or face revolution.

Saint-Simon, Fourier, and Owen were intent on improving the lot of the common people and reaching the perfect society through persuasion and education; only Owen hinted that violent revolution might follow if the authorities did not heed his advice. For Karl Marx and Friedrich Engels, both from well-off German families, the lack of realism in such men was the major reason they derided their socialist predecessors as utopian socialists. Revolution was the only way in which society could be transformed. Yet Marxism (the term undervalues Engels's contribution) owed much to the utopians. One of Marx's teachers at Berlin, Eduard Gans, was a Saint-Simonian whose scheme of history anticipated Marx's: "Once there was the opposition between master and slave, then between patrician and plebeian, and later still between feudal lord and vassal; now we have the idle rich and the worker."[4] When Marx moved to Paris in 1843, he entered the hotbed of socialist thought and lived for a short time in a Fourierist commune. The Marxist idea that human society has progressed through several stages of existence to the point that it is about to arrive at the summit of freedom and well-being came largely from the utopians.

Such a scheme of history was also found in another source for Marxism, Georg Hegel's theory of the dialectic. Its key concept is the unfolding of the spirit of the absolute in history. There have been four phases of history, beginning in the East with the Oriental system of despotism in which only one, the despot, was free. Just as the sun moves westward, so has history. The next two phases were the Greek and the Roman, in which a portion of the people was free. The final phase is the Germanic; at its end, the sunset of time, all will be free. What makes Hegel's theory of history different from several similar schemes is the presence of the dialectic, composed of the thesis, antithesis, and synthesis. All that makes up a society—religion, politics, economics, culture—forms its thesis, but the thesis does not fulfill every human need, and the efforts to achieve completeness will eventually generate the antithesis. The thesis and the antithesis are in conflict with each other, and the battle between them destroys the thesis, giving rise to the synthesis, a new society made up of elements of both. The synthesis becomes the new thesis, which then goes through the same process. It is the dialectic, then, that has moved history through time to the present, broadening the scope of freedom and human self-awareness and leading soon to the total unfolding of the spirit and freedom for all. Hegel is vague on what will happen thereafter.

Marxism took over Hegel's dialectic but made a significant change: It was the mode of economic production that determined the nature of a society, and class conflict was the force that has moved the dialectic through history. At the beginning of history, humans lived in a golden age of primitive communism, in which there was no private property and no exploitation of people. This primeval paradise ended when the population increased and the division of labor, original sin, was introduced. The division of labor, which benefited a few against the many, led to private property and class conflict. The first exploitive society was the ancient, in which a small number of masters dominated a vast number of slaves. The ancient thesis contained internal contradictions that formed the antithesis and led to its violent destruction. The resulting synthesis was feudalism, lords dominating serfs. The feudal thesis similarly created its antithesis and was destroyed in the early modern period by the rise of the bourgeoisie. The third mode of production is capitalism, in which the capitalists exploit the proletariat.

Although each succeeding mode of production has been less harsh in its exploitation of labor, Marx devotes most of his attention to the evils of the capitalist era, for it is both the current one and the final one before the great transformation. The proletariat, being more advanced than the preceding exploited classes, will recognize its common condition and will organize against the capitalists. The internal contradictions of capitalism will soon lead to a great depression during which the capitalists will seek to maintain their position by increased exploitation of the proletariat. The result will be the revolution of the proletariat, a truly violent and apocalyptic event. Capitalism will be destroyed and the dictatorship of the proletariat established to erase all of its vestiges. Once that happens, the state, which has always existed to protect the haves against the have-nots, will wither away; and humanity will enter communism. Then all will be equal in a society that will not require soldiers, police, judges, or any other groups that have controlled human behavior and set themselves up as the arbitrators of a class society. History will end since there will be no further change. Humanity will have permanently restored the Golden Age. As the German Marxist August Bebel wrote, "Human society has traversed, in the course of thousands of years, all the various phases of development, to arrive in the end where it started from—communistic property and complete equality and fraternity. . . . The 'Golden Age' that man has been dreaming of for thousands of years, and after which they have been longing, will have come at last."[5]

The similarity of Marx's theory to traditional Judeo-Christian millennialism is striking. Humanity has been thrown out of paradise by its acts and alienated from the source of the good. History is predetermined to move through a series of events until a great catastrophe signals the time to return to a golden age. There will follow a period of transformation until the endtime is reached, at which point history ends. Both Marx and the Bible are decidedly vague on what that golden age will be like; Marx felt that humanity will be so transformed that it was impossible to describe the future from the viewpoint of a corrupt bourgeois society. Marxists and millennialists urgently search for clues that the greatest event of history—the Revolution of the Proletariat or the Second Coming—is about to occur. For Marxists every economic downturn in the capitalist world has been seen as a signal that the great moment is close at hand. In both systems, the worse things become, the more certain the end is near. Each also has its chosen people who will help bring about the new age and have a privileged position in the new world. Marxists and millennialists alike are convinced of the inevitability of the foreordained events in their systems. The only question is when they will occur.

Just as millennialism with its certainty of the punishment of the evildoers and the reward of the saints has been so attractive through history because of that certitude, so Marxism has been attractive because of its certainty about the direction of history. The triumph of socialism must occur because Marx's study of history revealed the laws of nature and history that show that it will occur. Thus, Marx called his theory scientific socialism, for it was based on the reality of science, not the whimsical schemes of utopians. A major reason Marxism has been so influential in the century after Marx's death in 1883 is its guarantee that a Marxist revolution will be ultimately victorious. It is a law of history. Not only is Marxism uniquely a philosophy of revolution, it also pledges victory for its adherents. Most revolutionary leaders since 1900 have been rebels first, so profoundly dissatisfied with their society that they have resorted to violent revolution to destroy it. They became Marxists because that ideology promises that their revolutions will succeed. They also became Marxists because it accommodates to the fullest their thirst for vengeance on the exploiters and enslavers.

One significant difference between millennialism and Marxism is that the Marxist must take part in bringing about the revolution that will usher in the golden age. There is no such mandate in the Bible, and those millennialists who argue for the use of violence to bring about the Parousia have to ignore explicit statements to the contrary. Marxism allows no passivity in destroying capitalism, even if its overthrow is inevitable, and the obligation to be active can be highly attractive to many people. As Julius Caesar said about battle, it is not in the nature of men to wait for the enemy to attack; they want to take the fight to the enemy. A revolutionary does not have to be from the proletariat to help history achieve its goal. Marx, himself a bourgeois, argued that the revolutionary elite, who are that elite precisely because they will stop at nothing to bring about the socialist revolution, would have to lead the workers into the war to destroy the exploiters. It is ironic that for all their attacks on Christianity for its propensity toward violence, millennialists of reason, led by Robespierre and Marx, have been responsible for far more bloodshed in two centuries than Christianity has in two millennia.

X

THE BURNED-OVER
DISTRICT

T HE RISE OF SECULAR MILLENNIALISM certainly did not destroy the
Christian version, which became even more widespread as the
former appeared. Millennialism took on new forms and doctrines in part
through the cross-fertilization of ideas from the secular thinkers. The
spread of religious eschatology also was in part a response to the antireligious violence of its secular counterpart. Between the two approaches to the endtime, there were many more people committed to
some sort of millennial thought by the late nineteenth century than there
had been a century earlier.

Millennial movements appeared during the Enlightenment in
France under the absolute monarchy, despite the hostility of both to
them. Jansenism, a dissident Catholic movement, rose in the mid-sev-
enteenth century. It quickly caught hostile attention from the crown,
which could accept only conformity, and some Jansenists became involved in political dissent. The repression of the Jansenists never
reached the level of executions, but state action against them succeeded in reducing the movement to a small group by 1730. From
those who were left emerged the Convulsionaries, so-called from
their public displays of penance by which they hoped to hasten the
Second Coming. They were certain it was close at hand because of
the evil state of the world. The Convulsionaries believed that once a
time of trial purified the French church, it would serve as the means

of reunion for all Christendom prior to the end of the world. The Jews would be restored to Palestine and converted, and the return of the prophet Elijah would inaugurate all these events. Many Convulsion-aries at first supported the French Revolution because they expected a purified church to result, preparing the world for the endtime. As the revolution took a more radical and anticlerical turn, they backed off their support but remained convinced that it was the tribulation prior to the Parousia.

Most French Catholics denounced the revolution as the work of Antichrist, but some supported it on millennial grounds. Bishop Pierre Pontard argued that forming the republic, disestablishing the church, and granting citizenship to Jews were signs of a great regeneration of the world. The Jews would become Christians, regain their place as the chosen people, and assemble in Palestine. Then God would create the new heavens and new earth. Most prominent among millennialists who supported the revolution were two women, Suzette Labrousse and Catherine Théot. From humble provincial backgrounds they both had had hopes of becoming nuns but had been disappointed. By 1770 they had reputations as prophets and were predicting a regeneration of France and the Church. Both deviated from Catholic orthodoxy: Labrousse by demanding the pope give up political power before the purification of the Church could occur, and Théot by attacking clerical corruption. Labrousse gained attention at that start of the revolution by proclaiming that it was inaugurating the third age of the spirit. Some in the National Assembly discussed her predictions at its meetings, espe-cially her prophecy that a supernatural event would occur in 1790 to signal the regeneration of nation and religion. As the anticlerical Ja-cobins gained control over the revolution, Labrousse became con-vinced that her prediction had not come true because the pope had not given up political authority. In 1792 she went to Rome to tell the pope directly of his obligation and was imprisoned for antipapal agitation. Napoleon released her in 1798, and she returned to France, continuing to proclaim the Parousia's coming to a tiny group of followers until her death in 1821.

Théot, who was already over 70 years old in 1789, was then resid-ing in Paris, where she had acquired a cadre of disciples primarily from among female artisans and laborers. Like nearly every millennial group, however, it had some well-off members. When about seventy members were arrested in 1794, they were asked how they came to join her group, and all said that family and neighbors had brought them to it. They came to the attention of the revolutionary authorities because their meetings in a working-class neighborhood in Paris had been denounced as anti-revolutionary fanaticism. The police reports indicate that Mother Catherine proclaimed that she was the new Eve who would crush the head of serpent and that Paris would be the new Jerusalem after the revolution purified France and the Church. The group had a series of ritualistic kisses intended to protect the members from the tribulation and ensure that Christ would recognize the elect at his coming. The authorities apparently deemed them no threat, as none were executed. Neither Labrousse nor Théot had much influence beyond 1800, but as lower-class women they provide evidence of an important change in popular millennialism: Since 1750 women often have been millennial leaders.

The change also occurred in England, where millennialism continued to attract wide interest. Endtime calculating of the sort Newton did remained common, as demonstrated by another prominent figure in the history of science, the chemist Joseph Priestley. The more intense millennialism of the Puritan Revolution was little seen in the half-century after 1660 but then reappeared largely through French Huguenot influence. It had been rare among the Huguenots while the Edict of Nantes remained in effect, but when Louis XIV revoked the edict in 1685, it reappeared full force. A pastor, Pierre Jurieu, published a series of works declaring that all the signs for the endtime, which he predicted for 1689, were obvious, including the identity of Louis XIV as Antichrist. In southern France, where Protestantism had been strongest, a series of lay prophets arose, including a sixteen-year-old shepherdess, Isabeau Vincent, who proclaimed that the persecution would last only 42 months and then Christ would carry his saints to heaven. When 1689 failed to bring deliverance and Jurieu's recalculation for 1690 proved wrong again, some Huguenots turned to violence. A rebellion broke out in 1702. Some rebels believed that God would protect them against the royal troops as they went into battle. They were mistaken, and the revolt was crushed by 1705.

Some survivors fled to England, where they became known as the French Prophets. They gained a large audience in London and introduced a new style to the preaching of millennialism. The believers gathered in private homes to listen to Bible readings and sing psalms while waiting for one of the prophets to receive divine inspiration. When it came, after some hours, the prophets would shake and writhe, and then begin to speak in tongues. Scribes would take down what they were saying, and the meaning was later deciphered. Usually it involved predicting the time of the Parousia. As the Huguenots won converts among the English, some converts began to prophesy in the same manner, and they all became known as the French Prophets. What they predicted was a catastrophic end to the world in the immediate future. The death in 1707 of an English member, Thomas Emes, prior to the Parousia created a crisis. His death confounded the Prophets, and they responded by declaring he would rise from the dead in forty days. On the appointed day a crowd of about 20,000 persons gathered at the grave, but there was no sign of Emes. That prediction's failure did not chase off many members, and later the Prophets announced that believers had to wear a green ribbon so that the destroying angel of the Lord would recognize them when he came to end the world. They suggested that Emes had died because he had not been wearing one.

Female prophets were common among the Huguenots in France and the French Prophets in England. As the movement began to falter by 1720 because of the constant deferral of the Parousia, women assumed a greater role, and the majority of the followers were women. The French Prophets had some connections with the Quakers, another English religious movement in which women had larger-than-usual roles, and they had an impact on a Quaker couple, Jane and James Wardleys, from Bolton. The Wardleys left the Quakers in 1747 and formed the Bolton Society, which combined elements of both groups. Especially notable was the group's emphasis on waiting for divine inspiration; when the Spirit came upon them, all present, not just the prophet, would shake, shout, and writhe together. The Shaking Quakers, as the Bolton Society was called, were strongly millennial. What the Spirit usually announced to them was that the time for repentance was at hand since the end was near.

In 1758 an uneducated woman of twenty-two years named Ann Lee joined the sect. She was the daughter of one blacksmith and had married another when very young. Deeply unhappy in her marriage, repelled by sex, and distressed by the death in infancy of her four babies, she left her husband for the life of a prophet. In 1770 she and several followers were thrown into prison, and she allegedly went for two weeks without food. If true, it may explain her visions in which Christ revealed that celibacy was necessary to enter the New Kingdom, as sex was the sin that chased Adam and Eve out of the Garden. In her most important vision, Christ told her that since he first appeared to women after his resurrection, it was a sign that his Second Coming would be in female form. Her disciples later declared that Lee was this woman, although she seems not to have said it herself. Released from prison, she gathered around her a small group, called the United Society of Believers in Christ's Second Appearing. In 1774 Mother Ann, as she became known, had a vision in which Christ told her that there were chosen people in America who needed ministry. She and eight followers sailed for America, where her movement, better known as the Shakers, prospered for a century.

The decades surrounding 1800 in England were filled with millennial prophets, although the turn of that century was an eschatological marker for only a few. The profound social and economic changes wrought by the Industrial Revolution created a deep need for security, a need that millennialism answered for some by offering certainty in a world that had lost its stability. The French Revolution also was a source of uncertainty, sowing confusion in the minds of English millennialists. Many interpreted the fall of the French monarchy as the destruction of Antichrist, while others were convinced that the Jacobins were his agents, an opinion that was easier to hold as they grew more violent and antireligious. Matters became all the more confusing when Britain joined papist Spain and Austria in war against France in 1792. Napoleon also was identified as Antichrist once he seized power.

The revolution was of major millennial significance for Richard Brothers, who served as an officer in the British navy during the American Revolution. He resigned his commission after the war, and forming deep scruples about military service, he refused to take the oath to the king required for his pension. Destitute, he went three days without eating in 1791 and then had a vision in which God told him that he intended to burn London because its sins had made it the new Babylon. Brothers begged God to allow him to warn the people before it was destroyed, and God agreed to give it more time. Despite being in and out of asylums over the next five years, Brothers took on the task of saving London. He proclaimed that the new French republic would do God's work in destroying all monarchies. This would prepare for the coming end when, on May 4, 1795, Brothers would be acclaimed as the Prince of the Hebrews as a direct descendent of King David. He declared that his duty required him to lead the all the Jews, including the "hidden Jews"—the English—to Jerusalem in time for the Parousia. It was not a new idea, but Brothers helped popularize the notion that the English were the Lost Tribes, a belief that became known as British-Israelism in the next century. He spent the rest of his life planning for the heavenly city, even deciding what plants to grow there.

In the midst of the war with France, Brothers attracted many people, including members of Parliament and a prominent lawyer who sold his practice for £25,000 and spent it promoting Brothers's cause. Nathaniel Halhed, a member of Parliament and eminent scholar of Sanskrit, used Brothers's calculation for the date of the creation to conclude that the Millennium would begin on November 19, 1795, at the moment of sunrise in Jerusalem. Another luminary briefly in Brothers's circle was the poet William Blake. No other major literary figure has been as consumed by millennialism as he was. His works are replete with references, both obvious and covert, to apocalyptic books. He was fully committed to British-Israelism, as shown in these lines from his "Milton, A Poem in Two Books":

> I will not cease from Mental Fight,
> Nor shall my Sword sleep in my hand:
> Till we have built Jerusalem,
> In England's green & pleasant Land.

After 1800 Brothers lost much of his following. One phenomenon in millennialism over the past two centuries involves the movement of people from one prophet to another, as the first makes too many inaccurate predictions and the next provides a new sense of excitement and authenticity. (It probably was often true in earlier times as well, but evidence for such a conclusion is lacking.) Many of those who left Brothers joined Joanna Southcott. She was a farmer's daughter from Exeter who for years had worked as a servant. In 1792 she, claiming to be the woman of Revelation 12, began to prophesy, reflecting the fear over what was happening in France. When Napoleon took power, she publicized the conclusion reached by another woman that value of his name in Latin was 666. Southcott printed a pamphlet in 1801 that declared the opening of the seven seals was at hand. At the same time she found a seal with the initials IC that she used to seal letters declaring the bearer was an heir of God. Some 14,000 people received her letters by 1804 and became Sealed People. The Southcottians waited for Christ's return with little demanded of them except to believe in the imminent Parousia, although men were obliged to grow beards.

For the next decade the size of Southcott's following remained largely stable. She continued to make vague predictions about the evils that would befall England if the people did not repent. There were enough calamities in England for the Southcottians to proclaim that her prophecies had come true. An important part of her beliefs came from the passage of Genesis that describes the enmity between the seed of the devil and the woman. Southcott was that woman who would cast back on Satan the guilt of Eve. Thus, in 1814 she made an unexpected announcement that, despite being a virgin at age 63, she was pregnant with a son who would be the Shiloh, as she called the new messiah based on the verse: "The scepter shall not depart from Judah, until Shiloh come" (Gen. 49:10). Several physicians examined her fully clothed, for she refused to submit to a true examination, and declared that she was pregnant, setting the delivery day for Christmas. As it approached, Southcott, weakening rapidly, predicted that she would die after she delivered her son. That part of her prediction was true, as she died two days after Christmas but without giving birth. An autopsy revealed that she had not been pregnant. Disappointing as it was, it failed to break up her movement. Many continued to believe that she would return from the dead and give birth to the Shiloh; others, that he had been born but taken immediately to heaven and would eventually return.

Among the five prophets who claimed leadership of the Southcottians, the most successful was John Wroe. He emphasized that they were Christian Israelites and required adult circumcision, the use of Mosaic law, and distinctive dress. He demanded that his followers obey him absolutely and allegedly required that his young female followers submit to him sexually. Charged with seduction, he left England about 1840 and traveled to America and Australia. In both places he succeeded in winning converts and influenced several other millennial groups. The Australian Wroites alone raised enough money to build a mansion at Southcott's English birthplace 50 years after her death.

The most influential of the nineteenth-century English millennialists, John Nelson Darby, was less flamboyant and more virtuous. Born in 1800 and intended for a career in law, a spiritual struggle led him to the priesthood in the Church of England. When a fall off a horse required a lengthy convalescence, he was led to reflect on his growing discontent with the Church. Reading Acts, he was struck by its contrast with the church's present state, and he sought ministry outside it. Darby joined a group of like-minded believers in 1827 for Bible study. The group became known as the Plymouth Brethren; by 1845, they had grown to over 1,200 members. Darby spread the Brethren movement across Europe and North America until his death in 1882.

Darby was adamant in his belief that the Bible was the inspired, infallible word of God, absolutely authoritative and faithfully transmitted from its authors. He is credited with much of the theological content of the Fundamentalist movement so important in American Christianity for the past century. His belief in biblical authority carried over to his millennialism: One must go directly to the Scriptures and specifically to Revelation to understand the nature of the Second Coming. Darby and those who followed him rejected any symbolic meaning for Revelation. The events would occur in the order and manner as described there with all of its violence, blood, and vengeance on evildoers. According to Darby, the church was in a state of ruin, and thus Christ's return to establish the New Kingdom was imminent. While Darby's call for a radical change in the church had little effect, his teachings on eschatology were widely embraced. He argued that nothing was clearer in the New Testament than Christ's Parousia. Darby was adamant, however, that the Bible absolutely prohibited date-setting, citing the eight passages that explicitly do so. The good Christian does not know the day or the hour, but lives every day in preparation for Christ's return because today may be the day it happens.

Darby is called the father of premillennial dispensationalism. Dispensationalism refers to the idea that God has established seven stages or dispensations of salvation history. Five are placed in the Old Testament. For example, the age of the promise was from Abraham to Moses. The sixth and current dispensation is the age of the church, about which the Bible has little to say. It began at Christ's crucifixion and would end with the Rapture. It was almost certainly Darby who coined the term "the Rapture" for when the saints are taken into the sky to meet Christ as he descends (1 Thess. 4:17). He would take them to glory with him, to become the bride of the Lamb, while the reprobate would remain on earth to suffer the agonies of the tribulation. The unfolding of events after the Rapture is also clear. The tribulation will last 1,260 days, which is not a symbolic number a but literal number of days. Then will come Armageddon, when Christ and the heavenly hosts come down to defeat Antichrist and bind him in the pit. Christ's return will inaugurate the 1,000-year period of peace, when he will reign in glory from a site in Palestine. Satan will be released from the pit for the final battle against Christ. After Satan is defeated will come the Last Judgment. None of this is new to Darby, since it comes entirely from Revelation, but he presented it coherently, citing at great length the biblical texts without being distracted by previous theologians, Augustine in particular.

Premillennial dispensationalism, in its emphasis on taking all the appropriate biblical texts literally and consistently, accepts the view that there will be signs for the approach of the endtime that will be obvious when they occur. Part of the task of being a good Christian is to watch for them, although they will not reveal a date for the Rapture. One of those signs is the return of the Jews to Palestine to restore their ancient nation and rebuild the Temple. Darby rejected any idea that Amerindians or English might be the Lost Tribes. When the Bible speaks of the Jews rebuilding the Temple, it means the descendants of the Jews of

Christ's time. Those Jews had rejected Christ; their children must accept him as the messiah. That would occur, however, only after they suffer terrible persecution by Antichrist. The surviving Jews in the number of 144,000 will then convert to Christianity.

In the long term, premillennial dispensationalism was the major millennial theory to come to the United States during the nineteenth century, where its influence became ever more powerful in the twentieth century. It arrived at a time when Darby's emphasis on the literal interpretation of the Bible and its inerrancy attracted conservative Christians increasingly upset at new critical theories that considered Scripture as little more than history or folklore. His views also arrived in America shortly after other popular approaches to millennialism had suffered deep embarrassments.

Millennialism found its home in the United States after the War of Independence. There was a powerful sense that America was the chosen land. It was new and fresh, the place where the New Kingdom could be created, unlike the old corrupt lands of Europe. The disestablishment of the Anglican Church and the absence of any coercive authority to force people to conform to a particular interpretation of Christianity meant that sects could flourish in a manner impossible anywhere else in the world, even England. The developing democracy was instilling in many ordinary men the sense that their ideas were important and worthy of consideration. Everything was in flux; if an idea did not work, then one easily tried something else. The rapid transformation to the market economy, while making many people wealthy beyond their dreams, left large numbers far behind, ruining middle-class families and pauperizing workers. For all these reasons and more, the first half of the nineteenth century saw the flourishing of nearly every variation of millennialism. It should be noted, however, that one type absent was violent chiliasm.

One form of millennialism that reached its zenith in early nineteenth-century America was the apostolic community. One reason for the great number of communities, both millennial and utopian in inspiration, that sprang up especially between 1820 and 1840 was the availability of cheap land. Europeans who planned to create the new world by building a model community had to look to America because of the lack of land in Europe. The range of types of communities was nearly as vast as their numbers, and for purposes of brevity we will discuss only those that had long-term success or major implications for future millennial movements.

The most successful, both in duration and number of inhabitants, were the Shaker communities. Mother Ann Lee arrived in New York in 1774 with eight disciples and the intention of proselytizing among poor New Yorkers. The suspicion that the newcomers were British spies soon forced them out of the city, and they founded a settlement near Albany where they developed the distinctive Shaker lifestyle. In 1781 Mother Ann proselytized in New England and had surprising success, given that Shaker beliefs were difficult for most to accept because celibacy, communal living, and female preachers were rare in that place and time. Mobs frequently attacked the meetings where she preached. While the violence frightened off many people, it strengthened the commitment of the members against the wicked outside world. Mother Ann died in 1784, possibly a victim of mob violence, since Shaker legend has it that her skull was fractured when she was dragged down some stairs. Her death was one of many ways in which her followers claimed that she, the second Christ, paralleled his life. Some of her followers, who expected her to be immortal or at least live through the Millennium, were disillusioned and left the Shakers. It could be argued, however, that given her lack of interest in organization, she was worth more as a dead martyr than alive to her followers, for the movement began to expand only after her death. In 1787 the Shakers founded New Lebanon, also near Albany, to gather in the believers, and it became the Shaker mother house. It was there, largely under the leadership of first James Whittaker and then Joseph Meachem and Lucy Wright, that the final form of communal Shaker life was established. Active missionary work expanded their numbers greatly after 1800. There were nineteen communities from Maine to Kentucky; New Lebanon at 550 members in 1823 was the largest. The total number of Shakers reached its maximum at about 3,850 members, according to the 1850 census.

Shaker theology was based on the premise that both the promised revelation of God as Mother and the Second Coming of Christ had occurred in Mother Ann. The millennial kingdom had come down from heaven, and the world's indictment was underway. To live in Mother

Ann's spirit was to share in the reward of the saints, to be in the heavenly realm already. The New Kingdom with its perfect social order had to be clearly demarcated from the old profane world of sinners. It could be achieved only by living in separated communities of saints with a distinctive lifestyle and dress. The Shaker lifestyle was truly distinctive. It was totally celibate; membership grew by winning converts and taking in orphans, although many of the latter left when they grew up. To avoid sexual temptation, men and women remained segregated, although they lived in the same community and worshipped in the same room at the same time. Women and men had their own clearly marked spaces for work, worship, and other activities of life; there was virtually no mixing. The one area in which they worked together was the governance of the community: Female and male elders met to decide all matters. Women enjoyed as equal a share of authority in the Shaker communities as would be found in nineteenth-century America. Celibacy also solved the problem of mothers and babies, except for a few women who joined with their children. The maternal instinct usually has conflicted badly with communal upbringing of babies and has often been a major cause of dissension in other communities.

The Shakers practiced complete communal ownership of goods and labored diligently to make their communities entirely self-sufficient. Their commitment to craftsmanship—they are best known today for their Shaker furniture—gave their goods a reputation for high quality, and their communities earned large sums selling to outsiders. Unlike other communal societies that often collapsed in dispute over the use of resources, the Shaker communities had relatively few problems of that sort, although they had their share of defectors who could not live their lifestyle. Since theirs was a realized eschatology, the lack of any new revelation and signs of the Second Coming was not a serious problem for them or a cause of significant loss of members. Celibacy, on which the Shakers never compromised, always has had its attraction, especially for women prior to the development of reliable birth control. Shaker insistence on it, however, meant that there would be no self-propagation of members, and fewer and fewer were attracted to the Shaker lifestyle in the changing American society after the Civil War. Membership dropped below 1000 persons by 1905. New Lebanon was closed in 1947, and there is now one house with eight Shakers at Sabbathday Lake, Maine.

The issue of sex has always been a major concern for millennial communities, and the solution usually has not been celibacy. The most direct contrast to the Shakers in regard to sex was the Oneida Community in upstate New York. Its founder was John Noyes, born in 1811 in Vermont, whose relatives included President Rutherford Hayes. At age twenty, while reading for the law, Noyes attended a revival put on by Charles Finney. Finney's stock-in-trade as a revivalist included all-night meetings and terrifying descriptions of hellfire, but he was a postmillennialist who hoped to frighten his audiences into reforming their lives and becoming saints. Unlike for the Calvinists, for Finney humanity was not intrinsically depraved. Ignorance and self-interest led to sin, but the individual could be weaned away from sin through conversion and become sinless. Out of the pulpit, Finney was a reformer who was convinced that the Millennium could be brought about quickly by an extensive agenda of good works and missionary work. Sin must be confronted directly. Finney himself was not an active abolitionist, but many abolitionists, for whom slavery was the worst sin, heard his call for an onslaught against sin and concluded that eliminating slavery would mark the beginning of the Millennium. Finney became president of Oberlin College in Ohio, an abolitionist stronghold.

Finney was the most successful of the many revivalists who created the Second Great Awakening of the 1830s. It was widespread across New England but its epicenter was upstate New York, where the fires of revivalism and millennialism burned so hot that it became known as the Burned-over District, a term Finney may have coined. Noyes was hardly unusual in being whipped into religious frenzy on hearing Finney, but his response was unique. Finney tended toward perfectionism, but Noyes carried it to the ultimate: He simply could not find in himself a sense of sin. After a crisis of faith and mental health in 1834, he declared that Christ's second coming had occurred at the Temple's destruction. It had lifted the burden of sin from believers, abrogated the Ten Commandments, and replaced them with the gospel command: Love one another. Selfishness was the only sin, and Noyes intended to form a society whose members would be free of it. When the full number reached that level of perfection, God would establish the New Kingdom.

Noyes came to believe that traditional marriage was the worst form of selfishness, a truth he discovered because a woman with whom he had fallen in love had married another. He went to Ithaca, New York, to persuade her to leave her husband and marry him. Although his mission failed, he took up residence in the region, and thus at Oneida some sixty miles away his famous community took root ten years later. Noyes soon married as well, and while it appears that he and his wife rarely made love, it was certainly not because he was opposed to sex. The most notorious aspect of the Oneida community was its idea of marriage, which Noyes derived largely because he fell for another woman, Mary Cragin, and satisfied his longing for her by creating "complex marriage." According to Noyes, sex is good, one of God's great gifts to humanity, and sexual activity in the right relationship would enhance the love of God; but traditional marriage fosters a sense of attachment between the spouses, which is hostile to the love of God. Complex marriage allowed a couple to marry, but to ensure that the attachment between them was not selfish, others would be encouraged to have sex with them on the condition that Noyes and all the spouses involved consented. Only those who could make love to another's spouse without any sense of sin were allowed to enter into complex marriage.

Noyes was highly sympathetic to women, who had to face the pain of giving birth and the high possibility of death in childbirth but had little if any control over when they would become pregnant. Noyes argued that women should have the major say in that regard, and he was convinced women would enjoy sex as much as men if they did not worry about becoming pregnant. The solution was male continence: Men should have sex to give pleasure to their partners yet not climax. Such discipline required extensive training, and he argued that older women beyond childbearing age should train young men until they were capable of withholding their ejaculations.

Children, Noyes maintained, posed a similar attachment as marriage. A parent's attachment to a child was selfish. Once infants were weaned, they should belong to the community and be raised by it; children were told who their parents were and had special times set aside to visit with them. By 1866, with no sign that the New Kingdom was any closer, Noyes decided that it was necessary for his community to bring it about by creating a spiritually elite race through the selective mating of its members. Fifty-three women and thirty-eight men volunteered to serve as the parents of elite babies, although not all were allowed to mate because Noyes did not regarded them as spiritually advanced. Fifty-eight children came from those couplings, and Noyes, as the spiritual superman, had at least nine by as many women including a niece (he would have advocated closer forms of incest but thought the outside world would not tolerate it), along with three children by his wife and Mary Cragin.

The Oneida community was a communist society in material matters as well. Noyes drew extensively from Fourier in organizing his community. Unlike most Fourierists, Noyes was an astute businessman. With a balance between agriculture and industry, Oneida flourished and its members lived well. He overcame the problem found in most utopian communities—the refusal of many members to pull their full weight—by a system of mutual criticism. Adopting the latest technology, Oneida gained a reputation for high-quality but inexpensive goods, especially its tableware.

By 1870 a new generation was in place at Oneida, who had not experienced the revivalist fires of the Second Great Awakening. Noyes's complex marriage had not overcome the tendency toward monogamy or at least special relationships; when Noyes refused to allow certain couples to mate, hurt feelings spread discontent through the community. Unwilling to tolerate his authoritarian leadership any longer, several members cooperated with outside enemies of Oneida, mostly the local clergy, who for years had been looking for a way to shut it down. In 1879 a local newspaper announced that Noyes would be indicted for seducing teenage girls; unwilling to face trial, he fled to Canada and never was prosecuted. Without his leadership, the split between those eager to maintain his system and those who wanted change tore the community apart. In 1881 the 306 adult members, with Noyes's assent, agreed to form a joint-stock company for Oneida's properties. Some members lived Noyes's lifestyle in the great house for two more decades. Noyes died in Canada in 1886; the silverware business continues to flourish today.

The long-term success of millennialist communities like New Lebanon, Oneida, and those of the Amana Society in Iowa, founded by German communists with a realized eschatology, contrasts sharply with the almost immediate failure of the utopian socialist communities. It is easy to see how the Fourierists, with their impractical phalansteries, would fail, but explaining the quick collapse of the Owenite communities, especially the best known, New Harmony in Indiana, is more difficult. New Harmony had two major advantages: the presence of Robert Owen himself for two years and the incorporation of a flourishing village established by a religious society, the Rappites. George Rapp was a German Lutheran weaver who in 1791 announced that he was the prophet of the last days. He demanded celibacy of his followers in preparation for the Parousia. In the midst of Napoleon's wars, whom he deemed Antichrist, Rapp became convinced that the predictions in Revelation were coming true. The true church, the Harmony Society, had to flee into the wilderness to escape Antichrist. In 1805, 500 members founded a commune in Pennsylvania called Harmony. From the start, its hard-working artisans had success. Attracting more German immigrants and some Americans to Harmony, Rapp decided in 1814 to build a new village, choosing a site in western Indiana because of cheap land there. As the region's center of industry and agriculture, New Harmony and its 800 residents flourished. Yet because of its isolation from other Rappites, Rapp agreed to sell the village in 1825 when Owen offered a vast sum for it. Most Rappites moved back to Pennsylvania, where they founded a second village called Economy. Despite his attention to building villages, Rapp's millennialism had not declined. He announced that the present age would end on September 15, 1829. The failure of his prediction, while it led to a schism in the Harmony Society, did not discomfit Rapp. When he died in 1847, his last words were that if he did not know that he was divinely appointed to lead the saints into paradise, he would think he was dying. The Harmony Society lasted until 1916, when it was dissolved and its assets given to the state of Pennsylvania.

Owen thus had an established village when he issued a call for people to come to New Harmony and create his New Moral World. Owen visited Shaker and Rappite villages before purchasing New Harmony, but he failed to understand the nature of their success. Unlike the religious communities, there was neither a sense of a common cause nor any commitment to communal living among his recruits, many of whom had already met with failure in life. Owen made no effort to screen those who showed up. He had spent the prior year in America soliciting support among the wealthy, and some of them, eager to reform humanity, came to New Harmony, along with the workers and farmers needed to make the village function. Despite being largely useless in practical matters, the wealthy were better rewarded than the laborers, which sparked resentment among the latter. There was no sense of equality in the commune, as Owen had expected would naturally happen in his new society. Still another problem was that he based his social theory on the rationalism of the Enlightenment, which enhanced individualism, not communalism. By pressing his rationalist principles on his villagers, he only encouraged their individualism. New Harmony underwent eleven reorganizations before it disbanded in 1828. Despite this failure, twenty more Owenite communes were founded in North America. None endured for long, and the final one was dissolved five years after Owen died in 1858.

Both the collapse of New Harmony and Noyes's notion of complex marriage embarrassed millennialists, but their worst setback was the "Great Disappointment," the failure of the prediction that the world would end on October 22, 1844. William Miller, responsible for one of the most notorious episodes in millennialism, was a respected, sober farmer from Vermont. In 1816 at age 34 he attended a revival and converted from his youthful deism to active membership in the local Baptist church. His conversion led him to immerse himself in reading the Bible. Convinced of its literal truthfulness, he came to believe that the books of prophecy could be used to foretell the endtime exactly. Using the numbers found in Daniel and Revelation, he concluded that Ussher was wrong in predicting the end for 1996. Most significant for him was the passage that 2,300 mornings and evenings would pass before the Temple would be restored (Daniel, 8:14). Taking that to mean 2,300 years and dating the prophecy to 457 BC, Miller derived the endtime year as falling between March 1843 and March 1844. His views on what would ensue then came out of Revelation.

Miller reached his conclusion in 1818 but only made it public in 1831. He did so at the time when American optimism in the antebellum period had perhaps reached its height. Most Americans were convinced theirs was the promised land; progress seemed to be rapidly changing the character of humanity; and premillennialism with its images of the violent destruction of world had faded nearly out of sight. Yet Miller struck a highly responsive chord from Maine to Michigan, but little farther south. Millerites came from every Protestant denomination, in particular Methodism. There was no specific theological content to Miller's millennialism, although he did maintain the belief in the papal Antichrist. Miller's appeal came from insisting on a literal interpretation of Revelation. He claimed to have given at least 4,500 sermons on the topic, usually in revivalist meetings, and his pamphlets sold thousands of copies. A disciple, Joshua Himes, started newspapers in the major eastern cities with names such as *Signs of the Times* to spread the prophecy. It was the first time that a mass medium was used to disseminate millennialism. By 1843 some 100,000 people were expecting the endtime, and several times that number waited for the designated date with some trepidation. They were from every social level, and there is no evidence that the poor were involved in a proportion any higher than merchants and professionals.

When March 1844 passed, Miller, possibly the least assuming of millennial prophets, acknowledged that he had miscalculated, and in May he joined other leaders of the movement in resetting the date. They agreed that the end would occur the next October 22. This date was actively promoted as the right one, and perhaps because it was so specific, more people prepared for it. There were reports of farmers refusing to harvest crops because of their faith that they would not need them. As the day approached, evidence indicates that many Second Adventists, as Millerites preferred to be known, closed their shops, sold their properties, or forgave debts. The *Advent Herald,* in its last edition a week before the date, declared that it was making no provisions for another issue. Others continued their daily routine until the day arrived. They then jammed churches and meeting halls praying that they would be among those taken in the Rapture.

There was little fanaticism, and the only trouble, besides overcrowding in some churches, was caused by rowdies who ridiculed the faithful as they waited. Among the myths of American history is one that the Millerites, dressed in white "ascension gowns," went to the hilltops to wait for the Rapture; there is no evidence that any did this. The source of the story probably comes from the report that two scoffers donned white gowns and climbed onto the roof of a church in Maine where Millerites were assembled. Another story relates that as a congregation waited prayerfully for the end, a trumpet sounded outside and then sounded a second time. The Millerites rushed out in near hysteria, only to find that the town drunk was playing a trick on them. Another myth is that many Millerites went mad in their excitement waiting for the end or in disappointment over the failure. While they probably attracted their share of mentally unstable persons, there is no evidence that insanity was common among them. Much of the behavior of the Millerites, nonetheless, did strike outsiders as bordering on madness.

The only result was the "Great Disappointment." Hiram Edison described the reaction of the Millerites with whom he had assembled: "Our fondest hopes and expectations were blasted, and such a spirit of weeping came over us as I never experienced before. . . . We wept and wept until the day dawned. . . . Has the Bible proved a failure? Is there no God, no heaven, no golden city, no paradise?"[1] Despite such a black morning of the soul for the Millerites, many did not abandon hope that the end was near. Waiting for the Rapture was so psychologically powerful an experience—Edison called it "the richest and brightest of all my Christian experience"—that it was very difficult to give it up. Then too there was the problem of the scoffers, who took great delight in ridiculing the Millerites as they inconsolably left their churches. Vindication was sorely needed.

The Millerites showed the entire range of responses to the failure of prophecy except violence. Many abandoned their faith entirely; some returned chastised to their original churches; others joined the Shakers or similar communes. Probably a majority remained Adventists and sought an explanation for the failure. Some argued that Christ had come but in spirit and had closed the door to heaven, based on the parable of the marriage feast and the ten virgins (Matt. 25:6), and that only those who were among the saints on October 22 would join him when they died. All others, especially scoffers, were damned. Many of the Millerites organized Adventist churches, although Miller opposed that. He died in 1849 still convinced that the Second Coming was imminent. Second Adventism has been highly subject to schism, primarily over the issue of why the predicted dates for the end fail. Many sects have developed out of Second Adventism, including some of the most supercharged millennial groups of the twentieth century.

Millerism by no means disappeared from America after 1844, but it largely gave way to John Darby's dispensationalism. Darby made his first voyage to America in 1862 and found a receptive audience, returning six more times to 1877. His greatest impact was in winning several prominent theologians to his cause. James Brooks, a Presbyterian minister from St. Louis, was a major force behind the Niagara Conference, which met in summer to discuss millennial beliefs. The first conference was held in New York in 1868, attended largely by men associated with the millennial journal *Waymarks in the Wilderness*. After meeting elsewhere several times, the group settled on Niagara, Ontario, where it met from 1883 to 1897. It consisted of some 300 ministers from many Protestant denominations, who remained active in them, along with English members of the Plymouth Brethren. Premillennialism has always attracted people across the range of Protestant groups, including the Pentecostals, who were beginning to organize themselves in that period. The main theme at Niagara was proving premillennial dispensationalism from the biblical texts. Brooks argued that Christ would return twice: He would first come for his saints at the Rapture; then after the seven years of the tribulation, he would return with the saints to reign on earth for 1,000 years. This position, later called pretribulationism, was challenged by some who argued that the rapture would occur either midway through the tribulation, midtribulationism, or only at its end, posttribulationism. The first has been by far the most popular, since it allows the saints to escape the agony of the destruction of the current world. But the third has had a coterie of defenders on the grounds that the tribulation is to be a time of testing of Christians, and only those who stay steadfast through it will be worthy of joining Christ.

A second leader of dispensationalism was Dwight Moody, a Congregationalist Sunday-school teacher, who never formally became a minister but was probably the best-known American churchman of the late nineteenth century. Already a successful evangelist in Chicago, he met Darby and became a dispensationalist. He organized his own bible conference in Massachusetts, but his particular contribution to the movement was his bible institutes for training young people to read the Scriptures and become missionaries. The most important was one in Chicago that became known as the Moody Bible Institute after his death in 1899. Moody took very seriously the biblical charge to proclaim the gospel to every nation before the Parousia could occur, and his institute has been at the forefront of translating the Bible into every language and of training missionaries to bring the message to nonbelievers. Although it has not been obvious from his disciples' attitude and activities over the years, Moody did not expect many conversions. The obligation to preach the gospel to nonbelievers was to Moody the important point, even if the saints among them were few.

The second generation of American dispensationalists included Cyrus Scofield. After a dissolute youth, Brooks converted him and he became pastor of a Congregational church in Dallas in 1882. He was a prolific writer of premillennial works, and his major contribution was the Scofield Reference Bible, which has sold some 10 million copies since 1909. Its strength is its clear, concise style in turn-of-the-century American English, but more important for premillennialism are its notes, placed on the same page with the text and giving key passages a premillennial interpretation. Among the points he emphasized were the return of the Jews to Palestine and identification of Russia with Gog and Magog, both major elements in twentieth-century millennialism.

XI

FROM CIVIL WAR
TO WORLD WAR

B Y 1860 THE MILLENNIALIST SURGE of the previous half-century in America had largely spent itself. Both Millerite premillennialism and perfectionist communalism had suffered embarrassments. Throughout the lands of Western culture, the half-century before 1914 was a quiet period for millennialism, at least in comparison to what had gone before and would happen after. It was too ingrained in Christendom, however, for it to be submerged entirely. Events like the American Civil War continued to spark upsurges in millennial expectations, while the remnants of the Millerites reorganized themselves into distinctive sects that still flourish today. Societies faced with westernization and modernization also had millennial eruptions.

In the North, abolitionism, Protestant zeal, and millennialism were closely connected for 20 years before the Civil War; and after the war a similar relationship existed between the temperance movement and millennialism. Slavery was identified as one of the great sins that cried out to God for vengeance, and both pre- and postmillennialists could easily incorporate that idea into their theology. For premillennialists, its presence in America was one sign of the moral decline that would occur before the Parousia; many Millerites were outspoken abolitionists. For postmillennialists, eliminating slavery was one of the ways in which the world would be perfected prior to the Second Coming. Harriet Beecher Stowe's *Uncle Tom's Cabin* was a call for Americans to free themselves of the sin of slavery before God did it himself. Her symbols were drawn largely from the apocalyptic texts of the Bible, and most people of her time would have understood their meaning, although little of the book is explicitly millennial. The most outspoken of the abolitionists, William Lloyd Garrison, was a perfectionist who believed that if America could purge itself of slavery, the major barrier to achieving its perfection would be removed. He was willing to consider the dissolution of the Union to free the North of that sin's taint. There is no known evidence that abolitionist preachers denounced slave owners as antichristian, but in order to create the perfect society, some sanctioned violence against slave holders and the federal government that was seen as protecting them. John Brown ought to have been a millennialist given his beliefs and acts, but there is little specific evidence that he expressed himself in such terms. Many abolitionists, however, saw him as God's instrument for purging the land of slavery. Garrison spoke for many millennialists throughout history when he said in reference to Brown's raid that he, although a man of peace, preferred Brown's violence to a cowardly and servile spirit.

When Fort Sumter was fired on in April 1861, it was easy for some Northerners to see the approaching war as Armageddon before the Parousia. The victory of the Union was ensured because it was part of the divine plan for bringing about the New Kingdom. By purging the land of slavery, it would establish the divine glory of democratic institutions, and America would become the new Israel. When the pope lost control of the Papal States at the same time, it was further evidence that the Millennium would occur in five years according to Jonathan Edwards's often-cited calculation that the papal Antichrist had gained power in 606, and 1,260 years later would be 1866. While similar sentiments were expressed in the Confederacy, the South lacked as strong a sense of millennialism as the North. It was more difficult to give the same religious tones to a crusade to defend slavery, although some Southern ministers tried.

The millennial crusade is the theme of the greatest of the Civil War songs, "The Battle Hymn of the Republic." Julia Ward Howe moved in the religious and abolitionist circles of Boston and once hosted John Brown. Hearing soldiers singing the popular "John Brown's Body" in

1861, she decided to write more inspiring verses for the tune. It is difficult to imagine that the whole of apocalyptic thought could be summed
up better and in fewer words than the first verse of the hymn:

> Mine eyes have seen the glory of the coming of the Lord;
> He is trampling out the vintage where the grapes of wrath are stored;
> He hath loosed the fateful lightning of his terrible swift sword;
> His truth is marching on.

With the Union's victory, hopes were high that the Millennium was
at hand; the cause even had a martyr, Abraham Lincoln, without which
no millennial movement has been complete. Sadly, President Andrew
Johnson and the Republican Party were hardly ones to bring a people
into the New Kingdom. By 1871 a long-time abolitionist was demanding that a new political party, Jesus Christ's party, be created to bring
about the perfect society that the end of slavery seemed to promise. Although wartime millennialism lingered on in a few souls, most forgot it
quickly enough. There were fortunes to be made and lands to settle, and
the nation was back on track to reaching perfection through progress,
not by God's sudden intervention.

Although the Civil War led to an upsurge in millennial expectations, it was not a significant turning point in the history of American
millennialism. Trends begun before 1860 continued to shape the
decades leading to 1914. Millennial movements from the Burned-over
District proliferated long after the Great Disappointment. Of the many
divisions that had emerged from the Millerites, the largest was Seventh-
day Adventists. Its early leaders included Hiram Edison, James White,
the publisher of the *Second Adventist Review and Sabbath Herald,* and
Ellen Harmon. Harmon was a teenager in 1842, when her family was
ousted from a Methodist church for accepting Miller's prophecy. In December 1844 she had a vision in which she learned that Christ had not
returned because of Sunday worship. It was the mark of the beast, since
the horn of the beast in Daniel (7:25) is depicted as changing the sacred
times. As long as so-called Christians wore that mark, Christ would not
return. Returning to sabbatarian worship would ensure the Parousia. In
1846 she married White and as Ellen White became the long-time leader

of the Seventh-day Adventists. Her frequent visions serve as a major source of their beliefs and explain why they place less emphasis than most millennialists on the usual biblical passages.

At first the Seventh-day Adventists adhered to the "closed-door belief": Only those who had believed in Jesus' coming in 1844 were among the saints. They declared that he had gone into the sanctuary on the appointed day and would wait there for seven years before ending the world. After seven years with no sign that anything had changed, they renounced date setting and began to accept those who had not believed in 1844. Not only was the closed door abandoned, but the Seventh-day Adventists also became active proselytizers, which has remained one of their identifying characteristics. Another is their insistence on a strict dietary and behavioral code: Alcohol, tobacco, and caffeine defile God's temple, which always must be ready for Christ's coming. This view also was responsible for another major feature of the movement—its emphasis on healthful living. Seventh-day Adventism became identified with a meat- and medicine-free lifestyle, and one of its members, later excommunicated for his pantheism, was John Kellogg, who created cornflakes to provide a healthful alternative to meat.

By 1860 the movement had many members in the Midwest, and they held several conferences in Michigan to organize themselves. There was strong opposition to any formal church organization, which opponents denounced as going "back to Babylon"; Adventists regarded Protestantism along with the Catholic church as Babylon. Nonetheless, the drive to organize succeeded without many defections, although a group opposed to Ellen White's authority went its own way as the Church of God (Adventist). The name Seventh-day Adventists was formally adopted for the majority in 1863. The insistence on sabbatarianism created problems for them at a time when Sunday was the only legal day of rest. Frequently in the late 1800s members were arrested and fined for working on Sunday. This only confirmed their self-image as the persecuted saints of the true church and kept an edge on their millennialism. Theirs is a gathered church, and when the appointed number of prepared people receive the good news of Christ's second advent, he will return. These people live throughout the world, and it is the duty of those who already believe to bring the others into the fold; hence their strong emphasis on missionary work. By the time of Ellen White's death in 1915 the church numbered about 137,000 people around the world and was on its way to becoming a significant denomination still convinced that the end was at hand.

Another current millennial denomination that came out of Millerism, similar to the Seventh-day Adventists in important ways and often confused with them, is the Watchtower Bible Society, better known as the Jehovah's Witnesses, the name they have used since 1931. Its founder, Charles Russell, was converted to Adventism by one of Miller's companions by 1872, but he quickly developed his own unique millennialism. He concluded that each day of creation lasted 7,000 years, and thus the first act of creation took place 42,000 years before God created Eve, his last act of creation. God's day of rest until the end of the world must last 7,000 years from Eve's creation. Since Revelation indicates a period of 1,000 years from the return of Christ (who was not divine but the perfect man) to the Last Judgment, human history will last 6,000 years.

Russell worked out a series of events since 1799 that fulfilled prophecies found mostly in Daniel. When Napoleon captured the pope in 1799, it marked the end of the 1,260 days of Antichrist's domination of the Church that began in 539. Over the next 75 years several dates were reached. For example, in 1873 the 6,000 years of human existence were completed. The next year, 1874, was the end of 1,335 days since 539, when the saints were to rise to receive their reward (Daniel 12:12). Russell announced in 1877 that the second advent had occurred in 1874, when Christ returned to the upper air. The saints asleep in the Lord were resurrected and taken to the heavenly Zion. The total number of saints, some dating back to the first generation of Christians while others were still alive, came to 144,000. Since Revelation distinguishes the 144,000 saints from the great multitude from every nation (Rev. 7:9), Russell concluded that the latter would have a different fate. By living through the Millennium they prove themselves worthy of salvation and achieving perfection, and the world will become the earthly paradise. Thus, during the Millennium all people past and present will have a second chance to gain salvation. However, Satan also will have a final chance to win souls from the Great Crowd when he and his demonic hordes are released near the end of the Millennium and battle Christ at Armageddon. Some will fail this test and be destroyed; those who pass it will have eternal life in an earthly paradise.

In 1884 Russell incorporated Zion's Watchtower Bible and Tract Society, and two years later he published the first of his seven books, *Millennial Dawn*. Applying his millennial theory to his followers, he concluded that only a small number are "kingdom heirs"; the rest belong to the Great Crowd. The kingdom heirs have authority over the others whose major task is proselytizing. Jehovah's Witnesses preach two important themes that have strong appeal to nonmembers: There is no hell, because the wicked will be destroyed at the endtime, and "millions now alive will never die" because they join the Great Crowd by becoming Jehovah's Witnesses. Although Russell placed Christ's invisible return in 1874, the "time of the Gentiles" would end in 1914, when there would be visible signs of the Millennium's approach.

The Jehovah's Witnesses have always had a strong sense of alienation from broader society and have recruited largely from the discontented urban poor. Their antagonism to organized churches is so great that they refuse to be referred to as a church. Designating the pope as Antichrist remains in effect for them, while it has disappeared from most Protestant groups. Because Christ has already come and reigns over the earth, they reject all other forms of authority, principally the state's. Absolute rejection of military service and such practices as saluting the flag have made them the object of a great deal of popular resentment and the subject of much legal action; outsiders also have ridiculed their frequent changes in date setting. The Jehovah's Witnesses have used these attitudes to promote a sense of persecution, since being persecuted is a sign of being among the kingdom heirs. Because their focus is firmly on the coming age, the group is one of the best examples among millennialists of the lack of interest in education for its members, for what good is education when the present world will soon end? The genius of Russell and his successors lies in their sense of time and the relationship of the individual to it: The future time is already here, since Christ has returned; yet the individual believer must act as if it has not happened. Jehovah's Witnesses continue to live ordinary lives, no antinomianism for them with the few exceptions noted above. Being a Jehovah's Witness imposes a burden on the believer in respect to relations with nonmembers, but it is a lesser burden than most other sects with so powerful a millennialism. From its beginning, the Watchtower Society has had great success in winning converts, but the size of the society soon created its own problems, especially after 1914.

The most successful of the millennial movements that came out of the Burned-over District was the Church of Jesus Christ of Latter-day Saints, better known as Mormons. The millennial focus of their beliefs is made clear in their official name, since latter day refers to the New Kingdom. The first Mormons had ties to Millerism, but their founder, Joseph Smith, owed little to it; Smith's work largely predated William Miller's public mission. Smith was born in 1805 in Vermont but soon moved to upstate New York. As a teenager, he was caught up in the religious revival of the time and became deeply concerned about his salvation. Seeking divine guidance, he received a visitation from two spiritual beings, who told him not to join any existing churches but wait for the coming of the Church of Christ that was about to be reestablished. In 1823 an angel revealed the existence of gold tablets with the complete gospel as taught by Christ after his Resurrection to one of the Lost Tribes of Israel, the Nephites, who had migrated to North America from Jerusalem before the Babylonian captivity. Christ came to preach to them after his resurrection, and the prophet Mormon had compiled the tablets containing Christ's message. Smith, claiming descent from Joseph in Genesis, translated the tablets as the Book of Mormon, which was published in 1830. According to it, America is the Land of Zion, where the new Jerusalem will be built by the gathering of the Israelites before the Messiah's return. The Mormon statement of faith says: "We believe in the literal gathering of Israel and in the restoration of the Ten Tribes. That Zion will be built upon this continent. That Christ will reign personally upon the earth, and that the earth will be renewed and receive its paradisaic glory." Because members of the Mormon Church are the real Hebrews, nonmembers, including Jews, are termed Gentiles.

Having gained several hundred converts, in 1830 Smith organized the Latter-day Saints into a church, the name making a distinction from the saints of Christ's time. The members readily accepted being called Mormons. Smith was deemed first elder, prophet, seer, and revelator.

Because the purpose of the church was to gather the people of Zion in chosen places to watch for Christ's return, the Mormons were infused with proselytizing zeal and moved from New York to Ohio in 1831, since Smith had received a revelation that the chosen place was in the West. Efforts were made to establish The United Order, a communal system designed to make the church members equal in all things spiritual and temporal. According to the Book of Mormon, such an order had prevailed among the Nephites for two centuries after Christ's visit. While the communal aspect of the Mormons never reached the level of intensity of the Shakers, for example, there has always been a sense of sharing among the Mormons that has helped them weather hard times. Smith soon chose a site in Missouri for the new Jerusalem, and most Mormons moved there. In 1838 trouble arose between the locals and the Mormons. Armed mobs attacked them, and although Mormons are not pacifists, they were driven from Missouri. They retreated to Illinois, where they built the city of Nauvoo. By this time recruiting abroad had begun, and in 1839 Brigham Young and other missionaries visited England, preaching in all the principal cities. In England they founded a periodical called the *Millennial Star* and established an emigration agency. The first Mormons from abroad reached Nauvoo in 1840.

The state of Illinois allowed the Mormons to organize the Nauvoo Legion as part of the state militia, commanded by Joseph Smith. Local resentment over Mormon privileges soon led to trouble. The immediate cause of their flight from Illinois was Smith's promulgation of a revelation in 1843 establishing polygamy. The prophet had been practicing it personally for several years, having received a divine command to reintroduce plural marriage as practiced by the Hebrew patriarchs. Opposition appeared immediately within and without the church. Opponents among the Mormons published a newspaper setting out their objections, and Smith led his militia in destroying the press. In response a mob killed Smith and his brother in June 1844, providing martyrs for the church, always useful for a religion.

In the ensuing exodus, Young, back from England, led the first band of Mormons westward, reaching Utah in July 1847. A few days after their arrival they laid out Salt Lake City and designated it the New Zion; in 1853 they began building the great temple. Over the next years most

Mormons migrated to Utah. Those who remained in the Midwest were rift with schisms, and perhaps the most interesting was led by James Stang, who joined the church only four months before Smith was killed. Foiled in his attempts to take over its leadership, he led a band northward, eventually settling on Beaver Island in northern Lake Michigan. There he had himself crowned King in Zion and ruled over 3,000 people, who practiced polygamy. As the absolute monarch of the place where Christ was to return, Stang generated great resentment within his community, and in 1856 two followers murdered him. His following soon dissipated. Another splinter group of Mormons, the Reorganized Church of Latter Day Saints, formed by Joseph Smith's son, has flourished since 1852 and today has over 200,000 members.

In Utah the Mormons had far greater success, finding there the isolation they needed to found new Zion and wait for Christ's return. Consistent with the agrarian background of their leaders, they divided the desert of Utah into small farms, and cooperation and hard work made it bloom. In March 1849, the settlers in Utah formed a provisional government pending action on their petition for admission as a state. Congress denied the petition because of their practice of polygamy. Eventually, after some violence during the "Utah War" of 1857–58, the Latter-day Saints submitted to Congressional legislation and abandoned polygamy in 1890. Utah was admitted as a state in 1896. Not all Mormons accepted the renunciation of polygamy; many regarded the practice as the identifying mark of the saints precisely because of gentile objections. Schismatic groups continue to practice it up to the present, and several Mormon sects have resorted to violence in defense of what they regard as a divine command.

Mormonism has as its principal aim the gathering of a people who will build the new Jerusalem and there await the return of the Lord. Much of the money raised by tithing is used to keep thousands of missionaries in the field following the command to "preach the gospel to every nation." The Mormon Church is the most successful of the actively millennial denominations, with no sign that its zeal for proselytizing and millennialism has cooled. One reason for its success is the concept of baptism for the dead, by which one's ancestors, provided their names are known, can be baptized and entered among the saints.

There is no limit on the number of saints that can be gathered in the New Kingdom, nor is there any sense of when the end will come. Mormons live in anticipation of the New Kingdom yet are aware that it may come a long time in the future. Although Joseph Smith in 1843 prophesied the end for 1890, date setting has not been important for Mormons, nor has identifying individuals as Antichrist. He is anyone who, deceived by Satan, denies Christ and his church. Mormons must be educated and active in the world until the end occurs. Article 11 of the Mormon statement of faith proclaims: "We believe in being subject to kings, president, rulers and magistrates, in obeying, honoring and sustaining that law." The saints do not have to bear the burden of opposing governments or being regarded as traitors or unpatriotic, since they pay their taxes and perform military service. It is perhaps the most patriotic church in the United States, despite having come close to rebellion before 1890, because of its emphasis on America as the promised land where the new Zion will be built. Mormon missionaries abroad have been suspected of being American government agents because of this. Once polygamy was repudiated, Mormon doctrine remained largely consistent; Mormons do not have the problem of some millennial sects in which changes in key doctrines have caused defections.

Placing the Latter-day Saints in the broad context of millennial movements is difficult, because they incorporate aspects of nearly every approach to the endtime. They are a gathered and marked people, yet the number of saints is immense, coming from every nation. They must distinguish themselves from the Gentiles; yet, except for abstaining from alcohol and caffeine, they strive to be the most normal of people. It seems impossible that any other millennial group discussed in this chapter would support an academically respected university whose football team routinely competes for national honors. For the Mormons, time will come to a definite end, yet the human race will continue to improve until then. Modern inventions, especially those that improve communication, are God's contributions to humanity to ease the task of bringing the gospel to all nations. Although only Christ's return will bring about the earthly paradise, humans can bring the desert into bloom through their labor and with a strong emphasis on cooperation among men who have been highly successful as capitalists. Each side of these paradoxes has its appeal, and the success of the Mormon Church in large part lies in its ability to bind these contradictory elements into a coherent whole.

The Mormon movement into Utah was a major part of the European settlement of the West and the dispossession of the Indians, although the Mormons were less hostile to them than were most settlers. It should come as no surprise that the Indians, like most people under such pressure, developed their own apocalyptic forms. Discussing Indian approaches to the endtime poses a problem of determining the extent to which Christianity influenced indigenous concepts of the last days. Most non-European eschatological movements have occurred after contact with Christian missionaries. A good example is the Shawnee prophet Tenskwatawa, a brother of their leader Tecumseh. He was a triplet, which gave him unusual status from his birth in 1775 since multiple births were rare among Indians. As settler pressure on the Shawnee increased, he had visions in 1805 in which the Master of Life revealed to him the existence of paradise for the virtuous and hell for the sinful. He took the name Tenskwatawa (Open Door), and issued a call for virtue among his people, especially denouncing liquor, his vice before his conversion. He introduced new rituals and symbols yet called for a return to the traditional way of life. He drew from Christianity and acknowledged his contacts with French Catholics, Shakers, and the Moravian Brethren.

Tenskwatawa called for peace among the tribes to fend off the whites, and his new religion spread across the Midwest. Tecumseh used his brother's religious contacts to build military alliances, and as his alliance spread, so did tensions with the whites. As tensions built toward war, Tenskwatawa's beliefs took on a millennial tone. He declared that the Master of Life revealed there would be a great battle with the whites in which they would be destroyed. Then the earth would be renewed, restocked with game and fish, and the tribes would live in peace and prosperity. With Tecumseh off recruiting allies, Tenskwatawa led the Shawnee at the Battle of Tippecanoe in 1811. He told his warriors that the Master of Life had promised that the enemy's guns would not harm them because he would send rain to wet the gunpowder. The prophecy was wrong, and the Indians were routed. The outbreak of the War of 1812 reduced the impact of the rout on the Shawnee, as the British came to their aid, but Tecumseh died in battle in 1813. Tenskwatawa proclaimed that his brother would return from the dead and lead the Shawnee to victory, an idea that lingered well after they had been removed to Kansas. Tenskwatawa died there in 1834.

The pressures that the Shawnee faced were repeated among the tribes farther west as the settlers moved on, and so also were millennial episodes. The most famous episode was the Ghost Dance that first appeared among the Paiutes in Nevada about 1870. A shaman named Tavibo prophesied that while the earth would swallow up the whites, all dead Indians would emerge to enjoy a world free of their conquerors. He urged his followers to dance in circles, already a tradition in the region, while singing religious songs. Tavibo's movement spread across Nevada, California, and Oregon. Before fading away, it influenced another Paiute, Wovoka, born about 1856 and possibly the son of Tavibo, who developed its ideas further. Having worked for years on a settler's ranch, he learned about Christianity from the many local Mormons. He referred to Jesus as the messiah who lived on earth with the white men but was killed by them. In the late 1880s Wovoka began to make prophecies similar to Tavibo's. He announced the coming of a new age in which whites would vanish, leaving Indians to live in a land of abundance, renewal, and immortal life: "Do not tell the white people about this. Jesus is now upon the earth. He appears like a cloud. The dead are still alive. I do not know when they will be here; maybe this fall or in the spring. When the time comes there will be no more sickness and everyone will be young again."[1]

Like many millennialists, Wovoka stressed that salvation was not to be passively awaited but sought after in ritual dancing and virtuous conduct. In the ecstasy created by the whirling dance in which they could wear nothing made by whites, his followers had visions of the paradise promised to the Indians. The millennial content of these visions is clear in the description of one received by Little Horse, a Sioux:

> Two holy eagles transported me to the Happy Hunting Ground. They showed me the Great Messiah there, and as I looked upon his fair countenance, I wept, for there were the nailprints in his hands and feet where the cruel whites had once fastened him to a large cross. . . .

[He] promised me that no whites should enter his city nor partake of the good things he had prepared for the Indians. The earth, he said, was now worn out and it should be repeopled.[2]

As stories about Wovoka spread far from Nevada, he became identified as the miracle-working messiah, a claim he apparently did not make himself. He was a pacifist, urging his followers not to fight or hurt anybody. When his Ghost Dance spread among the defeated tribes of the Great Plains, the Sioux, who had recently been confined to reservations, gave it a militant tone. Sioux followers made sacred, bulletproof shirts for the dances. In late 1890, word spread among the Sioux that a great event brought about by the messiah would destroy the white men the next spring. That helped to persuade some Sioux to refuse to hand over their weapons to the army, which was trying to disarm them largely because of fears raised by the prediction. The resulting massacre at Wounded Knee, South Dakota, was cruel proof that the Ghost Dance shirts did not stop bullets and that an Indian millennium was not at hand. Some, however, continued to believe until the date set for the destruction of the whites passed uneventfully in 1891. Wovoka quickly lost his influence and lived quietly until he died in 1932.

In its promise to restore a defeated people to the golden age before the Europeans' arrival, the Ghost Dance is similar to many other nineteenth-century anticolonial movements. Events promising restoration occurred regularly among peoples whose cultures came under attack by western culture, whose religions were challenged by Christianity, and whose lands were controlled by European armies. One close parallel to the Ghost Dance happened in southern Africa among the Xhosa in 1818, at a time when they were under pressure from European settlers. A prophet, Makanna, adviser to the chief of one of the Xhosa tribes, organized a reaction against British incursions. He knew Christianity well and argued for a dualistic theology: The god of the blacks was good, with a moral code in which the only sin was witchcraft; the god of the whites was evil, whose perverted morality condemned most Xhosa practices as sinful. The god of blacks was stronger and would defeat the god of whites. Makanna proposed a special dance to bring back the dead Xhosa ancestors to help defeat the whites; it would also ensure that the whites' bullets would not harm the Xhosa. Once the British had been driven out, the land would become a paradise. His teachings helped push the Xhosa into the Fifth Kaffir War, in which they were badly defeated.

The Xhosa survived that defeat but remained under British pressure and were further threatened by drought in the mid-1850s. In 1856 spirits from the spirit world visited a girl, Nongquase, as she drew water at a river. When she returned with her uncle, a Xhosa leader, the spirits revealed that they had come to drive the British out. To do so required the sacrifice of many cattle and much grain, but when it was done, they would enter an earthly paradise, filled with fat cattle and towering grain stalks in which long dead members of the tribe would live again. Persuaded of the spirits' supernatural origins, the Xhosa destroyed most of their foodstuffs and cattle and built new barns for what was coming. The result was a devastating famine that made the final British occupation of their lands all the easier.

The movement most threatening to colonial rule was the Pai Marire in New Zealand. The Maori tribes had signed a treaty with the British in 1840 limiting land sales to settlers, but fraud and coercion led to ever increasing transfers of land to Europeans. In 1862, as tensions between Maori and settlers mounted and violence increased, the angel Gabriel appeared to a Maori named Te Ua Haumene with a revelation from "Peaceable God." He began to preach his "good and peaceful" religion, Pai Marire, to the Maori on the North Island. Like many Maori, Te Ua had accepted Christianity from Methodist missionaries but had not forgotten the traditional religion; his beliefs drew from both. Te Ua presented himself as the second John of Patmos and appropriated much of Revelation for his own. God, essentially the Christian deity, was about to cleanse the land of Canaan of the newcomers and return it to his people. A revelation from Gabriel informed Te Ua that he was to take the mast from a British ship wrecked on the coast and set it up as the center of worship. Te Ua composed chants, a mixture of Christian and Maori songs, to be sung as his followers danced around it. The word *hau,* divine wind, was used prominently; hence the derisive name Hau-Hau used by the British for the movement. Te Ua promised that the hau would deflect the British bullets. He sent apostles around the North Island to bring the Maori to the new faith and to ask the British to leave peacefully.

Te Ua expected the cleansing of the British to be done through divine intervention, not violence. At the end of 1864 groups of followers assembled at traditional sacred places to wait for God to act, proclaiming that the Maori who had not joined them and the British still in New Zealand would be killed. Disappointed when nothing happened, some believers began to act on the violence implicit in their beliefs. Marching against British outposts with their right hands in the air and shouting "hau, hau" to ward off bullets, they won several skirmishes. When a missionary was beheaded and his eyes eaten by a Maori in a traditional act of revenge for the murder of his daughters by British troops, the settlers joined the army against the Pai Marire. In two years time the island had been largely pacified. The millennial tradition among the Maori did not die out, however. Maori messiahs continued to appear well into the next century, drawing on Te Ua's beliefs, but as the Maori became more thoroughly Christianized, these movements took on more elements of Christian millennialism. For example, in 1905 a Maori laborer, Rua Kenana, declared that he was the new messiah whom God had chosen to lead the Maori, who were descended from the ancient Israelites, to the new Jerusalem. The failure of his prediction of the end of the world for 1906 did not destroy the movement, but a second failure for 1927 largely ended it. Some of Te Ua's symbols continue to be used today in the Maori autonomy movement.

Islam too had its revolts against European incursions influenced by messianism, which had been largely muted in the Muslim world since the early centuries of Islam but never forgotten. One major incident occurred in the Sudan in the 1880s. Muhammad Ahmed, a devout Muslim, became convinced that the Anglo-Egyptian incursions into his homeland, which were disrupting his world, were a threat to Islam and proclaimed himself al-Mahdi, the expected deliverer. Born into a family that claimed to be descended from the Prophet, Ahmed became known while still young for his commitment to the principles of traditional Islam. By 1881, 1298 in the Islamic calendar, rumors were rife that the Mahdi would return in two years at the turn of the century. Aware of the legend that the Mahdi would rise from his tribe, Ahmed became convinced he was the Mahdi and proclaimed himself to the local people. He called on them to flee with him from the corrupting influence of the Egyptians to southern Sudan. The Egyptians, alarmed at the unrest he was causing, sought to arrest him. Violence broke out, and Ahmed's followers, although badly outnumbered, were victorious in a brief battle. The victory was proclaimed a miracle, certifying him as the Mahdi. Two greater victories followed in late 1881. The failure of the Egyptians to crush the revolt brought the British directly into the fray, but for a time they had no better success. In January 1885, the Mahdi's army captured Khartoum, killing the famous General Charles Gordon in the process. The Mahdi was now the absolute ruler of nearly all of the Sudan and imposed a strict Islamic regime on it. He declared his intention to carry on the *jihad* against all enemies of true Islam. Six months later he suddenly died, probably from typhus. Led by a capable successor, the Mahdists retained control of the Sudan until a large British army defeated them in 1898 and established British rule there.

There were many similar movements but with fewer participants and less impact among nearly every non-European people faced with Western colonization. Examples include the Burkhan in western Siberia in 1904 responding to Russian control, the Njuli movement in Borneo of 1920–22 reacting to Dutch colonization, and the Tukanas in the Amazon region in 1941 responding to Brazilian settlers. All reflect in some way the influence of Christian missionaries. They show that millennialism is a widespread response among peoples faced with European disruption of their way of life.

Also common were millennial movements in Christian societies that were responses to modernization or encroachment on local autonomy by outsiders, often the national government. In Italy a Tuscan peasant, Davide Lazzaretti, declared in 1878 that Leo XIII was no longer the head of the Church, since he had replaced the pope as Christ the Leader and Judge who was inaugurating the Millennium. He was the only casualty when police broke up a meeting of hundreds of peasants demanding an end to changes in land-holding policies. Louis Riel, the leader of the Méti (mixed blood) Rebellion in Saskatchewan in 1885, took the name David to emphasize his role in bringing about the new Kingdom in Canada. Among the millennial elements of his thought were beliefs that he was the prophet of the new world, the new holy city would be Montréal, and a calendar he devised would be used in the new age. Captured by Canadian authorities, he was hanged, still convinced that he would rise in three days. At Tomochic in northern Mexico a group of villagers led by a local peasant, Cruz Chávez, and a young woman called Santa Teresa faced government troops in a bloody showdown in October 1892. Certain that they were fighting the sons of Satan and convinced by Chávez that they must be martyred to bring about the return of justice and peace to the world, nearly all the rebels died in a church that burned down around them and in the village hall during a firefight with the troops. A movement twenty years earlier in eastern Argentina required the death of the enemies of God—the foreigners and Freemasons in the region, 36 persons in all—to establish the new world. The largest number of such violent movements involving poverty-stricken peasants, eight clearly defined ones, occurred in Brazil. All reflect dissatisfaction with government policy and the incursion of new modes of business and industry. A popular ditty from one of them, the Canudos movement of 1893–97, nicely sums up their belief:

> The Antichrist has arrived to govern Brazil,
> But in the interior is the Conselheiro to free us from him.[3]

The theme of the return of King Sebastian of Portugal was present in most of the Brazilian movements despite the passage of over three centuries since he disappeared.

There is, however, one major exception to any generalization about the appeal of millennialism to impoverished peoples. It has been uncommon among African Americans; given their history, one might expect them to have been highly receptive to millennialism. The stripping away of African religions from people taken as slaves to America, leaving them without a golden past to restore, may have been a factor; but the strength of Christianity among the converted slaves and their descendants raises an unanswered question of why they have not responded in larger numbers to the appeal of the Book of Revelation. Nonetheless, blacks have occasionally been millennialists, such as Nat Turner, the rebel slave, whose uprising in 1831 was sparked by a solar eclipse as a heavenly sign of the impending endtime, and Sojourner Truth, the freed slave and abolitionist, who had been a member of a cult in New York, the Kingdom of Matthias, before her career as an abolitionist.

There have been only a few millennial groups that have arisen out of black society. The only one of significance in the nineteenth century was the community of Black Jews organized at Belleville in eastern Virginia. Its founder was a railroad cook, William Crowdy, who organized the Church of God and Saints of Christ in 1896 in Kansas and founded Belleville in 1906. He received a revelation published as *The Bible Story Revealed* in 1902: God intended his church to follow Mosaic law as well as the Gospels. The members of the Church regard themselves as the true descendants of the Ten Lost Tribes, believing that the ancient Hebrews were originally black. Modern Jews, who have lost their claim to be the chosen people, changed color by mixing with whites. There were over 120 congregations in the church, many of which still exist today, but only the one at Belleville, with some 300 members, was communal. There the full range of Mosaic law was followed, including the Jewish feasts and calendar, combined with Christian ritual. The saints, who cultivated the 1,000 acres the community owned, brought everything they produced to their Grand Father, who redistributed it to them. Belleville remains today the site of a prosperous black community and the home temple of the sect.

Belleville shows that millennial communalism, while less common than earlier, still attracted people after 1850. A German priest, Ambrose Oschwald, founded the only Catholic commune to appear in America at St. Nazianz, Wisconsin in 1854. He had lost his parish in Germany for too ardently predicting the arrival of the new Jerusalem by 1900 in his *Revelations of St. Methodius* (1848). Most of his parishioners followed him to America. Although married members were accepted, he emphasized celibacy. Oschwald's community, which had 450 members at its height, flourished for 20 years; but with his death in 1873 the group lost its rudder, and the communal property was sold to the members in 1898.

Celibacy was the distinguishing feature of the commune founded by Cyrus Teed, an eccentric physician from upstate New York. In 1869 he received a revelation from Divine Mother God, who informed him that the deity was equally male and female and that she had chosen him to complete the redemption of humanity. Along with declaring the unity of all substances in the universe, advocating alchemy, and denouncing heliocentrism, Teed argued that celibacy was necessary to reunite male and female in human persons and end the cycle of reincarnation. Convinced that celibacy could be maintained only in a communal society, he founded the Koreshan Unity in Chicago in 1886. *Koresh* is the Hebrew word for Cyrus, the Persian king who had been given the divine mission to save the chosen people from exile. Teed changed his name to Koresh and announced that soon the present states and religions would be replaced by a new state and religion. In 1903 he and 200 members built a commune in southern Florida at a place with great significance in his esoteric cosmology. Koresh claimed that he would rise from the grave, but much to his followers' dismay, he failed to reappear after his death in a boating accident in 1908. Disciples continued to live a communal life for over a half century after his death, and in 1968 their property was given to Florida for a state park.

Koresh/Teed was accused of breaking celibacy with several of his female followers, but his community was the model of propriety compared to the House of David. Its founder, Benjamin Purnell, was an itinerant preacher born in 1861; about 1890 he joined John Wroe's Christian Israelites. The American Wroites, having gained many converts among the Millerites, acquired a talented leader in James White, who changed his name to James Jershom Jezreel. His key doctrine involved the gathering of the third and final church, The New and Latter House of Israel, with 144,000 members from the Ten Lost Tribes. Once gathered, they would redeem their bodies and souls to become immortal. In 1882 Jezreel and his prophet wife, Clarissa, established a permanent base on a disciple's farm near Detroit. To the shock of their followers, the couple died a short time apart. When Queen Esther, as Clarissa styled herself, died in 1888 at age 28, the movement's leadership fell into dispute, and Prince Michael Mills, a Canadian, briefly made good his claim. He soon was jailed for statutory rape for persuading a fourteen-year-old girl that he was the son of man who must sow good seed for the purification of the race. Purnell then emerged as the new leader.

In 1895 Purnell received a vision revealing that he was the seventh and final prophet; the prior ones were Brothers, Southcott, Wroe, and

three others in the Christian Israelite tradition. He fit well into their tradition, having been involved in a bigamous situation when he left his
first wife for Mary Stoddard without first getting a divorce and was accused of adultery with several female disciples. The accidental death of
one of two daughters he had by Mary created a major scandal in the
Ohio town where they were living, because the couple refused to see to
her burial. Her death showed that she was a sinner: "Let the dead bury
the dead!" The townspeople's outrage forced the Purnells to move to
Benton Harbor in western Michigan, which had become the Christian
Israelite stronghold. In short order the Purnells were acknowledged as
dual Shilohs. In 1903 they legally incorporated the community as "the
Israelite House of David, the New Eve, the Body of Christ." By 1915
the prosperous colony had over 400 members, including many Wroites
from Australia.

Purnell's millennialism involved both an imminent endtime and
perfectionism. He emphasized 1915 among several dates for the destruction of the world. The 144,000 gathered would alone survive it and
live through the Millennium without tasting death. Purnell said that by
1915 all 144,000 would belong to the House of David, but the early
members would have a head start on achieving perfection. Perfection involved obedience to the Shilohs, communalism, and celibacy. Communalism was based on the need to assemble the 144,000 by the last days.
The Purnells ruled their commune with an iron hand, and a system of
informers was set up to enforce discipline. Dietary rules included no
meat or alcohol. Members' life savings and labor were directed toward
reaching those not yet gathered-in and bringing them to Michigan, but
it was also necessary that the saints have a home appropriately luxurious for God's elite. What Purnell called the virgin law was based on the
idea that original sin was Eve's sexual intercourse with Satan. She then
corrupted Adam by sex, who passed sin on to all humans. Celibacy
would purify one's blood until the original sinless nature of Adam and
Eve was recovered.

The idea that Shiloh's home should be a pleasant place to live
meant that Purnell emphasized music, entertainment, and sports. Since
there was no obligation to be separated entirely from the world, the
House of David became a lucrative tourist spot with a miniature train

among its attractions, where outsiders mingled with the oddly dressed, long-haired members. Perhaps the strangest aspect was its baseball and basketball teams that traveled about playing against all comers, including major league teams. In 1936 a former member offered Babe Ruth $35,000 to play for the House of David, but he declined. The bearded, long-haired players caused as much amazement for their talent as for their appearance. On the other hand, Purnell had no use for education. He compared it unfavorably to manure, which, he said, at least could be used to grow crops.

Through the hard work of its members and shrewd dealing on Purnell's part, the House of David flourished for 20 years. The failure of Purnell's 1915 prediction discomfited few members, and membership reached 800 by 1920. Yet there was trouble in paradise. The Purnells, like so many other cult leaders, did not feel that the rules specified for their followers applied to them, especially in regard to sex. Benjamin was seducing his young female disciples, while Mary was allegedly involved with a lesbian. He was successful in keeping his behavior secret from most members and the outside world by paying off those he seduced or arranging sham marriages for them. The couples were expected to remain celibate. In 1923 a family leaving the colony sued for the money they had handed over upon joining and for back pay for their years of unpaid labor. At the trial, it came out that Purnell was having sex with underage females. The state issued a warrant for his arrest, but he disappeared before it could be served. It turned out that he was hiding in a secret room in the central mansion, attended by devoted women, although staying in the dank room undermined his health. After four years someone informed on him, and he was arrested in a dramatic night raid. At his trial, extensive information about the House of David and embarrassing testimony about the sexual behavior of the Purnells came out, albeit largely from hostile witnesses. Most members remained loyal.

Purnell's death in December 1927 made moot the November verdict banning him from the colony. His disciples expected him to rise in three days, but even when that failed to happen, they did not lose faith in him. A greater problem was the struggle for leadership between Mary Purnell and Thomas Dewhurst, a former judge and recent recruit. In

1930 a settlement divided the colony's property between them. Mary, who died in 1953, set up the City of David across the street with about half of the remaining members. The colonies remain separate today with an aging membership of under ten people each, living off the property accumulated in the House of David's heyday. In that respect, the House of David is in much the same situation as the Shakers.

As of August 1914, attitudes in the United States and most of Christendom were more receptive of postmillennialism than premillennialism. Most people in western culture were satisfied to live in a society where the expectation of the endtime largely meant a time when the human race, led by science and technology, would become perfect. The behavior of the House of David, the polygamy of the Mormons, the date setting of the Adventists and Jehovah's Witnesses, the violence of the Ghost Dancers—all had made it easy to dismiss as crackpots the small number of people for whom millennialism still burned brightly. The outbreak of World War I would shatter that optimism and provide new opportunities for premillennialist prophets. In respect to millennialism, we are still living in the aftershocks of the guns of August.

XII

WAR AND
RUMORS OF WAR

UMEROUS PROPHECIES HAD LOOKED to 1914 for the Parousia.
When war broke out in July 1914 and spread across Europe, the
belief was widespread that the tribulation had come. The nature of the
war with its enormous casualty rolls and use of such apocalyptic
weapons as poison gas, zeppelins, and airplanes convinced many who
had not paid much attention to earlier predictions that the endtime was
at hand. Letters, poetry, and literature from the soldiers, movies and
photographs taken in the war zones, and news reports helped to spread
the image of the war as Armageddon. The terror of the Great War provided moviemakers with apocalyptic themes that the new medium of
cinema was able to depict in a manner more compelling and effective
than traditional media could.

One of the most powerful movies of the period was Abel Gance's
film *J'accuse,* made in 1918 but released after the armistice. Partly anti-
German propaganda since Germany was deemed responsible for starting the war and for numerous atrocities, it uses the image of the return
of an army of dead soldiers to indict the living and demand an end to
war before the world destroys itself. More obviously apocalyptic was
The Four Horsemen of the Apocalypse, released in 1920 and starring
Rudolph Valentino. Based on a novel by Blasco Ibáñez, it is both a
maudlin love story and a vivid portrayal of the horrors of war. The opening scene, set at the beginning of the war, has a Russian prophet telling

Valentino's character: "It is the beginning of the end. . . . The world will behold the Four Horsemen—enemies of mankind; those who go before the Beast—the Four Horsemen of the Apocalypse." Images of the Four Horsemen appear in the sky above the two men. The movie ends with the burial of the hero, killed in the last days of the war, while the souls of the countless dead appear in the sky along with the Four Horsemen.[1] The movie was a great commercial success, as was Eric Maria Remarque's *All Quiet on the Western Front*. It too has a final scene of the ghosts of dead soldiers, although the apocalyptic elements in it are not as obvious.

In literature, soldier-poets such as Wilfred Owen, Siegfried Sassoon, and Ernst Jünger applied apocalyptic images to the horror of the war in the trenches. After the war, writers continued to express in novels and poetry their belief that the events of the endtime were at hand. The theme of Karl Klaus's play *TheLast Days of Mankind* (1922) is evident from its title. An Austrian too old to serve, in 1908 he had written *Apokalypse* in which he tied recent technological developments such as the airplane into Revelation's description of the endtime. The stage directions for the final scene call for "Total darkness. Then, on the horizon, the wall of flames leaps high. Death cries off stage."[2] Several poems full of apocalyptic symbolism from the twenties are now regarded as major pieces of modern literature. In T. S. Eliot's "The Waste Land" (1922) the extensive use of symbolism and allegory requires great effort on the part of the reader to decipher the millennial meaning. His "The Hollow Men" (1925) is more obvious, especially its famous final line: "This is the way the world ends, not with a bang but with a whimper."[3] William Yeats's "The Second Coming" (1921) contains what is surely the best-known millennial couplet in western literature:

> And what rough beast, its hour come round at last,
> Slouches towards Bethlehem to be born?[4]

While the outbreak of war in 1914 was a cause of despair for postmillennialists, some premillennialists, convinced that the time of trial had begun, were almost giddy with excitement. Did not Christ say "You shall hear of wars and rumors of war" (Matt. 24:6) before the endtime? For premillennialists in the Allied countries, the German empire matched up well with the beast of Revelation, although not perfectly, since it had not been part of the Roman empire. As the war widened and casualties mounted, they became ever more convinced that scenarios predicted in Daniel and Revelation were being played out. The dispensationalist Arno Gaebelin, following closely to Darby's script, wrote in 1916 that events clearly were moving toward the end, and the terrible war in Europe was only a foretaste of the trials to come. The saints, however, would be taken in the Rapture before matters became much worse.

The Jehovah's Witnesses were probably the most anticipatory of those groups in late 1914, the year that Charles Russell had designated for the end. In October 1914, he happily announced to applauding followers: "The Gentile times have ended; the kings have had their day."[5] When the world, and the war, continued, the idea of Christ's invisible coming served well to explain the prophecy's failure. The war, however, created problems for the Jehovah's Witnesses, who adamantly refused to serve in the armed forces of the warring countries, which they deemed were under Satan's control. Imprisonment was the usual punishment for refusing military service, but some members were conscripted and then punished severely, even executed, for refusing orders. When the United States entered the war in 1917, it exacerbated the problem because most Jehovah's Witnesses were American. Being so unpatriotic brought down opprobrium on their young men and the entire membership. Despite their neighbors' rage, the Jehovah's Witnesses continued to win converts, in part because many people were impressed with their firm stand on their principles. In general, American premillennialists faced suspicion if they did not support the war. In 1918 a hostile periodical accused them of taking German money to spread their unpatriotic nonsense. They were forced to emphasize their patriotism and, as usually happens under such circumstances, made claims of being the most loyal of all.

Premillennialists took particular interest in events in the Middle East. When the Turkish empire entered the war in 1914, fighting spread to Palestine. The old notion that the Turks were agents of Antichrist was revived, and their defeat was taken as a signal for the endtime. From the first battles against the Turks, some premillennialists called for the restoration of the Jews and the rebuilding of the Temple. While a major reason for British Foreign Minister Balfour's declaration calling for a Jewish homeland in Palestine was the hope of winning support for the Allied cause from German Jews, pressure from some British religious leaders was also a factor. The British capture of Jerusalem later in 1917 was seen as the opportunity to make good on the old prophecy. Among the Jews themselves, who had seen little messianism since the seventeenth century, the issue of a nation in Palestine was a point of contention. For most the reestablishment of a Jewish state was an apocalyptic matter: the Messiah would bring it about in the last days. Theodor Herzl and his Zionists, however, were inspired more by the nationalism of nineteenth-century Europe. Most Jews considered the Zionists too secular and irreligious, and Orthodox Jews regarded a nonmessianic Jewish state as blasphemous, a position that some ultra-Orthodox Jews still hold today. Thus, the Balfour Declaration did not stir a wide response from the Jews, although some migration began once Britain took control of Palestine after the war.

For premillennialists the idea of a Jewish state in Palestine created enormous interest. To be sure, some wondered whether Zionists could really be God's instrument, but for most it made no difference what the motivation was of those who sought to build the Jewish state. The key point was that the prophecy was about to come true, and God could do it with whomever he might choose. The most outspoken of the American Christian supporters of Zionism was William Blackstone, Dwight Moody's disciple. In 1891, even before Herzl organized his first Zionist group, Blackstone sent a petition to President Harrison signed by over 400 prominent politicians and businessmen asking that Palestine be given to the Jews for a homeland. He continued such efforts up to his death in 1935, which led the Jews to honor him as a Father of Zion. Blackstone and other premillennialists, however, did not forget that the second part of the prophecy about Jews returning to Palestine required their conversion to Christianity. They actively evangelized among American Jews but with little success.

Since little progress was made toward a restored Jewish state in the decade after 1918, for most Christians, such a possibility paled in comparison to apocalyptic events taking place in Russia, which elicited a great response from millennialists of all types. Russia in the century before 1917 saw an increasing level of millennial anxiety. The Raskolniki had continued to grow in numbers since 1700, while their millennialism hardly declined. In 1820 the government raided one of their communities and found a portrait of Czar Alexander I done up to look like Antichrist with horns and tail and 666 written on his brow. It was his successor, Czar Nicholas I, who more truly merited being deemed Antichrist by the Old Believers. He pushed an active campaign of repression against them that succeeded in breaking up most of their communities. Such repression simply confirmed the Raskolniki belief that the endtime, delayed for 200 years, was now close at hand and reinforced their faith. It took the more systematic repression of the Soviet state to destroy the Old Believer movement.

Two intriguing Russian groups that gained notoriety in the nineteenth century were the Castrates and the Doukhobors. Both had their origins in the Spiritual Christians of the 1760's, who, rejecting the worship services of the Orthodox Church, worshipped God in spirit and truth. The first group split off under the leadership of Kondratii Selivanov (d. 1832), who proclaimed himself Christ reincarnated. He demanded the fiery baptism of castration for his followers, including clitoral circumsion for the women. When 144,000 persons had thereby proven their rejection of the world and Satan, the last judgment by Selivanov-Christ would take place. The Doukhobors gained their name about 1785, when a Russian prelate gave the group its name, which means Spirit Wrestlers, implying that they were wrestling against the influence of the Holy Spirit. They took up the name but changed its sense to indicating that they were wrestling with the Holy Spirit against Antichrist. They believe that Jesus was not divine but fully human, who had died in the flesh and rose in the spirit. His spirit has continued to promote the commandments: Recognize and love God, and love thy neighbor as thyself. Fulfilling these commandments requires the renunciation of all violence and war. When finally all receive the spirit in their souls, then the world will be transformed into heaven on earth. The most notorious part of their beliefs was the nude parade, when they would march naked like Adam and Eve around their fields, homes, and barns to make the world fertile again like the Garden of Eden.

In 1895, under the influence of Peter Verigin (d. 1924), several Russian officers dropped their weapons and stripped off their military insignia, following the command: "Resist not him that is evil." When Verigin and the officers were sent off to Siberia, the Doukhobors held a bonfire of their weapons. The government's hostile reaction to this act led over 7,500 to migrate to Canada, attracted by the Canadian government's homesteading policy in the prairie provinces and aided by the Quakers, with whom they shared some beliefs. In western Canada the Doukhobors created communal villages, and their hard work and mutual aid made them flourish. The resentment of their new neighbors and their odd behavior, including nude parades and burning barns as symbols of the new life to come, led to conflict. A few Doukhobors reacted with violence, using arson and dynamite against their antagonists as late as 1980. Their transformation into a violent millennial sect was prevented by the active commitment to pacifism from the great majority, but they have successfully resisted assimilation into Canadian society and continue to exist as a distinctive group.

Within mainstream Russian society, there was a growing anticipation of the endtime as the nineteenth century ended. Elsewhere the turn of the century sparked little millennial anxiety, but in Russia there was a sense that something cataclysmic was about to happen. Vladimir Solovyov, a prominent theologian of the Orthodox Church, wrote to a friend: "The approaching end of the world strikes me like some obvious but quite subtle scent - just as a traveler nearing the sea feels the sea breeze before he sees the sea."[6] In 1900 he wrote *Three Conversations and . . . a Short Story of the Antichrist,* in which the Japanese are identified as the hordes of Gog and Magog. In the story Antichrist, aided by leaders of the three major Christian churches and the Jews, creates a vast empire, but when the Jews realize that he is not the Messiah as he claims, they revolt. Events lead to the final battle at Armageddon. The Japanese figured prominently in apocalyptic novels by other Russian authors such as Andrei Bely. He wrote *Petersburg* in 1916 when the enormous defeats and casualties of the war gave increased anxiety to the sense of impending doom.

Apocalypse came, but not in the way most Russians expected. In 1917 the situation in Russia was so dreadful that for both millennialists and Marxists, the moment of the great transformation of the world had to be at hand. Marx had not envisioned Russia as the place where the Revolution of the Proletariat would begin, but Russian revolutionaries, filled with hatred for the czarist regime, were attracted to the Marxist promise of certain victory and a better world to come. That was true of Lenin himself, who became a Marxist only after he had become a revolutionary. Lenin and his Bolsheviks violated Marx's scheme of history, in which the dialectic follows a predetermined road to communism, and argued that peasants could serve as the masses needed for the socialist revolution. Thus, they put special emphasis on the role of the revolutionary vanguard, the Bolshevik Party. Like Robespierre, Lenin was convinced that he knew best how to bring about the new golden age; any moderation in the party's use of extreme violence to gain its goals was counter-revolutionary and worthy of death.

Most Bolsheviks had a devout Christian or Jewish upbringing; Stalin, for example, had been a seminary student. Thus, they were familiar with biblical apocalyptic, and their rhetoric and expectations drew heavily on that literature. The idea that revolution could create a new age was well expressed in the antiphon sung by the Russian revolutionaries of 1905: "After the bloody battle, there will be the sun of truth and eternal love." John Reed's memoirs of the Russian Revolution reveal his belief that he was living through the transitory period to the new age, and he recorded statements from the Bolsheviks to the same effect. He quoted Maria Spiridonova, the most powerful of the Bolshevik women: "There is no force in the world which can put out the fire of revolution. The old world crumbles down, the new world begins." And Trotsky: "A new humanity will be born of this war."[7] The Bolsheviks had to burn the present world in the fire of revolution to create a new and better place. They were certain in the first months after their takeover of the Russian state that revolution would spread across the world in a matter of months. Lenin expected that within six months the capitalist regimes would collapse, as the laws of history worked their inevitable will in human society. In another perhaps unwitting millennial touch, Lenin organized the Third Socialist International, the final, perfect means of bringing about the new age, after Marx's First International and the moderate socialists' Second had failed.

For the second time, millennialists of reason had gained control of a large state. Much the same Jacobin program of antireligion, free love, and violent repression of the slightest disagreement with the will of the people was put into effect, along with the Marxist program of a society without private property. What makes the Russian Revolution different from the French was the long-term control of the revolutionaries over Russia. Historians have debated for seven decades whether the death of Lenin in 1924 was the equivalent of the Thermidorian reaction and whether Stalin's rise corresponded to Napoleon's; but unlike the French government after 1795, Stalin's regime remained committed to the idea that it was creating the new age. The rhetoric of the Soviet state pronounced that its citizens were the new people living in the new age; the golden age had come with communism.

Just as people outside of France, both supportive of and hostile to the French Revolution, had viewed it as evidence of the coming end-time, non-Russians similarly evaluated the developments in Russia. Communists outside of Russia saw the new world rising there and knew that it was good. According to an American Marxist, Mike Gold, the revolution was on the winning side of history; there was no doubt that when communism replaces capitalism, which is as certain as the sun rises, "there will be all that we have dreamed of."[8] On the other hand, the communist campaign promoting atheism affirmed its antichristian status for those with any millennial inclination. There was an old tradition of identifying Russia as the source of the hordes of Gog and Magog. Not only did Russia lie north of Palestine, but according to an early nineteenth-century interpretation, the Hebrew term *nesi rosh*—in the passage in Ezekiel (38:3) that mentions Gog and Magog—referred to the prince of Russia. Darby picked up on it for dispensationalism, and the Crimean War spread the idea in Britain and France, Russia's foes in that war. Cyrus Scofield emphasized it in his works, and thus it came as no surprise to many that Antichrist would establish himself in Russia as communism.

While the Protestant premillennialists since 1917 have been the most determined to see the Russian Revolution as evidence for Antichrist, it also sparked a millennial response among Catholics in the form of Mary's apparitions at Fatima. Although Jesus' mother has no role in the biblical sources for millennialism, except for often being identified as Revelation's woman in the wilderness, her apparitions have usually included a strong millennial message. The earliest known one with such a message occurred in 1476, when a young German, Hans Böheim, better known as the Piper of Niklashausen, attributed his radical millennial message to a visit from Mary. The message was highly similar to that of more recent apparitions: God had intended to punish mankind for its sins and destroy the world, but she begged him to relent. He agreed, but only if men proved that they could amend their ways and show proper respect to Mary at her shrine at Niklashausen. At first Hans simply called for repentance, but soon he turned to denouncing the clergy and the pope for their avarice, and the secular rulers for the burden of taxes and feudal dues on the peasants. In the New Kingdom, he proclaimed, there would be no taxes or tithes; all would be equal; the clergy would practice apostolic poverty. The local bishop arrested him, and after his followers failed in an attempt to rescue him, he was burned as a heretic.

Marian millennialism, common in the late Middle Ages, was again rare until the nineteenth century. By 1840 the idea had emerged among some Catholics that there would be a Marian golden age before the Parousia, in which Mary would reign in preparation for Christ's return. In 1846 the prototype of modern apparitions occurred at La Salette in the French Alps. A beautiful woman appeared to Mélanie and Maximin, cattle herders in their early teens from impoverished families. The woman spoke of the great effort she had to make to restrain her son from chastising sinful humanity. It was not the children but another person who suggested that the woman was Mary, but they and most villagers accepted the idea with enthusiasm. The spot on a mountainside where the Virgin allegedly stood became a pilgrimage site, and miraculous healing was associated with it. It soon was said that the children had been given warnings about four chastisements in 1847—war, disease, famine, and flood. Although that year saw little in the way of disasters, it failed to halt keen interest in such prophecies, which became all the greater when it was disclosed that Mélanie and Maximin had each received a secret message from the woman. At first they refused to divulge the messages to anyone, but after considerable pressure from the local clergy, they agreed to write them down for the pope's eyes alone. Although Pius IX reportedly read them, the Vatican has never released their contents.

That did not stop others from proclaiming that they had in one fashion or another gained access to the messages. These reports give them a highly millennial content: The arrival of Antichrist and the Parousia are at hand. Maximin died in 1875 adamant that no one except the pope had ever learned his real message, but Mélanie, who died in 1904, allowed hers to be published in a pamphlet in 1870. Although critics pointed out that the published secret was too long to have been written on the three pages sent to the pope, it attracted numerous devotees. The "Secret of La Salette" was unrelentingly apocalyptic. The corrupt Catholic clergy, a "cesspool of iniquity," was to be replaced by an "Order of the Mother of God," whose members would be the apostles of the last days and preach the gospel to the ends of the world. The pamphlet's endtime scenario came out of Revelation, except its assignment of a larger role to the Archangel Michael in the defeat of Antichrist.

The next important Marian apparition, at Lourdes in France in 1858, had little millennialism connected with it. Its association with miraculous healing explains why it remains the most popular of the apparitions, while the millennialism connected with the apparition at Fatima in Portugal in 1917 probably explains why it is a close second to Lourdes in importance. The three young seers at Fatima, siblings Jacinta and Francisco and their cousin Lucia, had much in common with the two at La Salette in respect to their family situations. The site at Fatima, however, attracted far larger crowds, even while the apparitions were still occurring. Early on there were secrets associated with Fatima, but the children insisted that they pertained only to them. Two years later, Jacinta and Francisco died in the flu epidemic, which Mary is supposed to have foretold, and Lucia, who is still alive, became the keeper of the secrets of Fatima. In 1925 she became a nun and under pressure from her superiors began to reveal the secrets. It was only in 1941 that a full account of the first two secrets was printed. The first involved a vision of hell; the second, that the present war—World War I—was about to end and another great war would break out during the reign of Pope Pius XI, as it did. The key was Russia, which was to be consecrated to the Virgin. If that were done, Russia would be converted and world peace would ensue; if not, Russia would continue to spread error throughout the world, leading to a bloody persecution of the faithful and annihilation of many nations.

Lucia refused to divulge the third secret until she became seriously ill in 1943, when she decided to write it down, and it was later sent to the pope, supposedly with the injunction "not to be opened until 1960." In the midst of the cold war, the third secret of Fatima became the object of an enormous amount of speculation, largely dealing with nuclear war and the victory of atheistic communism prior to the Parousia. The intriguing aspect of the Fatima secrets is how well they fit into the ancient tradition of apocalyptic literature. A prophetic secret is revealed well after it supposedly had been given to the prophet; part of the message is confirmed by events since then, which makes the rest of the message, in this case never revealed, seem fully credible or of crucial importance.

Within Catholicism, where millennialism has always been muted, Fatima and dozens of apparitions since it—in places such as Ezkioga in northern Spain on the eve of the Spanish Civil War—have provided a way for pious Catholics to give expression to their anxiety that the great evils of their time, especially communism, were the prelude to the Second Coming. Other religious groups responded in their own way to the same pressures and fears. The Jehovah's Witnesses, however, faced a crisis largely of their making—the failure of the prediction of the end of the gentile nations and the beginning of the reign of Christ for 1914. Russell confidently maintained that the outbreak of war in 1914 was the first of the events that would lead to the Millennium; his death in late 1916 freed him from having to explain the Peace of Versailles. It was left to his successor as president of the Watchtower Society, Judge Joseph Rutherford, to deal with the problems created by the failed prophecy, the death of Russell prior to the Rapture, and a schism in the group caused by Rutherford's election. He was an effective administrator who exemplified the sort of second leader needed for a millennial movement to achieve permanence. In 1920 he published *Millions Now Living Will Never Die,* which set 1925 as the date for the Millennium. He also maintained that the patriarchs Abraham, Isaac, and Jacob would be resurrected and lead the saints into the new order on earth. Using much of the society's treasury, he built a mansion in San Diego for the Hebrew worthies who would return to life. Until they did, he would live in it.

Rutherford made several significant changes in the Watchtower Society. He emphasized more than Russell the need for members to proselytize and largely created the popular image of them as people going door-to-door to give out free religious literature. More austere than Russell, he insisted that members not celebrate holidays such as Christmas, Mother's Day, and birthdays, which he regarded as pagan in origin. To emphasize the distinction between his group and several schismatic ones, he changed its name in 1931 to Jehovah's Witnesses. It gave the members a greater sense of identity, being involved in a work of immense importance. The Jehovah's Witnesses needed the great commitment that the name change fostered because the next two decades were an era of persecution for them. The Nazis denounced the German members as enemies of the German people for their refusal to serve in the German military. In a 1938 law they mandated death for conscripted men who refused to serve and severe penalties for anyone encouraging their refusal. The Jehovah's Witnesses faced the same fate in the Soviet Union, Italy, and even Greece, where three were executed in 1940. In countries such as Britain, Canada, and the United States, they suffered penalties for refusing to salute the flag, which led to an American Supreme Court decision in 1942 recognizing their right to refuse. Rutherford had died the previous year, leaving his movement in much the same circumstances as Russell had, in the midst of a world war that he had designated as the last event before the Millennium. His movement, with about 200,000 members in 1942, had been thoroughly institutionalized by then, and it easily made the transition to a new leader. Thus, the Jehovah's Witnesses, still insisting that they were not a church, took on most of the identifying characteristics of one.

In 1926 the addresses given to an international Jehovah's Witnesses convention were broadcast live on a network of 53 radio stations worldwide. Despite a conservative stand concerning popular culture, millennial groups have generally been quick to use new forms of popular media, as the sixteenth-century Anabaptists did with the printing press.

For one cult the radio became so important as a means of proselytizing that the group took on the name The Radio Church of God. Its founder was Herbert Armstrong, born a Quaker in Iowa in 1892, who moved to Oregon after he married. His wife, Loma, joined an Adventist sect, the Church of God-Seventh Day, and instead of refuting its beliefs as he intended, he joined it. The church dated back to a schism in the Sabbatarian Adventist movement in the 1850s, and schism has continued to be a feature of it and its offspring.

The Church of God had a powerful sense of being the faithful remnant of Israel. It insisted on the observance of Saturday as the day of worship, tithing, Jewish dietary laws, and Old Testament feasts. It too had experienced a strong sense that the biblical prophecies were being fulfilled in 1914, and the failure of the predictions cost it a larger portion of its membership than was true of similar sects. The group, headquartered in Missouri, had no minister in Oregon until Armstrong was ordained in 1931. By then, disputes in the church's general conference over doctrine and practice were leading to another schism. Armstrong joined a dissident group based in West Virginia and became one of its seventy elders. In early 1934 he purchased air time from a small radio station in Eugene, Oregon, and made the first of thousands of broadcasts over radio and, later, television. He rejected door-to-door proselytizing in favor of broadcasts and mass meetings. By 1937 when his followers reached 1,000, he felt emboldened to challenge his church on several points of doctrine, and the next year he was asked to return his credentials as a minister.

Among the key points of dispute were Armstrong's enforcement of absolute shunning of those members deemed to have cut themselves off from the truth, the obligation to avoid unclean meats as determined by Mosaic law, and a great emphasis on celebrating the eight-day Feast of Tabernacles as the major religious event of the year. Armstrong's demand for a triple tithe, or 30 percent of members' income, also caused dissension. The most significant matter, however, was Armstrong's definition of God as a family, rejecting the Trinity. He taught that the elect would be reborn at the endtime into the Family of God. When Christ returns to earth, he will give immortality to the members of the true church alone, who will reign with him forever. Armstrong adopted

British Israelitism, according to which Britain and America were two of the Lost Tribes of Israel. When war broke out in 1939, he denounced Hitler as Antichrist and identified the Germans with the Assyrians, who would invade "Israel," that is, the United States. Church members would be whisked away to Petra in Jordan to wait for the final victory of Christ. Even after 1945 he continued to predict a German invasion of America for 1975. By then he had gained a much larger audience for his radio sermons, having moved to Los Angeles in 1947 and in 1953 getting airtime on Radio Luxembourg, the most powerful radio station in the world. He had become a wealthy man, and the contrast between his lifestyle and that of his largely impoverished members caused some to leave the Worldwide Church of God, as it had become known. Most members, however, regarded it as appropriate that God's representative on earth lived well. Accusations of incest with his daughter and the failure of several predicted dates for the endtime discomfited only a few. But his death in 1986 and accusations of sexual misbehavior leveled against his son and chosen successor, Ted Garner Armstrong, have resulted in undermining the faithful, and membership is well down from its peak of the 1960s.[9] The son has since begun his own schismatic movement.

Millennialists like Armstrong were quick to conclude that fascist dictators Mussolini and Hitler were Antichrist. In Italian fascism, Mussolini's call to rebuild Rome's golden age was the only millennial element, striking many as fulfilling Revelation's prophecy. Hitler's National Socialism, on the other hand, incorporated millennialism deeply into its ideology. Unlike Marx, who hid his debt to millennialism under the rhetoric of his theory, Hitler openly drew from a variety of eschatological sources. It is plausible to argue that much of the Nazi appeal came from the great success Hitler and other Nazi leaders had in framing their ideas in millennial rhetoric and apocalyptic symbolism. One eschatological source was the ancient Germanic myth, *Götterdämmerung,* the twilight of the gods, which was familiar to Hitler and the Germans of his era through the operas of Richard Wagner. Wagner was hardly faithful to the old myths, but he did succeed brilliantly in depicting the twilight of the gods in his opera cycle, *Ring des Nibelungen.*

Wagner's music is often described as being the epitome of romanticism in music. As is true for nearly all cultural and intellectual movements in Western history, romanticism had a large millennial element. Reacting against Enlightenment rationalism that found truth in the conquest of nature through science and technology, romantics saw these fields as leading humanity to destruction. Numerous pieces of romantic literature depict the endtime as being a result of the arrogance of those who believe that they can control nature and thereby violate it through scientific research and machines. Nature strikes back by destroying most or even all of humanity. The prototype novel with that theme is Mary Shelley's *The Last Man* (1826). Set in 2093 when modern science and technology seem on the verge of reestablishing the Garden of Eden, a plague is brought to Europe from the East, reducing humanity to one man. Her book is not truly millennial, for it conveys no hope of the new world, but it established the genre of futurist science fiction, or what in this case might be called anti-science fiction. Perhaps the best known romantic novel is Herman Melville's *Moby Dick* (1851). Replete with apocalyptic symbolism, the novel relates how Antichrist-Ahab's arrogance toward nature takes all but one of his crew to destruction by warring against the great white whale, the force of primal nature. Ishmael survives by clinging to a coffin floating free from the sinking *Pequod;* it is a symbol of the resurrection and the new world to come out of the old. Thus, Melville, while reducing the world of his ship also to one man, is more hopeful than Shelley about the promise of the new age. Shelley, Melville, and most other romantics had a powerful sense of the loss of innocence caused by the sin of humanity's violation of nature. Most of them looked back to the Middle Ages when society was purer and closer to nature. This half-mythological medievalism inspired Wagner's operas, and it is the element of romanticism that had the greatest appeal to Hitler, although he certainly did not repudiate modern military technology.

Wagner also has been described as a Social Darwinist, a political philosophy that applied Charles Darwin's theory of evolution to human societies. Its major exponent, Herbert Spencer, coined the phrase "survival of the fittest." Social Darwinism differs from most types of millennialism in arguing that human society did not begin in paradise but in a primitive state; it agrees with secular millennialism in seeing history as progress and the steady improvement of the human condition. Spencer maintained that the competition among societies has led to progress, as the stronger societies that survive are those that are improving. He argued that as societies improved, the competition would take on more peaceful forms and war would decline. He did not envision a static golden age in the future, but looked for progress to continue indefinitely. Spencer's views only tenuously can be called millennial, but others gave Social Darwinism interpretations more millennial in tone. According to them, the struggle among races was leading to the creation of a superrace, which would dominate the world and usher in a golden age. Although war would eventually disappear, it was good or at least morally neutral because it was the means by which the fitter races and finally the super race would achieve nature's goal for humanity. Those in the late nineteenth century who made this argument were mostly the British, who applied it to their empire, but it had its advocates elsewhere, especially in Germany.

Hitler adopted Social Darwinism and pushed it to its extremes. A race becomes great by purifying itself of alien elements and warring against weaker races. War is good, because it is the means by which the fittest struggle and survive. The more war the races engage in, the stronger they become, until one race, the German, will emerge as the superrace. When that happens, a golden age, the Third Reich, will be established and last for a thousand years. It was a law of God himself that guaranteed it would happen. The use of the term *Third Reich* was natural enough for Hitler, since the earlier German reichs he had in mind were the medieval Holy Roman empire and the German empire of 1870–1918, but it also tied into the Joachimite tripartite division of history. Figures from Europe's millennial past such as Charlemagne and Frederick Barbarossa were made into Nazi icons. For most Germans, their nation becoming the Third Reich meant that they were entering the final millennial age. The era before the Nazis took power was seen as an age of corruption and decadence; German culture and all of Western civilization were in severe decline. Hitler declared that the world should be changed "thoroughly and in all its parts."[10] The old age had to be destroyed in fire, blood, and violence, a *Götterdämmerung,* before the new age could begin. The great enemy the Germans had to destroy to achieve their golden age was not Antichrist but the Jews. Yet Nazi rhetoric against the Jews was remarkably similar to that about Antichrist. The Nazis looked for the marks to identify a Jew as thoroughly and eagerly as any premillennialist did for Antichrist. The great war against Jews and Jewish-inspired Bolshevism would be as cataclysmic as the apocalyptic wars in Daniel and Revelation. Piling up the dead bodies of their enemies in the numbers given in those books appealed greatly to the Nazis. Hitler did not reject Christianity entirely, but he worshipped the avenging God of the apocalyptic books, which are often overlooked as sources for the Nazi cult of the glorification of war.

It would not be stretching matters too far to define the Nazis as a millennial cult. Although their millennialism was far from systematic, traditional millennial images and concepts were an important part of their repertoire. Hitler acted as a charismatic cult leader in most respects, even if he did become the political leader of a large state. It can be argued that Hitler is the model of what many cult leaders might have become had they ever gained his power. Nazi propaganda shrewdly used millennial images as part of their campaign to win the support of the German people. Hitler on horseback in armor, holding sword and standard, drew on numerous symbols that played to the German imagination, but in particular he was the crusading last emperor who will begin the Millennium by defeating the Jewish Antichrist.

As Hitler's plans for the Jews, Jehovah's Witnesses, Gypsies, and other enemies of the German *volk*'s destiny became clearer by 1938, millennialists became more certain that he was Antichrist. An enterprising soul among them discovered that the name Hitler added up to 666. Some Jews saw the Nazi anti-Jewish measures and such atrocities as *Kristallnacht* in 1938 as signs of the imminent coming of the Messiah. With the outbreak of World War II in 1939, millennialists who designated Hitler as Antichrist became more common, but, given the enormity of the evil committed by his regime and the destructiveness of the war, it was not as common as might be expected. One reason was that for many premillennialists, Stalin loomed equally large as Antichrist; another was that the dates of the war did not coincide with millennial dating as 1914 had for the previous war.

One aspect of Nazi policy, the effort to destroy the Jewish people, probably would have raised the apocalyptic expectations of premillennialists had the full extent of it been known earlier in the war. Among those who knew all too well about Nazi aims, the Jews in the death camps, there was little organized messianism, certainly no movement like Sabbatai Sevi's in the seventeenth century. The nature of the camps meant that it was impossible to form a movement of any size or duration, but those caught up in the Nazi atrocities could not have failed to think that the endtime truly was arriving. At the beginning of the war many Jews held that the Messiah was coming in 1940, the year 5700 in the Jewish calendar. When the year ended with no sign of the Messiah, some efforts were made to recalculate for 1941; but by the end of that year the Nazis were beginning to implement the Final Solution, and the Messiah seemed more distant than ever. Since the prophets had predicted an incredible chastisement of the people of Israel for their sins before the faithful remnant would be restored to Jerusalem, perhaps the only way that the victims could retain faith in God in the horror of the Warsaw Ghetto and the death camps was to give it an apocalyptic interpretation. As one survivor put it, "When we stop sinning God will stop punishing us and we may enjoy the rewards and benefits of being His chosen people. That will be the days of the messiah."[11] Yet others lost their faith in the Messiah: If he did not come during this war, when would he come? Why should he bother to come later?

The limited messianism among the Jews caught up in the Nazi machine of mass murder was part of a more general phenomenon during World War II. Despite its greater destructiveness and death rate, this war did not elicit the same sort of millennial thought and literature as the first war had. World War I, even with its enormous casualty rate, could still evoke traditional images from religion, art, and literature to explain and comfort; this war could not. Apocalypse as metaphor came too close to reality.

"The Archangel Michael defeating Antichrist," based on Revelation 12:7 - 9 (Fifteenth Century) from K. Boveland, et al., from K. Boveland, et al., *Der Antichrist und die Fünfzehn Zeichen vor dem Jüngsten Gericht,* 2 vols., Hamburg: Friedrich Wittig Verlag, nd, II, 24. Reproduced by permission of Friedrich Wittig Verlag.

"Jerusalem," the Main Building (c. 1905) at the House of David, Benton Harbor, Michigan. Photographed by author.

Opposite: Detail from Hieronymus Bosch (c. 1450–1516), "Garden of Earthly Delights, Museo Del Prado, Madrid. Reproduced by permission of Art Resource, New York. Note the superabundance of nature during the Millennium.

Spot where the Virgin Mary first appeared to Mary Ann van Hoof in 1949, Necedah, Wisconsin. Photographed by author.

Opposite: "The Rapture." Reproduced by permission of the Bible Believers' Evangelistic Association, Sherman, Texas.

XIII

ANTICHRIST HAS THE BOMB!

O N JULY 16, 1945, THE FIRST DETONATION of an atomic bomb occurred, an event that has defined millennialism and so much else
in the past half-century. The atom bomb greatly raised millennial anxiety, both religious and secular, by providing a device through which the
end could happen in a manner very close to that described in Revelation.
In particular it stimulated nonreligious apocalypticism, since it was now
possible for the human race to destroy itself, perhaps even the entire
world, by its own agency, without requiring an act of the deity. The nuclear clock of the *Bulletin of Atomic Scientists,* set a few minutes before
midnight, symbolizes especially well the sense of humanity's responsibility for its coming end. As a result, in the post-1945 era the ordinary
person's fear and awareness of the possible end of the world have been
greater than at any time in the past, including the darkest of the Dark
Ages.

The first detonation of the bomb provided apocalyptic images that
set the tone for the next fifty years. The physicists who designed the
first bomb and set it off drew heavily on the Bible and other sacred literature to describe what they saw happen. The most famous statement
on the first nuclear explosion came from Robert Oppenheimer, the lead
physicist in the Manhattan Project. When William Laurence, the only
reporter permitted to view the detonation, asked him what his thoughts
were during the explosion, he replied that a passage from the Hindu

epic *Bhagavad-Gita* had leapt to mind: "Now I am become death, destroyer of worlds."[1] Most observers thought of doomsday and the Second Coming, but Laurence's own reaction is especially interesting, because he thought of Genesis and the creation of the world. The bomb's great flash of light reminded him of "Let there be light!" and its awesome roar was for him the cry of a newborn world.

Laurence's view that the atomic age was a new beginning for the world reflected his participation as a teenager in the 1905 revolution in Russia, which he had expected would create the golden age. After its failure, he fled to America, where he became a science reporter and discovered science as a new means for transforming the world. He was convinced that an advanced civilization existed on Mars that would someday make contact with the earth and bring it into the new kingdom of peace and progress. The idea was not original with Laurence. Earlier writers of science fiction had expressed it often, and the idea had an increasingly important impact on millennialism after 1945, although it also had an anti-apocalyptic aspect: the hope that the aliens from outer space could show the human race how to avoid catastrophic nuclear war. Laurence also became a vocal advocate for the idea that nuclear energy would bring humanity into utopia. It would provide an endless source of amazingly cheap power and the means to level mountains and fill valleys, control the weather, and eliminate disease. In the decade after the war popular magazines were filled with predictions about the golden age to come when the atom would be harnessed for the good of humanity—if it did not destroy the world first.

In August 1945, two atomic bombs were dropped on Japanese cities. World War II was over, but the world had seen the destructive potential of nuclear weapons; and the fear that the inevitable next war would end in a nuclear apocalypse became rampant. Books about planning for the next war had titles like "Wizards of Armageddon," or "Preparing for Armageddon." Both secular and religious millennialists began to sketch out scenarios of how it would happen. Statements about the incredible destruction of nuclear war made by scientists and others seeking to prevent use of nuclear weapons played into the hands of millennialists by providing them with a scientifically validated endtime scenario. Science fiction had long fantasized about how an epidemic, natural catastrophe, or some superweapon might destroy most of humanity, leaving a few people to create a new world. A good pre-war example of the genre as apocalyptic is *When Worlds Collide* (1932). After August 1945, such fiction seemed all too real. Numerous novels and films depicted the aftermath of nuclear war. The first such film was *Five* (1951), about survivors in a destroyed New York. As most examples of the genre, it presented the new world as antinomian; the rules of the old society, especially about sex, did not apply in the new world. The best-known work on nuclear war, *On the Beach* (novel, 1957; film, 1959), was entirely pessimistic: The few survivors face certain death from radiation poisoning; yet they remain conventional in their morality. Antinomianism does not rear its ugly head. Such an ending does not really qualify as millennial because of the absence of hope for a new world.

For premillennialists, scenarios of nuclear holocaust appeared to match amazingly well the descriptions of the last days in the Bible, especially 2 Peter and Revelation, in which fire, the all-consuming breath of God, serves as the principal means of the world's destruction. The speed with which the destruction of the human race by atom bomb could occur also seemed to affirm the Bible. Evidence of recent German, Japanese, and Soviet atrocities proved that the world was under Antichrist's rule. Yet many premillennialists had a sense of satisfaction that their views had been vindicated. It was especially strong among the pretribulationists, who expected to be taken in the Rapture before the bombs were dropped and thus escape nuclear destruction.

The most prolific among the premillennialists immediately after 1945 was Wilbur Smith from the Fuller Theological Seminary in California, which along with Dallas Theological Seminary has been the principal center of premillennialist scholarship since 1945. In 1946 *Reader's Digest* published Smith's article "This Atomic Age and the Word of God," which appeared as a book with the same title in 1948. He sought to prove that nuclear energy had been described in the Bible, arguing that God may have used it to destroy Sodom and Gomorrah. In September 1949 the Soviet Union exploded its own atomic bomb: Antichrist has the bomb! Two days after the news broke in America, Billy Graham, then an unknown evangelist, described the coming end of the world in terms of a Soviet nuclear attack on the West. Graham's career took off at this point, although his premillennialism has been more muted in the past two decades.

Since the cold war was in full force by then, the apocalypticism of nuclear war merged with anticommunist premillennialism. Christians from denominations that had long been amillennial were filled with millennial anxiety and looked to long-ignored biblical texts for an explanation of God's design for the world. In particular, millennialism became common among Catholics during the cold-war nuclear standoff. It mostly took the form of Marian apparitions, and the importance of Fatima increased exponentially, largely because of the secret third message. Mary's messages to Lucia as published in 1941 included what many saw as a prediction of the atomic bomb: "When you see a night illumined by an unknown light, know that this is the great sign given you by God that He is about to punish the world for its crimes."[2] Protestant premillennialists, despite their deep hostility to Marian apparitions as a source of millennial prediction, also influenced many Catholics. The Catholic Church had largely ignored the Rapture as an event of the endtime, but in the postwar era, some Catholics began to emphasize it in response to the anxiety created by the threat of nuclear war. In general, however, Marian apparitions provided a more active response to the threat of nuclear apocalypse than passively waiting for the Rapture. The conversion of Russia could be achieved through prayer, especially the rosary and other Marian devotions: If Catholics prayed hard enough, they could avert nuclear destruction.

In the decade after 1945 there were 114 Marian apparitions reported in Europe alone, including 48 in 1947 and 1948, with Italy the principal center.[3] Usually they involved young girls who received messages from the Virgin revealing how to prevent the coming nuclear war and Russian victory. Among the more important were apparitions at Necedah, an isolated town in central Wisconsin, that began in November 1949. The seer was a forty-year-old farm woman, Mary Ann van Hoof, who in May 1950 began to publicize the messages that she was receiving from Mary. They were similar to those of Fatima, with emphasis on America's role in the fight against communism. On August 15, a Marian feast day in the Catholic calendar and a month after the Korean War broke out, at least 100,000 people from across America gathered at the van Hoof farm to hear messages from Mary transmitted through van Hoof. They received what they had come to hear—a gloomy assessment of the state of the world and of America. Three-quarters of the nations of the world would be destroyed. Antichrist and his minions were readying an attack on America; it would include not only flying machines dropping destruction from the air but also chemicals placed in food and drink to weaken American will to resist. Yet not all was lost. If Catholics, and indeed all Christians, prayed to Mary, and prayed hard, she would intervene with Christ to prevent the coming apocalypse.

Despite the popularity of the Necedah apparitions among ordinary Catholics, the church hierarchy remained suspicious of their authenticity and refused to recognize them as credible. Without the high clergy controlling the phenomenon as they did at Fatima and Lourdes, van Hoof began to fall under the influence of conservative Catholic laymen, who used her visions to promote their strident anticommunist, conspiratorial views. She became adamant about a conspiracy of communists, Freemasons, and Zionists to destroy the United States and create a world government. Van Hoof also received a secret communication from an angel, which she never revealed, about the endtime and the renewal of the earth after the great chastising. She died in 1984, still receiving messages from Mary. Necedah remains today the center of a small but vocal group of Catholics opposed to Vatican II, who are still convinced that Russia is the great enemy and the events foretold in Revelation are about to unfold.

The messages Mary gave to another middle-aged woman, Veronica Lueken, are so similar to van Hoof's that some accused her of plagiarism. Lueken was a housewife in Bayside, (Queens) New York, in 1970 when Mary began appearing to her, which Mary continued to do with amazing frequency until Lueken's death in 1995. Bayside became a center of pilgrimage for thousands of Catholics, but as at Necedah, the church hierarchy was decidedly hostile to recognizing it as credible. There too the seer's death has not broken the faith of many of her followers, who remain active in spreading the word. The key difference between the two sets of Marian messages is that Lueken's has a place for the Rapture, reflecting premillennial influence on her. Mary promised

Lueken that her faithful would be taken off the earth before World War III and a comet hitting the earth would destroy it in flames. She also maintained, as did other discontented Catholics, that a conspiracy had removed the real Pope Paul VI and replaced him with an antipope, who might well be Antichrist replacing traditional practice with the innovations of Vatican II.

Included in the Marian messages has been an attack on the United Nations, as the evil One World Government to be created by the beast with ten horns and seven heads (Revelation 13:1). Attacking the UN was common among premillennialists, who had rejected the League of Nations on the same grounds. The greater strength of the UN made it a greater threat for many premillennialists, although others argue that the UN is of no significance in prophecy since it does not correspond to the borders of the old Roman empire. The hostility to the UN from many Americans comes not only from opposing many of its decisions as contrary to American interests but also from viewing it is a tool of Antichrist. American millennialists were surprised in 1950 to find the UN voting to support a police action against the North Korean invasion of the south. They explained it as Antichrist fooling Christians into supporting him by opposing atheistic communism. He would use the credit he would win among Christians when the Soviet Union was overthrown to establish his world government. The fact that the UN had organized the counterforce in Korea, although the forces there fought under their own flags, raised fears among premillennialists that it would create its own military force to implement Antichrist's designs. When, a decade later, forces drawn from member nations fighting under UN command with UN insignia appeared in trouble spots around the globe, premillennial suspicion became all the greater.

Because of the UN's role in the Korean War, premillennialists gave it limited support for several years after 1950, but it eroded largely because of Security Council resolutions regarding the Arab-Israeli conflict. The creation of the modern Jewish state has had perhaps as much impact on premillennialism as the atom bomb. Jews and Christians alike could agree on its significance in the divine scheme. Even before World War II, some Jews were prepared to see the Messiah as being other than a person. During the nineteenth century, Reform Judaism began to argue for replacing the traditional belief in a personal Messiah with a messianic age. In 1937 a conference of American Reform rabbis defined the age as "the establishment of the Kingdom of God, of universal brotherhood, justice, truth, and peace on earth. That is our messianic goal."[4] During World War II it had been difficult to believe that such a messianic utopia might be at hand, although Jewish apocalyptic is similar to the Christian in requiring a time of evil before the messianic promise can be fulfilled. For a majority of Jews, the creation of Israel was the ultimate messianic moment. At the founding of Israel, the chief rabbi commissioned a prayer for its well-being, which refers to "the commencement of our redemption."[5] Israel itself was the Messiah. Yet for many ultra-Orthodox Jews, including some living in Israel, the idea that the messianic kingdom could be established without the coming of the Messiah was sacrilegious. They refuse to recognize Israel even while they live in it.

Although Christian premillennialists had only a limited role in creating the state of Israel, they have emerged as the most outspoken of its non-Jewish supporters. They are convinced that it confirms the prophecy of the return of the Jews to the Holy Land before the endtime and thus is the most important sign that the Parousia is close at hand. Since 1948 they have concentrated on the meaning of this event for the timing of the Second Coming. As John Walvoord, a widely read premillennialist and president of the Dallas Theological Seminary from 1952 to 1984, wrote in 1964: "The formation of the nation of Israel is of tremendous significance, for what is now being witnessed by the world seems clearly to be a fulfillment of prophecy that there was to be ultimately a complete and final ingathering of Israel in connection with the second coming of Christ."[6] For a brief time when the First Arab-Israeli War of 1948 broke out, it seemed as if fate had been only teasing Jews and premillennialists alike, but the quick Israeli victory was taken as proof that biblical prophecy was being fulfilled. Even more significant was the 1973 Israeli occupation of East Jerusalem, the site of the ancient Temple. Some religious Jews and premillennial Christians began to plan the rebuilding of the Temple on the Temple Mount in Jerusalem, which would require demolishing two of Islam's most sacred mosques on the site. Had any of several schemes to blow up the mosques succeeded, apocalypse might have already come. In fact, apocalypse should have already arrived, since many premillennialists designated 1988 as the beginning of the endtime, based on Jesus' statement that a generation would not pass before the events foretold would occur (Matt. 24:34). The length of a generation has been vigorously debated, but for millennialists the most common period is forty years, the time the Israelites spent in the wilderness until the generation of the Exodus died.

The most successful, in book sales if not prophetic accuracy, of those premillennialists who see the events in the Middle East as proof of the fast-approaching endtime was Hal Lindsey. A graduate of the Dallas Theological Seminary, he published *The Late, Great Planet Earth* in 1970, which has sold nearly 30 million copies to date. It also was made into a popular movie in 1977, narrated by the noted actor Orson Welles. Not only has *The Late, Great Planet Earth* remained in print; but Lindsey has also continued to publish extraordinarily successful books that update it, such as *The 1980s: Countdown to Armageddon* (1980). Far behind Lindsey in sales but still successful by any other count are Salem Kirban's premillennial works. In *666* (1981) he describes how Antichrist will force people to bear the mark of the beast on their foreheads. It did a great deal to bring 666 to popular attention as Antichrist's symbol. The 1991 movie *The Rapture* provides as authentic a premillennial vision of the endtime as Hollywood is probably capable of producing.

Although premillennialists have been outspoken advocates of Israel, it is hardly from any deep love of Jews or Judaism but from the prophetic necessity that the Jews return to their ancient homeland, long a key part of millennialism. The rest of the prophecy concerning the Jews is far less favorable to them. According to the prophecy, they will have to suffer through trials even more devastating than those inflicted by the Nazis. Russia will attack Israel in alliance with the Arabs and wreck immense casualties on the Jews before a coalition of Christian nations from Europe defeats Israel's enemies. Only then will Christians and Jews alike realize that the leader of that coalition is Antichrist. He will gather his forces for the final showdown at Armageddon against Christ and the forces of good. Two-thirds of the Jews will be killed in these events; most of the survivors will accept Christ as the Messiah and join the saints in the New Kingdom. The Israeli leaders are well aware of the basis on which these Christians support their state, but having no belief in the prophecies themselves, they are willing to accept their political aid as part of realpolitik necessary in the modern world.

Since 1948 some groups of Jews both in Israel and elsewhere have made preparation for the coming of the Messiah the focus of their lives. They argue that Israel must be made into a Torah State, from which secular influences have been eliminated, and have used their political clout to force the Israeli government to take steps in that direction. More dangerous for the world is their tendency to look to the example of the original Hebrew conquest of the Holy Land, whose inhabitants are exterminated at God's order: "So Joshua defeated the whole land; . . . he left no one remaining, but utterly destroyed all that breathed" (Joshua 10:40). There is a strong messianic element among the Israeli settlers in the West Bank, who intend to reclaim all of the land of greater Israel and purge it of its people, as Joshua did, so that the Messiah might come. The most dangerous aspect of Israeli messianism lies in the expectation that the Temple will be rebuilt soon. It is not in Israel's interests to allow the destruction of the mosques on the site, but given the strength of Israeli messianism, one must wonder when an official will look the other way as radicals plot to blow them up, as several groups have tried to do since 1973.

The Arab response to the creation of Israel and the Arab-Israeli wars contains its own element of messianism. The Sudanese Mahdi of the 1880s demonstrated what could be accomplished by a Muslim leader who used the Islamic messianic tradition. The Palestinians began to draw on it soon after 1948, but it took over 20 years before a full-fledged movement developed among them. Jews do not have a major role in that tradition, but there is a *hadith* (saying) from the Prophet that states the final hour will not come until the Muslims fight the Jews and defeat them. When that time arrives, Muslims and Jews will be arrayed east and west, which naturally is taken to refer to the Jordan River. The belief that the Palestinian struggle against the Israelis is an apocalyptic event became significant only in the late 1970s, as the Islamic calendar approached another turn of the century. Hamas (the Islamic Resistance

Movement) draws heavily on that tradition. Its ideology starts with the principle that in these last days the situation of true Islam has returned to what it was under Muhammad—a small number of believers arrayed against the world. Not only Christians and Jews but most Muslims are agents of the Dajjāl, who now rules Israel. This tradition helps to explain the setbacks that the Islamic cause has had, since Satanic power is at work in support of the infidels. True Muslims must struggle against the Dajjāl in the final *jihad,* and those who die in the process are assured of paradise. The presence of suicide bombers in Hamas is a strong sign that it is apocalyptic.

Both the Sudanese Mahdi and Hamas are examples of anticolonial, national liberation movements that combine political motivation with apocalypticism. The number of such movements since 1900 has been astounding, although we will limit our discussion of them to two examples. There is little that is new about them, since the Bar Kokhba, Hussite, and Apu Inca revolts serve as good models among many pre-1900 examples, but they have become much more common in this century. One of the most intriguing movements is the Rastafarian, which began in Jamaica in 1930. The Rastafarians claim Marcus Garvey, the Jamaican-born organizer of the Back-to-Africa movement as their founder, although it is less certain that he regarded them as his progeny. He drew heavily on a long tradition of Ethiopianism, which maintains that David, Solomon, and the Queen of Sheba were black and that the Ethiopians were the Lost Tribes of Israel. He proposed the hymn "Ethiopia, Thou Land of Our Fathers" as the anthem of his movement and regarded Africa as the New Kingdom. According to the Rastafarians, Garvey, prior to going to the United States in 1916, declared: "Look to Africa for the crowning of a Black King. He shall be the Redeemer."[7] When in 1930 the Ethiopian prince Ras Tafari was crowned Emperor Haile Selassie, King of Kings and Lion of Judah, continuing a dynasty that claimed the Queen of Sheba as an ancestor, some of Garvey's followers, struck by the use of those titles in Revelation (5:5; 19:16), saw the fulfillment of his prophecy. They declared that the new emperor was divine, and they took his previous name for their group.

A powerful millennialism appeared immediately among the Rastafarians, who came mostly from the lowest levels of Jamaican society.

They declared that Africans, the Lost Tribes, had been forced into slavery and taken to hells such as Jamaica, where the white agents of the devil degraded them as a punishment for their sins. The time was at hand for them to return to Africa with the aid of the divine emperor. When they all arrived there, Africa would become Paradise, and whites would serve the blacks as their servants. The authorities soon accused the Rastafarians of sedition, and several leaders were jailed for two years. The remainder, numbering over 500 persons, took to the mountains and organized a commune. There they adopted a set of rituals including the use of marijuana, rejection of tobacco and alcohol, a kosher diet, and a distinctive appearance, especially dreadlocks and beards that characterize the Rastafarians to the present. The police, pushed into action by the complaints of the commune's neighbors, raided it twice, and the second raid in 1954 ended its existence. The Rastafarians, forced back into Jamaican society, which they designated Babylon, became politically radical. In 1960, goaded on by black revolutionaries from the United States, they turned to violence, and deaths occurred on both sides through 1964.

By then Jamaica had gained its independence from Britain, and although the Rastafarians were suspicious of the new government, relations improved. They toned down their militancy, and the government largely tolerated their marginal behavior and antigovernment rhetoric. Haile Selassie visited Jamaica in 1966, and the Rastafarians were accorded an honored place in his welcome, gaining them respectability. His death in 1975 failed to discomfit their belief that he was divine, but it had the result of redirecting their emphasis from repatriation to Africa toward reforming Jamaica. Never a formal organization, the Rastafarians have become divided into one group moving toward becoming an organized church and another being coopted into the political system as a leftist party. Rastafarians have appeared in other Caribbean islands, the United States, and England. When Rastafarian musician Bob Marley and reggae became wildly popular among middle-class American young people in the 1980s, the Rastafarians had come far from their millennialist origins.

The most numerous third-world movements in this century have been the "cargo cults." It is a term used for a series of some thirty millennial groups that appeared across New Guinea and the islands of the south Pacific from 1890 to 1960. A small majority of them were true cargo cults, which believed that the Europeans had stolen cargo from the islanders' ancestors. Cargo referred to the goods, especially guns, that Europeans brought to the islands. The cults believed that the divine ancestors would return in a ship loaded with cargo and distribute it to their descendants, the rightful owners, thereby inaugurating a golden age. This idea drew heavily on native beliefs that the beloved dead will return to renovate the earth and restore it to its original state of freedom from want and death. In most cases, a native prophet proclaimed that the cargo ship was coming soon but only after catastrophic earthquakes or tidal waves. The hostility to the whites found in these cults often was evident in predictions that only they and their lackeys among the natives would be killed in these calamities. The prophet usually demanded that his people purge themselves of European ways and goods. In response, the cult members refused to labor for the whites and did other acts that frequently led to violence. They often destroyed or gave away their animals and supplies of food in anticipation of the endless quantities that the cargo ship would bring. Often the islanders would build a special dock or depot in anticipation of its arrival.

Christianity won converts among the islanders with relative ease because they could identify with Christian doctrines of the resurrection of the dead and renewal of the world. They sometimes identified Christ as the captain of the cargo ship with the returning ancestors and looked to Revelation for clues to its coming. During and after World War II, airplanes often substituted for ships in their beliefs. The prophecy's failure led the prophets sometimes to declare that the ancestors could not return as long as Europeans and natives who did not belong to the cult remained on the island. That led to violence until the Europeans quashed the uprising and imprisoned or executed the prophets. In some cases, a new leader appeared who claimed to have had a supernatural visit from the earlier prophet telling him to reestablish the cult. Several islands had a cycle of cargo cults in this pattern that lasted for a half-century or longer.

The other type of millennial cult found in the South Sea islands was highly similar to the cargo cult but lacked the idea of the cargo ship or plane. The dead were waiting in a mountain or inside the earth until the time to return to the living. The most intriguing of these cults began in 1933 in northeastern Papua New Guinea. A prophet named Marafi announced to his people that Satan had taken him to the center of the earth to visit the spirits of their ancestors. Satan told him that he had replaced God as the supreme being, and that Marafi must win his people over to worshipping him. When he did, there would be earthquakes, volcanic eruptions, floods, and a terrible fire. Believers were to build large houses where they were to take refuge when the first signs of the disasters occurred; persons not in these houses would be killed. Then the dead would return with huge quantities of European goods and food, and the people, who would become white while the Europeans became black, would never have to work again. Marafi commissioned apostles to preach Satan worship throughout the region, and their success gained the attention of British authorities when many natives refused to work or pay their taxes. Their efforts to undermine Marafi received a huge boost when it became known that Marafi was persuading girls to leave their families and become his wives, since Satan had indicated that he could have as many as he wanted. Discredited, he was arrested with little difficulty, although remnants of his cult survived for several more years. What makes Marafi so intriguing was that his was one of the few anticolonial movements that took the logical ultimate step of inverting the European religion, making Satan the supreme being, as a way to reverse European hegemony.

The idea of using Satan worship as a means to overthrow the imperialism of Western society also found expression within that society during the 1960s. It is impossible to mention all the cults and movements of the sixties' counterculture that have a millennial component, to say nothing of discussing them fully. In a sense the entire counterculture was millennial, since its professed goal was to create the new age of peace and harmony, but we will restrict our discussion to those groups with an important place in history or with clear ideas about the coming new age. Arguably, the belief in the new age is best expressed in the play *Hair* (1967) and a song from it, "The Age of Aquarius." The play's staging calls for the presence of the tribe, which gives its members the means to find an alternative to the establishment's standards, goals, and morals. The tribe, having its own morality, dress, and behavior, illustrates the emergence of a "new-ancient culture among the youth." Except for identifying the chosen people as simply the young, it is difficult to sum up better what is meant by an antinomian cult. Like many millennial cults, *Hair* became notorious for its nudity, intended to signal the "new man."

For astrologers an astronomical event called the precession of the equinoxes—the sun's location at the moment of the spring equinox moves through the zodiac signs over 24,000 years (not the actual time)—marks major changes in history. For the last 2,000 years the sun has been in the sign of Pisces; for the previous 2,000 years, in the sign of Aries. By 1966, the time for the sun to move into Aquarius was close at hand. It often was placed in 1987, but dispute over the exact boundary between the two signs caused disagreement when the Age of Aquarius would begin. For some astrologers, the three zodiac signs mark a Joachimite division of time, the ages of father, son, and spirit. The Sun's movement into Aquarius would begin a new age of wisdom and renewal, ending the present age of war and repression. The Age of Aquarius will have:

> Harmony and understanding, Sympathy and trust abounding,
> No more falsehoods or derisions, Golden living dreams of visions,
> Mystic crystal revelation, And the mind's true liberation.[8]

The theme of Hair, speaking for the hippies of the sixties, is that young people can create the new age if they "Tune in, turn on, and drop out," but "new-agers" include many other approaches to transforming the world. Some of the new-agers, such as UFO-millennialists, became important after 1980 and will be discussed in the next chapter. A prominent voice among new-agers since 1965 is Ruth Montgomery, a reporter assigned for many years to the White House. She has described the new age through what she calls walk-ins, when the spirits of dead persons take over her hands and type messages with them. Her millennialism combines traditional Christian and new-age ideas: Christ's birth began the age of Pisces, which will end around the year 2000 and will usher in the Age of Aquarius, the true Millennium of Revelation. In her early books Montgomery spoke of a World War III begun by Antichrist, who she claimed was already alive and attending an elite university in the northeastern United States; her later books rarely mention him. Now Montgomery maintains that the present age will end in a dramatic event called the polar shift. Shifting on its axis so that the two poles will take different positions, the earth will undergo a tremendous cataclysm in which much of the current dry land will slip into the sea while land from past eons such as Atlantis will rise out of the water. There will be vast casualties from floods, earthquakes, and volcanic eruptions that will both precede and accompany this event and the vast climatic changes to follow. Once all this tumult has ended, humanity will enter a new age of peace and brotherhood. The human mind will be so improved that education will not be necessary. Humanity will live in harmony with nature; illness, famine, war and other causes of human misery in the current age will disappear.

Montgomery, like most new-agers, also looks to the Amerindians for wisdom and prophecy. The most influential Amerindian eschatology for new-agers is that of the Hopi. According to Hopi belief, when Taiowa created the world, it was perfect, but the appearance of evil brought by sorcerers led to its destruction and the re-creation of a new one. A few righteous humans lived through its destruction and repeopled the new world. There have been three worlds before the present one that is now manifesting the problem of mounting evil. The Hopi expect that sometime soon Taiowa will become so dissatisfied with the world, he will destroy it and create a fifth one. A few pious people will survive the apocalypse and live in perfect harmony in the new world, but the Hopi do not expect that it will be the final one. The cycle may go on indefinitely. The extent to which Christians influenced the Hopi, with whom they have been in contact since 1540, is impossible to answer, but the concept of the Bahana, the True White Brother, who will act as a redeemer to save the righteous few seems to reflect Christ. It can also be argued that the Bahana is the Hopi version of the Quetzalcoatl myth of the Aztecs, with whom the Hopi had close ties in the pre-Columbian era. For some new-agers it follows that the Aztec calendar determines the coming of the Hopi new world, and the Aztec calendar in turn is essentially identical to the Mayan. The Maya also thought in terms of old worlds destroyed and new ones created, but they supposedly set a date for these events: Their calendar ends on the winter solstice in 2012. For many new-agers this will mark the present world's end and the creation of the new one of perfect knowledge and peace.

The new-agers also draw on theosophy for much of their thought. This "divine wisdom" has as its early sources the German mystic Jakob Boehme and a Swedish engineer-turned-theologian Emmanuel Swedenborg (d. 1772). The latter at age 53 had a vision of Christ who informed him that he was to reveal the true spiritual meaning of the Bible. Swedenborg discovered different spiritual eras in human history. He called them "churches," referring to phases in the developing relationship between God and human beings. The next and final age involved a new approach to Christianity, which he called the New Church, and a key part was his understanding of the new Jerusalem. The new era will not begin through the destruction of the current world but through its spiritual re-creation by the presence of God in the hearts and minds of all people. A few Swedenborgians kept his thought alive into the mid-nineteenth century, when it attracted a Russian, Madame Helena Blavatsky. Married at age 17 to a much older man, she quickly left him and spent the rest of her life traveling in Asia, Egypt, and the Americas, becoming learned in ancient religions and philosophies. She claimed that she was in contact with a great spirit of the past she called the Master, who revealed to her the secrets of the universe. In 1875 she founded the Theosophical Society to spread her message that all major religions are derived from one original religious philosophy. She drew heavily from Hinduism including the ideas of karma and, especially, reincarnation. Blavatsky declared that theosophy's first objective was universal brotherhood. She also created a close connection between theosophy and spiritualism through her claims of making contact with the dead.

If new-agers like Montgomery still draw partially on Christianity for their endtime scenarios, others reject or, more correctly, reverse it by promoting witchcraft and Satan worship. Counterculture repudiation of Western society, modern feminism's declarations that the new age will come only when women are given equality to men, and theories postulating the existence of a mother goddess religion that predates Christianity—all have led some, mostly women, to take up the worship of the great Goddess. They argue that what Christians condemn as witchcraft is really the folk survivals of an older religion called Wicca. Loosely organized small groups called covens practice what they regard as ancient rituals at nighttime on key dates such as mid-summer's eve. The two largest such groups, the Church of the Circle Wicca and the Covenant of the Goddess, were both organized in 1975. Wicca's most prominent advocate is a woman called Starhawk, who published *Spiral Dance: A Rebirth of the Ancient Religion of the Great Goddess* in 1979. Although the Wiccans identify themselves as witches, they deny that witchcraft is malevolent. What it really involves is an intimate connection with nature, impossible in Christianity or Judaism, that will bring about the unity of the female and the male.

Most Wiccans are active in the ecological movement, and their idea of the new age looks toward a time when humanity is in harmony with the earth and all forms of life. Eco-millennialism is a term used for the view that humanity is rapidly bringing earth to an ecological apocalypse that will probably destroy human life if not all life on earth. It can be averted if people come to realize the role they have in depleting the earth's resources and take steps to moderate their consumption. The group Earth First! is willing to use radical steps such as spiking trees in wildernesses to make sawing them dangerous, thereby preserving the wilderness. In September 1998, the movement had its first casualty when an Earth First!er was killed when the tree he had climbed was cut down.

Wiccans honor a horned male god representing the masculine side of nature whom, they argue, the medieval Church turned into the devil, but his place in their belief hardly constitutes devil worship. The 1960s, however, did produce a few unabashed devil worshippers who reveled in their deification of evil. It is difficult to say how many of these Satanists truly believe in devil worship and how many are simply acting out to get attention or spoof traditional beliefs. Tales, not all of them unfounded, of secret satanic cults date back to the Middle Ages, but the first modern effort to create a public cult began in 1966 when Anton LaVey organized his Church of Satan in San Francisco. He reversed Christianity by worshipping God's adversary, writing a *Satanic Bible* (1969)—"If a man smite you on the check, SMASH him on the other!"—and using parodies of Christian rituals; but his emphasis was largely on hedonism and egotism. Included among some 300 members at its height were several celebrities such as Sammy Davis, Jr. and Jayne Mansfield. A disciple organized the smaller Temple of Set in 1975, named for the god of chaos in Egyptian religion. Satanism takes its millennialism directly from Christianity but reverses it. Antichrist's coming will begin the new age, and the time for his appearance is looming. Satanists expect an apocalypse in which the earth will be purged during an Age of Fire. Then Christianity will crumble away, as people at last will recognize its lies, and finally God will fall from his throne. Humanity will then evolve into its true nature, although little is said about what life would be like in a satanic Millennium. LaVey died in late 1997, and according to recent reports his church has fallen into chaos because of disputes over his will and the absence of an effective second leader.[9]

Perhaps the only mark LaVey made in American culture was in serving as an adviser (even that is disputed) on the hit movie *Rosemary's Baby* (1968). The film has sparked a whole genre of movies about Antichrist. The character Rosemary is tricked into giving birth to Antichrist (the film leaves open the possibility that it is a hallucination on her part) by her husband who has joined a coven. It uses millennial symbols but quite subtly; it is, for example, easy to miss the significance of the baby's birth in June (the sixth month) of 1966. The movie ends with Antichrist's birth, but others following in the genre, such as *The Omen, Damon,* and *The Seventh Sign* follow Antichrist's career to his final showdown with God, giving legions of viewers Hollywood's vision of the last days.

Despite great attention in the popular media about satanic cults engaging in ritualistic orgies with child abuse and even child murder, modern Satanists seem more interested in enraging traditional Christians than engaging in amoral behavior. There was one group, however, where Satanism's influence was not so benign. The extent to which the notorious Manson family had contacts with Satanists in San Francisco probably always will remain unclear, but there is no question that somewhere Charles Manson picked up the satanic beliefs that helped to inspire his group's violent murders. Manson, the illegitimate son of a Kentucky teenager, spent half of his first 33 years in detention for petty crime. After his release from jail in 1967, he drifted to the counterculture's center, the Haight-Ashbury district in San Francisco. There he found that his notoriety as a criminal and convict gave his views great authority among hippies eager to reject the society they so hated.

Manson had little trouble attracting followers among rootless young women on the fringes of the hippie movement. They believed that he was Christ, and although he may not have claimed it directly, his followers reenacted the crucifixion with him in the title role. He changed the names of those who joined his mostly female family, which numbered about 25 in 1969; perhaps double that number drifted in and out of it. Living by their wits and petty thievery at isolated sites in California, entirely antinomian in regard to sex, drugs, and even killing, the Manson family waited for the violent apocalypse that he predicted was close at hand. Out of a mélange of sources including the Bible, Satanism, Hitler, the Beatles, and science fiction, Manson developed a millennialism requiring violence to cause the endtime. Race hatred between blacks and whites would lead to black revolution in which all whites would be killed except for the Manson family, which would enter a bottomless pit in Death Valley before the violence began. Emerging after the race war, they would take over rule of America from the blacks, who would prove incapable of governing. The Manson family would be the model for a new world. There would be no inhibitions about sex; women would service men sexually and have children; the only loyalty would be to Manson.

Manson became obsessed with the Beatles' foreboding "White Album" and believed the song "Revolution #9" referred to Revelation, chapter 9. Especially fascinated by the term helter-skelter from another Beatles' song that actually refers to a ride in an English park, Manson used it for the coming black revolution. When it failed to occur, he concluded that his family had to bring it about by murdering several prominent white people and making it look as if black militants were responsible. Frightened whites would then increase their repression of blacks, which would lead to helter-skelter and the apocalypse. In August 1969, the Manson family put the plan into action by killing eight people in Los Angeles including the actress Sharon Tate. Revealed to the authorities by the boasting of family members jailed for another crime, Manson and five followers were tried and convicted of murder. The willingness of some followers both in and out of prison blindly to accept Manson's words more than 25 years after he was imprisoned says much about the control that a charismatic leader can exercise over followers. It is easy to see from the example of the Manson family how the words of martyred cult leaders, who have even more cachet than incarcerated ones, can continue to excite and incite long after their deaths.

The Manson family was the most radical and violent of the vast number of utopian communes that sprang up as part of the counterculture's efforts to form a new world. All were antinomian because they were founded precisely to free themselves from the rules of society; some were caught up in violence, whether as victims or perpetrators. But none had the impact that the Mansonites did. Several commentators have suggested that the Manson murders mark the beginning of the end of the counterculture. That probably is giving Manson too much importance, but there is no question that he struck a severe blow to its ideals of peace, harmony, understanding, and the mind's true liberation.

XIV

FROM JONESTOWN
TO WACO

FOR THE AVERAGE AMERICAN IN 1978, millennialism was off the
radar screen. The ending of American involvement in Vietnam reduced the volume of the apocalyptic voices arising from the antiwar
movement; Jimmy Carter's presidency lowered anxiety over the likeli-
hood of nuclear war with the geriatric crowd in the Kremlin. Millennial
cultists seemed to be little threat because the counterculture was in decline and Manson's millennialism was not well known. In late 1978, the
first in a series of violent episodes brought millennialism crashing back
to public attention, which has remained focused on it ever since.

In November 1978, millennialism seized the world's attention with
the news flash that a United States congressman and four members of
his party had been murdered in Guyana and hundreds belonging to an
obscure cult had committed suicide. What happened in Jonestown has
remained to the present a major subject of both scholarly research and
morbid fascination. The cult involved was the Peoples Temple, and its
founder, Jim Jones, remains for many the classic image of a cult
leader—a demonic face, eyes hidden by the sunglasses that he always
wore, even indoors. He was born in 1931 in Indiana, the only child of
poverty-stricken parents who were largely irreligious. Friends and
neighbors took young Jim to virtually all the churches in their small
town, making him familiar with the style of many denominations. As a
teenager he gained attention from his peers by imitating a revival

preacher, yet he had hopes of becoming a physician. After vacillating between these career goals, he settled on being a Methodist minister, gaining his first pulpit in 1952. Jones early on befriended blacks and worked for improving race relations. Married, father of a son, he also adopted several children from different races. Feeling out of place with the Methodists because of his practice of faith healing and involvement in civil rights, he organized a Peoples Temple in Indianapolis in 1956 to provide shelter and medical care for the poor and homeless.

Two years later he went to Philadelphia to visit an established version of his temple that had been created by Father Divine, a black minister who had been enormously successful in rising from poverty to run a vast movement called the Peace Mission. Father Divine was millennial in a limited way: Since 1915 he had been asserting that he was divine and that his presence on earth was ushering in the new world. His businesses catering to blacks brought him vast wealth, but he avoided taxes by putting it all in his church and using it to enjoy a luxurious lifestyle. He established a communal lifestyle for his followers, who included blacks and whites, for whom celibacy, a simple lifestyle, and the transfer of all wealth to Father Divine was mandatory. For him, none of that was necessary, and he had numerous lovers among his female disciples. Impressed with Father Divine's movement, Jones sought for years to be named as heir apparent and when Divine died in 1965, to take it over. As Jones waited futilely to be called to lead the Peace Mission, he used Divine's techniques in the Peoples Temple and lured away some of his members.

Meanwhile, Jones became affiliated with the Church of the Disciples of Christ in 1960 and was ordained a minister in it largely because it had a reputation for liberalism and local autonomy. Soon Jones abandoned any loyalty to the denomination. He had long been interested in faith healing, and his cures became ever more extravagant and numerous. Several defectors later described how they helped Jones pull off his fake cures. He spoke of being a hundredfold filled with God and did nothing to contradict his followers who said he was divine. By 1965 the Peoples Temple had gained a good reputation for interracial harmony and good works in Indianapolis. Over half of its members were black, and some blacks held positions of authority, but most of Jones's lieutenants were white. Jones's stand on civil rights created enemies, although he is suspected of sending some of the nastiest attacks to himself as a way to bind his disciples tightly to him.

The decision to move to California, however, grew largely out of Jones's millennialism. The world, at least capitalist America, was hopelessly corrupt and about to end, he believed. Jones predicted that nuclear war would break out on July 15, 1967, and only those in safe zones would survive. One such zone was northern California, since the prevailing winds off the ocean would keep away radioactive fallout from any bombs that hit San Francisco or Portland, and the expanse of the Pacific would greatly reduce any fallout from eastern Asia. In 1965 he announced the move to his congregation. It was a true test of loyalty on the part of his followers, making Jones sure of the commitment of 86 persons who moved and several dozen more who followed later. The small town of Ukiah also provided Jones with the opportunity to exercise rigid control over his flock. As outsiders practicing interracial living, they had little chance of fitting in among the locals and became ever more dependent on their pastor. In Indiana, Jones had already talked of "apostolic socialism," but here he could implement it. Members turned over all of their wealth and income to him, since those who could work were expected to have outside jobs, and the Peoples Temple took in welfare payments for the elderly and orphans among its members. Jones's politics turned more socialist, and he spoke glowingly of Cuba and the other communist states.

Jones continued his extensive outreach program in California, and it served as a valuable recruiting tool, as many of those who made contact with him did so through the vast range of social work performed by its followers. Those who came to the temple to learn more were usually impressed with the sense of love and sharing among its members and with the charismatic Jones. When sure of the commitment of new members, he had them sign a highly incriminating statement that they were communists or guilty of some sexual perversion or in the case of one family, the Stoens, that Jones was the real father of their son. The members regarded these signings as a test, but they would soon find that Jones used them to keep members in line and to threaten them if they wanted to leave. Nothing upset him more than the defection of members, and he used every technique of persuasion and intimidation, often successfully, to keep them with him. As were so many other cult leaders, Jones was obsessed with sex and avidly controlled the sex lives of his followers. At first he had advocated free love, but after the move to Ukiah, he demanded celibacy even of married couples, although there were about 30 babies born to the cult in Guyana. He, however, was free to engage in sex with whomever he pleased, male or female. He was proud of his sexual prowess and the size of his penis. While Jones had a powerful sexual appetite, he used sex as a means of controlling his followers, especially the men with whom he copulated, some of whom would have never contemplated homosexual acts in any other circumstance.[1]

Even as Jones became deeply involved in California politics, his millennialism became more urgent. A former member quoted him as saying in 1969:

> I have seen by divine revelation the total annihilation of this country and many other parts of the world. The only survivors will be those people who are hidden in the cave that I have been shown in a vision. . . . It will be up to our group to begin life anew on this continent. Then we will begin a truly ideal society just as you see it here in this room today. . . . This church family is an example of what society will eventually be like all over the world. There will at last be peace on earth. I have seen this all by divine revelation.[2]

By 1973 Jones had expanded his operations to San Francisco, about 100 miles from Ukiah, and his following reached 3,000 people. While the membership in Indiana had included a good number of poor and poorly educated people, their proportion increased substantially in California, as did the proportion of blacks (nearly 80 percent), but his lieutenants remained mostly middle-class whites. Jones took a strong interest in San Francisco politics, and with his involvement in the black community, he became an important ally for the city's Democratic politicians. Jones's growing influence had caught the press's attention, and not all of the reporters were as easily conned as the politicians were. A flurry of bad publicity persuaded him to look for a possible refuge outside of America, and he found it in black-ruled, socialist, English-speaking Guyana. In 1973 he bought land 130 miles south of the capital, Georgetown. A bitter custody battle over the Stoens' son and accompanying bad publicity precipitated the decision to move to his land in Guyana, which he called Jonestown. By late 1977, some 1,000 people had migrated there, although several of those closest to Jones remained to supervise affairs in California. Without Jones's presence, most members who refused to go to Guyana drifted away.

Jones slipped out of California with the Stoens boy, putting himself in contempt of court. The move also forced the hands of those relatives of temple members who were trying to get them to leave the cult. Both factors persuaded Congressman Leo Ryan of California to go to Jonestown in November 1978, accompanied by several reporters, to investigate charges that the members were being held against their will. There he found conditions overcrowded but less harsh than he had been led to believe. Still, some 20 members asked Ryan to take them with him. The betrayal by so many was a severe blow to Jones, who had always worked strenuously to keep even one from leaving. As Ryan's party prepared to board planes at a nearby airstrip, some of Jones's followers killed Ryan, three reporters, and a defector. Meanwhile, Jones was preparing his people for "revolutionary suicide" in what he called " the white night," which he had rehearsed with his followers many times previously. A tape recorder captured the voices of Jones and others, including a woman who bravely but futilely objected, as he set the plan in action. Nearly all the 637 adults and 276 children who died were poisoned with cyanide in a flavored drink. Some took it willingly; others were coerced. Several people including Jones died from gunshots; whether he committed suicide or was killed by another's hand has never been settled. Three young men made a run for it and escaped, and an elderly woman slept through the entire event and survived. A member in Georgetown killed herself and her two children when the order came from Jones; another member committed suicide several months later. About 200 members, mostly those who had remained in California, survived.

A great deal is known about the Peoples Temple. Dozens of surviving members and defectors have been interviewed, and thousands of hours of Jones lecturing his faithful are preserved on tape. Yet all this information has not resulted in a proper understanding of him or the temple. Too much emphasis has been on Jones as malevolent cult leader and too little on his millennialism. Of all the personas that he took on, the most important was that of a messiah leading his people into the promised land. The idea of a migration into the wilderness has always been a powerful one for those with millennial inclinations, and Jones was no exception. It was his great success in California after his first migration that led to the move to Guyana. By recruiting so many members, Jones found himself facing the problem of defectors and lawsuits, and his budding political career threatened to expose his many shady dealings. A millennial group usually does not stand and fight against the forces of evil; it flees them for the wilderness where it can isolate itself from those forces. In the Guyana wilderness, however, the internal problems facing the group, evident earlier, were exacerbated. Isolation became severe, and the difficulty for discontented members of leaving was made worse; their discontent created a cancer in the group. Jones controlled all the sources of information and made sure all believed that the forces of evil were deployed against them. He did not need to say much against Ryan when he and the reporters appeared; all knew who they really were. Their arrival made a crucial point to Jones and his close advisers: The hostility of the corrupt world could not be shaken simply by flight to a remote land. It became clear that suicide was the only way to the promised land: To die in revolutionary suicide is to live forever.

The world had little time to digest the events in Guyana as it was quickly faced with another movement with greater political importance. In January 1979 the shah of Iran was overthrown, and an Islamic fundamentalist government was installed. A majority of Iranians are Shi'is, a branch of Islam with a strong messianic component. It contains a potent martyr complex, a reflection of the death of the Imam Husayn in the battle of Karbala in 680, to whom Muslims attribute the statement: "Death is better than life under oppression." As Shi'is, the Iranians are prepared to be long suffering until the time is right to fulfill the prophecies about the return of the twelfth imam, who will then lead them to victory over the forces of evil. This attitude is an important reason why for years there was little open resistance to the modernizing policies of the shah, who was compared to Yazid, Husayn's vanquisher and embodiment of evil for Shi'is. The approach of the century's turn in the Islamic calendar precipitated revolt. Ayatollah Khomeni, the most zealous opponent of the shah, timed his return from France to coincide with it. In exile for sixteen years, where he had been stoking the fires of messianic zeal, he now emerged as the leader of the Iranian Revolution. He made no claim to be more than a true Muslim, zealous for Islam, but some followers proclaimed him to be the Hidden Imam or, more often, his special messenger. The goal of the Iranian Revolution was to establish a true Islamic state that would set the stage for the return of the twelfth imam and begin the events of the endtime. That required eliminating the agents of the Great Satan, thus the attack on the American embassy in 1980. Since the victory of the Islamic fundamentalists, Iran has existed nearly 20 years as a messianic society under strict observance of Islamic law without evidence that the endtime is any closer. It is now showing signs of normalizing its society. No society long can endure the style of life dictated by messianism or millennialism; Iran has survived that way for a surprisingly long period.

The Iranian hostage crisis was a major factor in the election of Ronald Reagan to the American presidency in November 1980. For the first time a president was a strong believer in millennialism, although the depth of Reagan's belief was not understood until after he left office. (Ironically, it was once proposed by a fundamentalist preacher that he is Antichrist because his full name, Ronald Wilson Reagan, consists of three names of six letters apiece and when badly wounded, he made a miraculous recovery.) He was raised in the Disciples of Christ (Campbellite), a premillennialist church, and once he left acting for politics, his interest in the endtime seemingly returned. Both as governor of California and as president, he commented several times in public forums about the approach of Armageddon. In 1971, while discussing with Reagan the prophecies in Ezekiel naming the enemies of Israel, a California politician noted that Ethiopia was numbered among them and commented that no one could expect that it would become communist. Reagan replied that the prophecy required it and it would happen, as it did three years later. Little wonder that Reagan and other premillennialists mused that the last days were at hand. Perhaps his best known remark came in a meeting with an Israeli diplomat: "I turn back to your ancient prophets in the Old Testament and the signs foretelling Armageddon, and I find myself wondering if we're the generation that's going to see that come about."[3] Several cabinet secretaries made even more explicit comments on the approach of the Parousia.

The support of America's premillennialists was a significant factor in Reagan's election, and their leaders gained political influence far beyond what could have been imagined a decade earlier. Pat Robertson's political clout reached so high that he made a serious run at being nominated as the Republican Party's presidential candidate in 1988. The son of a U.S. senator, founder of a flourishing university and television network, and voice of a powerful Christian political movement, he is not the sort of person that has usually been associated with ardent millennialism; yet prior to 1988 his premillennialism was explicit. In 1980 he declared: "If the approximate dating of events is even close and if Anti-Christ is yet to come, then we must conclude that there is a man alive today, approximately 27 years old, who is now being groomed to be the Satanic messiah." Robertson predicted nuclear war for late 1982, bringing about the events of the endtime. "One scenario seems capable of fulfillment at almost any time: A major war erupts in the Middle East, with the Soviet Union leading a force into Israel." [4] Once he threw himself into politics, however, Robertson began to back away from his explicit premillennialism. The belief that one is waiting until Christ comes to destroy this corrupt world is inconsistent with the goals of a political career, nor is it likely to win many votes among the majority of Americans who are not premillennialists. In late 1984 Robertson called for a society with a Spirit-filled president and a godly Congress that would take on the features of the Millennium. His change toward postmillennialism was so sudden that a dumfounded premillennialist proposed that he was Antichrist, leading the faithful astray. Since 1988 Robertson seems to have returned to premillennialism, at least in his novel *The End of the Age,* one of many novels published in the past three decades with fictionalized accounts of the last days. His device of an asteroid crashing into the sea to begin the tribulation is justified by Revelation (8:8) but rarely used in premillennialism.

Jerry Falwell, another successful television evangelist and founder of a Christian university with broad political influence in the 1980s through his organization, the Moral Majority, was not as systematic in his premillennialism, but he had the panache to preach about Armageddon from the site of Megiddo in 1983. He was able to do it because he has been the most outspoken and influential supporter of Israel among American Christians. If the statement of a former aide can be taken as accurate, Falwell also bluntly expressed the view common among premillennialists that nuclear war is not to be feared, because "I ain't going to be here," expecting to be taken in the Rapture before the devastation begins.[5] In early 1999, he created a stir with his public comment that Antichrist had to be Jewish. Those who charged that this was anti-Semitic failed to understand that it is an ancient tradition in millennialism, not Falwell's personal opinion.

There was some discussion in the press during Reagan's presidency whether the strong premillennial element in his administration might result in reduced efforts to prevent nuclear war: If the end would come through nuclear destruction, it was presumptuous to try to thwart God's will by working for arms control. Fears raised in such discussions might have become more urgent if the research published in 1986 on the beliefs of workers in the plant assembling nuclear weapons in Amarillo, Texas, had become better known.[6] Interviews indicated that the workers were mostly premillennialists who accepted the possibility that the world might end in nuclear war as part of God's plan. The research did not address the question of whether those workers were already premillennialists and took their jobs because they did not find them threatening to their beliefs or had they become premillennialists as a psychological defense mechanism because of the terrifying implications of their work.

As influential as American premillennialists were in the 1980s, their clout pales in comparison to that held by their coreligionists in South Korea. Despite being a largely Buddhist nation, close to a majority of its government and military command belong to Christian churches that emphasize the impending Parousia. It is plausible that the influence of Buddhist eschatology, one of the strongest among non-Christian religions, explains the strength of premillennialism in Korea, but the country's division in 1945, the subsequent war, and the constant fear of invasion from the North also are significant elements. The most notorious episode of date setting in Korea involved the Hyoo-go movement, known as the Mission for the Coming Days by its American members, which targeted October 28, 1992 for the Rapture. The date was based on the calculation that the millennium would begin in 1999, 6,000 years after Adam's creation, and the tribulation would start seven years prior in 1992. The 20,000 members of the sect expected that before midnight of the appointed day they would rise into the heavens to meet the Lord, while everyone else left on earth would suffer the tribulation beginning after midnight. Discomfiture at the prophecy's failure was compounded when it was revealed that the sect's leader, Lee Jang Rim, had invested in bonds that matured in 1993.

The Korean movement best known in the West is the Unification Church, or Moonies, founded by Sun Myung Moon in 1954. Its first missionaries to America arrived in 1959. Moon, born in 1920, received a vision as a teenager that he would complete Jesus' work. His thought took a strongly millennial turn after his second marriage when he declared that fulfilling Jesus' work required marriage and children. Since Jesus had remained unmarried, he could offer only a spiritual renewal; a coming messiah will provide physical salvation as well. When Moon's twelfth child was born, he took the title of Lord of the Second Advent and announced that he and his wife were the True Parents who would restore the earth to perfect harmony. Three different dates, most recently 1981, were selected as the time when it would be achieved. The failure of all three predictions did not damage the movement to any great extent, but it has moved the Moonies from expecting an immediate fulfillment of the millennium to building gradually toward it. Moon has been vehemently anticommunist, and the most controversial aspect of the Moonies, besides the control over members' lives, has been their financial contributions to conservative American politicians.

When Mikhail Gorbachev began his policy of glasnost, many premillennialists were highly suspicious of him. To them, the birthmark on his forehead marked him clearly as Antichrist, and glasnost was Revelation's great act of deception. In *Gorbachev! Has the Real Antichrist Come?* (1988), Robert Faid gave the arguments for an affirmative answer, including the fact that sum of Gorbachev's name totals 1,332 or 666 times 2. As Gorbachev gave way to Boris Yeltsin and the Soviet Union was dissolved, many premillennialists refused to relinquish Russia's role in the endtime. Some argued that since Russia, not the Soviet Union, is identified in Daniel, it would still play its role in the invasion of Israel. Others looked to the Islamic successor states in Central Asia, as Hal Lindsey did in 1995, or the coming One World Government to serve as Antichrist's tools. The addition of Greece as the tenth member of the European Economic Union sparked interest because it fit the prophecy (Rev. 17:12) of the ten horns of the beast making up ten realms in a new Roman empire. The practice of searching out Antichrist was so ingrained in some Americans that as the danger of war with Russia receded in the early 1990s, they quickly found others to serve the part. Thus, during the Gulf War of 1991 against Iraq, Saddam Hussein made a fine fit, since as ruler of Babylon he was alleged to be the new Nebuchadnezzar. The belief that Islamic rulers would serve as Antichrist's agents had one advantage over the earlier fixation on Russia: It was never clear why Russia would want to invade Israel, but Muslim hostility was well known and apparently implacable.

As Russia faded out of the picture in the search for Antichrist, some Americans found him in an unexpected place—their own government. A combination of anger at high taxes, prayer bans in public schools, and abortion; of fear of the growing size and influence of minorities; and of economic difficulties in rural America led to the formation of groups usually referred to as right-wing militias. Most members of such groups have a powerful millennial belief called Christian Identity. It is an offspring of British-Israelism of the nineteenth century. The belief that the Anglo-Saxon people were descendants of the Ten Lost Tribes reached America in the late 1800s and gained a number of committed adherents. They never formed its own denomination but continued to belong to mainline Protestant churches. Most earlier British-Israelites expected to join the Jews as the chosen people in the New Kingdom, but in the 1920s several Americans had added an anti-Semitic element. Advocates such as William Cameron, editor of a weekly paper published by Henry Ford, declared that the Jews were not true Israelites at all. They argued that by interbreeding with Asian peoples Jews had lost all claim to be descendants of Abraham. Anglo-Saxons were the only true Israelites and would alone join Christ in reigning during the Millennium. In the 1940s books with titles such as *When Gog Attacks* introduced the claim that the Jews were the offspring of Satan through Cain and used terms such as the "synagogue of Satan." By 1960 adherents broadened the identity of the Lost Tribes to all Teutonic peoples, claiming that "As a White Person YOU ARE A DESCENDANT OF THE TRIBES OF ISRAEL or Judah and as such are THE CHOSEN PEOPLE OF GOD [*sic*]."[7]

Although British-Israelites had long been involved in the Ku Klux Klan and similar groups, they had never had a unified organization. After 1970 they began to coalesce into a religious-political movement called Christian Identity. It has no central statement of doctrine, leaders, or headquarters but is made up of a large number of groups with similar views with names like New Christian Crusade, Church of Israel, and the Covenant, Sword, and Arm of the Lord. The last existed as a commune in Missouri from 1971 to 1985. It defined its purpose as building an ark for God's people at the coming tribulation. The community broke up in 1985 when a man on his way to join it killed a state trooper, and police raided the commune. Members of Christian Identity usually belong also to political groups that include Aryan Nations, Patriots Council, and the Freemen; the distinction between the religious and the political organizations is very difficult to make.

Christian Identity groups claim that with the help of the Jews, Antichrist has taken over control of the American government, which they call the Zionist Occupied Government (ZOG). According to them, nearly everything the government has done in the past several decades is intended to destroy the truth and the people of God. Civil rights laws, for example, are part of Antichrist's plan to corrupt the white race by racial interbreeding, which the Bible prohibits. The time is rapidly approaching for the showdown between ZOG and God. True Christians must prepare for it by weapons training and learning to live off the land, since the economic infrastructure will be destroyed in the coming days. Thus, they emphasize survivalism and retreat into remote areas of the mountain West. Christian Identity is posttribulationist: Members expect to endure the tribulation before Christ comes to reign on earth. They denounce pretribulationism as "a myth invented by the enemies of Christ and of His Church to neutralize Christian people and render them useless in the fight for Christian dominion of the Earth."[8] They must battle the forces of Antichrist and ZOG to win the right to share in Christ's glory, a fight that they seem to anticipate with relish. While there is no perfect correlation between Christian Identity and the militias that have sprung up in the past two decades, a high proportion of the memberships overlap.

The Christian Identity groups found all the proof they needed for their case that the federal government was antichristian in one of millennialism's most violent and tragic episodes, the destruction of the Branch Davidian commune at Waco, Texas, in April 1993. Unlike Jim Jones's esoteric blend of Christianity and Marxism, the millennialism of its leader, David Koresh, was entirely within the Christian tradition. Born Vernon Howell in 1959 to a fourteen-year-old girl, Koresh was raised in a dysfunctional family loosely affiliated with the Seventh-day Adventists.[9] A barely literate high-school dropout, he became exceptionally well-versed in the Bible and later surprised biblical scholars with his command of the texts. Despite being a talented mechanic and guitar player, he was adrift when at age 20 he joined a Seventh-day Adventist fringe group and found his niche.

Seventh-day Adventists, rift with schisms since their founding, have become more torn in the past half-century as they have had to accommodate themselves to the constant delay in the fulfillment of prophecy and the need for the three million members to live in the world. Many who join because of the belief in the imminent Parousia grow disappointed that the church is less interested in preparing for the second advent than they expect. Fringe groups with a stronger millennial focus spin off and recruit members largely from among other Adventists. The sect that Howell joined had been founded in 1929 by a Bulgarian immigrant, Victor Houteff, in Los Angeles. Houteff, declaring that he was Ellen White's successor as prophet, made enough change in Adventist doctrine for the church leaders to expel him. His major point of deviance was arguing that the Parousia had not yet occurred because the Seventh-day Adventist Church had lost its zeal for the truth and proselytizing. He proclaimed that when 144,000 saints were identified, Christ would return to earth in Palestine. Because Christ would soon return to sit on David's throne, Houteff's followers were called Davidians. In 1934 he selected a site near Waco, where the saints would gather to wait for Christ. The commune was called Mount Carmel for the place where according to one tradition Christ would return to earth. By 1940 the population had reached 64 members who strove to be as self-sufficient and distinct as possible. One source of distinction was an insistence on marrying within the commune; a married newcomer whose spouse did not join had to get a divorce. Despite internal disputes the small society flourished in Waco under the benevolent reign of Houteff, prophet and king.

In 1955 Houteff died, creating a crisis in the sect. As the new Elijah he was supposed to live until Christ's return. The membership of about a thousand, mostly living away from Mount Carmel, split between Houteff's wife, Florence, who retained control of Mount Carmel, and Ben Roden, whose followers called themselves the Branch Davidians because Christ came from the branch of Jesse, the father of David (Isaiah 11:1). Florence immediately predicted that Christ would return at Passover in 1959, 1,260 days after Houteff's death. Over 900 people assembled in Waco to wait. Many sold their property or came great distances. After a month of futile waiting, most drifted off in bitter disappointment. Florence Houteff returned to California and disappeared from sight. The failure of her prophecy is one of the few times where such a failure has deprived a millennial leader of all authority and following.

The Davidian movement, however, was not dead. Many of the discomfited joined Roden, who gained control of Mount Carmel. He sought to reproduce Christ's perfection in the 144,000 saints and was interested in migration to Israel, arranging for six families to settle there. While that experiment soon failed, he introduced traditional Judaic rituals and feast days to his sect. Although Roden was proclaimed prophet and king, he soon gained a rival for influence in his wife, Lois. She had a vision in 1977 revealing to her that Christ would return in female form. When Roden died in 1978, the struggle for control of Mount Carmel involved Lois and their son George. She gained the upper hand but became involved in a protracted lawsuit with George. This was the environment in which Vernon Howell arrived in 1981. Lois Roden began to groom him as her successor. When she died in 1986, George gained control of the commune, but his eccentric ways and contempt toward the court lost him both his followers and a lawsuit to Howell, who became the leader of Lois Roden's group. In March 1988, Howell claimed Mount Carmel, while Roden ended up in a mental institution.

Howell set about reestablishing the community of Branch Davidians. He restored financial stability by soliciting large donations from members and establishing several successful businesses, most notably selling firearms and hunting equipment. He traveled to England and Australia to proselytize, winning recruits mostly from among Seventh-day Adventists. Surviving members have indicated that what attracted them the most was Howell's extraordinary knowledge of the Bible, which they felt could only have been divinely inspired. Some new recruits immigrated to Waco. In early 1993 the Branch Davidians were a multiracial, multinational group of about 130 members in residence consisting mostly of young couples with children (of the 80 who died at Mount Carmel 28 were black; only 5 were over age 50). Those in Howell's commune found themselves in a different situation than was the case under the Houteffs and Rodens. It had been made up of integral family units living a common life; under Howell it became a true commune, with gender and age segregation for the members.

In 1989 Howell changed his name to David Koresh. As David he was making his claim to being the new King David and a messianic figure; as Koresh he announced his mission to save the chosen people from exile. He had read several of Koresh/Teed's books, but his main sources of doctrine were the Bible and Adventist tradition, albeit with his own unique interpretation of both. His basic premise was that Christ had died only for those who had lived before him; Koresh was the messiah for the generations since. He was a "sinful messiah," because he had sinned, but that made him more effective in saving souls because he had experienced their weaknesses. He, not Christ, is the Lamb "that has been slaughtered" (Rev. 5:6) who opens the seven seals, hence his preferred name for his followers—Students of the Seven Seals. They will have a special place in the new kingdom above the 144,000 saints and will be taken to heaven before them, Koresh affirmed. That time was rapidly approaching, since the world had entered into the tribulation. Soon the Branch Davidians would emigrate to Israel, which Koresh visited twice, and convert the Jews. That would prompt Antichrist's appearance, who would lead an American army in an invasion of Israel. His defeat at Armageddon would be the signal for the consuming angel, Koresh himself, to purify the world for Christ's return, which would transform it into paradise.

Most important in bringing about the tragedy of Mount Carmel was Koresh's New Light doctrine. God had revealed to him that he was to father a new people of God, the House of David. Chosen women among the Branch Davidians would be sown with the seed of the Lamb. Koresh was to be their only mate on earth, although they would be united with their husbands or future husbands in a perfect union in heaven. In short the only sex allowed in Mount Carmel was between Koresh and his "spiritual wives." Everyone else was celibate. In 1987, three years after his marriage, Koresh took as a spiritual wife one of the teenage girls in the commune, telling her and her parents that she was having a baby for God. For a time only the unmarried women were privileged to be spiritual wives, but by 1990 Koresh was also mating with married women. He had at least fifteen children besides two he had with his legal wife, Rachel. She seems to have consented fully, usually preparing the spiritual wives for their nights with him.

Having sex with female members and their teenage daughters was the most powerful way in which Koresh bound both his partners and their relatives to him. It was the means of making absolutely clear the distinction between the chosen few in the commune and the condemned many outside, who regarded such behavior as sinful and illegal. Koresh was antinomian not only in regard to the law of the outside society but also in respect to his own law, imposing strict rules in such matters as diet and then flaunting his violations of them. It was his way of proving that he was above all law. His antinomianism, however, led to his downfall. Not every follower acquiesced in Koresh's sexual behavior. Several couples defected because of his demands on the wife or daughters; in other cases only the husband left in a jealous rage, leaving his family behind. It often happens that defectors become extremely hostile to the sect and provide ever-present outside opponents with rhetoric and legal evidence against the charismatic leader. Custody battles, the bane of Jim Jones, also erupted for Koresh. One accusation made against him in these custody suits was that he was having sex with underage girls, and there is evidence that at least three of his partners were between the ages of 12 and 14. A twelve-year-old girl had a daughter by Koresh; she was expected to grow up to marry his legitimate son and found a royal dynasty for the new kingdom.[10] These explosive charges of child sexual abuse were the key reason why the matter of Koresh's alleged gun-law violations, which if true should have been quickly resolved with a fine, led to the deaths of 84 people.

Mount Carmel's flourishing gun business put Koresh on the edge of the law controlling firearms sales. Largely though the efforts of defectors, the Bureau for Alcohol, Tobacco, and Firearms (BATF) had become aware of his activities. Persuaded by the defectors that the Branch Davidians were armed and dangerous and would violently resist any attempt to arrest Koresh, BATF planned an armed raid on the commune for February 28, 1993. About 80 heavily armed agents carried out the raid despite learning that secrecy had been breached. The Branch Davidians were prepared for them, and as the BATF agents approached the commune's buildings, gunfire erupted. It remains unclear who fired first, but when the shots ended, four agents and six Branch Davidians were dead. The government responded by rushing hundreds of FBI agents and massive amounts of military equipment to Waco to place Mount Carmel under siege.

Our purpose here is not to detail the 51-day siege nor dwell on the government's errors and misconceptions during it; it is rather to point out how Koresh's millennialism led him to misinterpret the actions of the federal officials. For some time, Koresh had been selling firearms at gun shows and talking with militia members present. While there was little in his lectures to his people that was hostile to the federal government—he was too involved in interpreting Revelation for that—he could not have avoided learning about ZOG and its role in the endtime. Everything about his background and business activities suggests that he was sympathetic to the militia ideology, and mistrust of government is an Adventist tradition. A year before the raid Koresh had given up hope of moving to Israel and began to talk of Mount Carmel as Ranch

Apocalypse, the site of Armageddon that he expected in 1995. He prepared for the coming battle with Antichrist by stockpiling weapons and supplies, and building defensive works in the commune. The federal officials played their role as the Babylonians to near perfection.

In the days after the failed raid, BATF justified it by stating that Koresh had imprisoned himself in the compound and made himself inaccessible for serving a warrant; but in fact he had been coming and going regularly. The BATF raid recalled nearly exactly Christ's word at his arrest (Luke 22:53): "Have you come out with swords and clubs as if I were a bandit? When I was with you day after day in the temple, you did not lay hands on me. But this is your hour, and the power of darkness!" Koresh believed that he would reenact Jesus' life and death. The coincidence between Christ's words and his situation could only prove that he was about to suffer the same fate. The deaths of six Davidians in the raid also confirmed the prophecy of the fifth seal of Revelation (6:9 - 11). When it is opened, John sees the souls of the those killed for the word of the Lord. They cry out for vengeance and are told that they should rest a little while until the number of those to be killed is complete. Given Koresh's deep concern with the seven seals, it is easy to see how he and his disciples would regard themselves as the saints yet to be killed.

Once the FBI took control of the siege around Mount Carmel, it tried a combination of negotiations and psychological warfare, using such tactics as blasting the compound with loud rock music or the bleating of dying rabbits and shining powerful spotlights into the windows at night. Encouraged by the Davidian defectors and anticult activists who served as advisers to the FBI, agents claimed that they were dealing with a violent, dangerous man who was holding women and children hostage. The FBI negotiators were ill-equipped to deal with Koresh. All he wanted to talk about was Revelation, while many of them were Catholics for whom that book was largely alien terrain. They ignored the advice of scholars of millennial groups, who advised them to meet Koresh on his own terms and persuade him that Revelation called for a peaceful resolution; nor did they grant his request to communicate with biblical scholars. The media, which was denied access in every other respect, were given full transcripts of Koresh's discussions with negotiators, "Bible babble" as the agents called it. By making available to the media those transcripts only, the authorities apparently wanted to make Koresh appear as a maniacal cult leader, another Jim Jones. Certainly that is the way most Americans perceived him.

Could Koresh have been persuaded to come out peaceably? Some who have studied the tragedy are adamant that it was possible if he had been allowed to finish his work of opening the seven seals. Over forty members, mostly women and children, to be sure, but also ten men, were allowed to leave. Koresh did not react to those leaving with the deep sense of betrayal that Jones did, providing hope that all would eventually come out. Yet there is little reason to believe that the stand-off could have been resolved peaceably. If Koresh were indeed Christ, the act had to be played out according to the script. Koresh knew that the men outside were Antichrist's agents; they had only one purpose: Kill the Lamb and his saints. He knew that eventually the government would lose patience and assault Mount Carmel, giving him the martyr's death he craved. It took 51 days, but on April 19 the FBI acted.

Was the fire that destroyed the compound an unintended result of actions taken either by the FBI or the Branch Davidians, or was it intentionally set as an act of apocalyptic suicide? Either scenario is plausible based on both forensic evidence and an understanding of Koresh's millennialism—he was obsessed with cleansing the world with a purging fire. When all the bodies were counted, 59 adults and 21 children had died, some by gunshots, while 8 people escaped. Of the 50 surviving members, about half are bitter toward Koresh while the others still regard him as the messiah. They expect his resurrection after 2,300 days, in August 1999, to open the sixth seal and begin the cleansing of the temple.

Even more than Jonestown, Waco is the definitive millennial event of our time. It was played out on television over two months and ended in a horrific catastrophe. The federal agencies involved and Congress made extensive investigations of what happened. Charges for killing the BATF agents were brought against the male survivors, and in the ensuing trial Branch Davidian beliefs and the government's acts were rehashed at great length. (The defendants were acquitted of most charges but given long sentences for those on which they were convicted.) Millennial beliefs were publicly discussed as never before in America, giving a crash-course to a large part of the American people who knew little or nothing about them. Despite the tragic deaths at Waco and the high probability that they were part of the motivation behind the bombing in Oklahoma City in 1995, Waco has perhaps one positive consequence. For some time to come, the government will be more careful of how it deals with millennial groups. It can be argued that that has been true in regard to Christian Identity groups, as shown by the 1996 Freemen episode in Montana that was resolved without bloodshed after a long standoff. It seems unlikely that there will soon be another violent clash between a government and a millennial cult anywhere in Western society.

XV

BEYOND THE
MILLENNIUM

M ILLENNIAL GROUPS HAVE RARELY BEEN VIOLENT entirely of their
own accord.[1] Outside interference has almost always been present before millennialists resort to violence in response to it. Such interference has been more common in the late twentieth century than in any other period except the sixteenth, which also saw several extremely violent events. If governments of the Western world have indeed learned a lesson from Waco, then there should be a period of time without significant violence associated with millennialism.

The absence of state-sponsored violence, however, creates a problem for those millennialists who regard collective death at the hands of Antichrist's forces as the instrument of their redemption and the world's end. If the saints cannot count on antichristian governments to provide that escape, then suicide is the only recourse. It may be mere coincidence that there have been three episodes of collective suicide in millennial groups since 1993, but mass suicide may become more common, as the beliefs of the cults move farther away from Christianity and its strong stand on God's sole right to decide when one dies.

The first of the suicide cults was the Order of the Solar Temple, which ended its existence in collective death between 1994 and 1997. Its founder was Luc Jouret, a Belgian physician, but Joseph Di Mambro, a Frenchman interested in the occult, emerged as co-leader. In 1984 they founded the Chivalric Organization Solar Tradition in Geneva, and two years later they set up a branch in Québec. Its membership, which peaked at about 100, comprised almost all middle class, French-speaking former Catholics, who handed over all property to the cult. Female members were available to the two leaders for sex. Their doctrine was eclectic, drawing on the medieval occult, Catholic tradition, and new age ideas. Both men claimed that they were reincarnations of knights Templar, the crusader order, and that they and 31 other male members had also been Ascended Masters of a centuries-old sect, the Roscrucians, who reveal themselves when Apocalypse approaches. The two men saw the world rushing toward ecological catastrophe, and only a small handful of the elect, the cult members, will be spared the coming all-destructive fire. Members will be purified through a ritual death and the burning of the body by "Christic fire." They will then be taken to "the Great White Lodge" on a planet of Sirius to live forever.

Di Mambro, who had largely supplanted Jouret by 1993, was in trouble over illegal firearms, and police raided the cult's Canadian site but found little evidence. He believed that the authorities intended the same fate for his group as the Branch Davidians had met and declared that Waco and other instances of what he regarded as state harassment were signs of the coming endtime. Accordingly, he proclaimed that his daughter Emmanuelle was the "cosmic child" who would lead the purified to Sirius. Di Mambro allegedly was enraged when a member couple in Québec, who were becoming disaffected from the cult, named their son Emmanuel; he declared that the baby was Antichrist. In October 1994, Di Mambro arranged for the ritual murder of the couple and their son, who was killed by a stake driven through his heart, and the three bodies were burned. Two members who had set the fire threw themselves into it, while the two assassins fled to Switzerland, where they joined the two leaders and 43 other members in ritual suicide in two locations. The buildings were set with incendiary devices that failed to go off. In December 1995, sixteen members committed suicide in France, and in March 1997 five more did in Québec although three teenagers escaped. There is evidence that many of the seventy people who died were killed by another's hand. Knowledge about the cult remains limited because the few surviving members have not been eager to detail its beliefs. Generally those who commit suicide do it as an entire group. What makes

Solar Temple unusual is the fact that two groups committed suicide separately from the main body and after the leaders' death.

Perhaps because the Solar Temple suicides occurred in remote sites outside of the United States, they received only a fraction of the publicity given to mass suicide by the Heaven's Gate cult in 1997. Heaven's Gate is the best example of a new phenomenon in millennialism—the UFO cult. The idea that the deity communicated with humanity through some sort of vehicle descending from the heavens dates back at least to Ezekiel (1:4–28). UFO believers often cite Ezekiel's description of a domed object that made a sound like thunder as evidence that earth had been visited by alien beings in ancient times. The modern concept of the UFO arose in 1947 with a rash of sightings, which have numbered in the hundreds every year since. Novels like Arthur Clarke's *Childhood's End* (1953) quickly appeared, in which benevolent aliens arrive to save the world from nuclear war and help create a perfect society. In other novels the aliens come to destroy the earth; sometimes they succeed; other times they force humanity to learn to cooperate against them. There soon followed the UFO abduction phenomenon, in which aliens supposedly take people into their spacecraft to experiment on them or warn them of a coming catastrophe. Those who have interviewed abductees have been struck by the heavy apocalyptic content in the descriptions of these experiences. Many Christian premillennialists, such as Hal Lindsey, believe that UFOs are real and their presence is satanic, signaling the endtime.

Any concept so freighted with millennialism will surely give rise to cults, and the UFO movement is no exception. What was probably the first such cult arose in the early 1950s; it was the subject of a notable book, *When Prophecy Fails* (1956).[2] The people involved and their cities were given pseudonyms; but nonetheless, the description of the cult's beliefs conforms closely enough to those of later UFO groups to allow its use as a model for such cults. "Mrs. Keech," whose husband never became a believer, began to receive messages (no year given) from Guardians from the constellation Cerus. They told her that nuclear explosions had transformed the upper atmosphere, allowing them to break through and make contact. They said they were only interested in bringing enlightenment to earth now in darkness. They revealed that flying saucers were real and provided a detailed history of the universe.

Humans originally lived on another planet that was destroyed when the forces of good and evil had battled using their equivalent of atomic bombs. Lucifer had brought his followers to earth with all knowledge of their previous home forgotten. The forces of good had gone to other planets, where they have worked to recover humanity from Lucifer. Christ was a Guardian whose mission was only partly successful, but he left behind enlightened humans like Mrs. Keech.

Mrs. Keech was told that at the next winter solstice there would be a great flood in which most of humanity would be destroyed, but a small group would be "evacuated" beforehand. She and her handful of followers began to spread the word but with limited success. By December they had about thirty disciples. Nearly all had a religious upbringing but were disenchanted with their churches; many had experience with spiritualism and knew theosophy. They gathered in Mrs. Keech's house on the evening before the solstice, expecting to be taken away in flying saucers before the flood hit the next day. Of course, the prophecy failed, and the members were left to deal with its failure. About half quickly abandoned the group, but the others rationalized the failure, recalculating to find a new date and proselytizing more actively than before. As of the study's end six months later, nearly all of some 15 true believers, still expecting the arrival of UFOs to whisk them from earth, had left their hometowns because of the ridicule they were receiving.[3]

The beliefs of Heaven's Gate were similar in most respects but included collective suicide. By a stroke of good fortune, its founders also were the subjects of a study on charismatic leadership soon after the cult had been formed in 1972.[4] Its author had no idea that his subjects would rate headlines two decades later, but because he chose to study them then, he had access to letters and other materials since destroyed and to their relatives and friends when memories were still fresh and, most importantly, before the events of 1997 colored perceptions. The founders were Marshall Applewhite and Bonnie Nettles, who first called themselves Bo and Peep and later Do and Ti. Both were in their forties and respected professionals, a music professor and a nurse, when they founded the cult, which went by several names before they settled on Heaven's Gate. Both also were in the midst of personal crises when they met in 1972 at the propitious time of the spring equinox. Applewhite's marriage had broken up over his homosexuality, and perhaps trying to prove his heterosexuality to himself, he became involved in a messy affair with a female student that led to the loss of his position. Nettles's marriage also was breaking up. Interested in spiritualism and theosophy, she introduced Applewhite to them. Soon he began to hear voices from other-worldly beings. Over the next three years the pair broke off all ties with their former lives and began to attract a few disciples to their new beliefs. What struck those who came into contact with them was how utterly inseparable they were in their platonic relationship. He was the "mouthpiece" and she, the "battery." They had an antinomian streak, as they regularly defrauded the motels where they stayed, and Bo spent eight months in jail in 1974 for not returning a rental car.

By 1975 Bo and Peep, shepherds of a flock, or the Two (a reference to the two witnesses of Revelation) had completed the process of creating a cult with about 150 members. There was a great deal of turnover in the membership, and the Two made little effort to keep defectors from leaving. They proclaimed that they would soon be martyred, rise from the dead, and be taken by UFO to a paradise on another planet. Those who would accompany them to this new world were obliged to give up all attachments of this world to begin the process of metamorphosis, which would be completed when they boarded a UFO. Sex was regarded as drawing energy away from the Process, so celibacy was mandated, although a man and a woman were always paired as partners in the Process, following Christ's example of sending out his disciples in pairs. On their new planet, soul and body would be melded into an indestructible being, ending the cycle of death and reincarnation that was the lot of souls on earth. The cult had no permanent home but stayed for weeks on end in campgrounds.

In late 1975 the group, which had been proselytizing mostly among college students, suddenly dropped from sight. Membership dropped below fifty persons. Members, but not Bo and Peep, spent most of the next twenty years proselytizing among the people with whom they came into contact on the backroads of the western states. They demanded strong commitment immediately from would-be members, who were expected to abandon their present lives and often travel for hundreds of miles to join the main group. Once there they were expected to embrace fully the group's lifestyle upon arrival. While Heaven's Gate had good success in attracting recruits, few stayed for long, but those who did were in it for life. Tracking their movements is most difficult, although it is known that the cult dashed from place to place expecting to be picked up by UFOs. The pathos of individuals in that situation, hardly unique to Heaven's Gate, is summed up in a member's comment: "Everytime I go to buy toothpaste, I buy a small tube, thinking I'm going to be here just a little longer. But I always wind up buying another tube."[5]

In 1985 Nettles, now Ti to Applewhite's Do (indicating they were mere notes in the symphony of the universe), died of cancer or, in Do's terms, "left her borrowed human vehicle." In 1996, the group surfaced in a suburb of San Diego and rented a mansion with funds from their business of creating web pages for the Internet. They also had their own web page on which Do presented his beliefs in detail. In early 1997, Comet Hale-Bopp, one of the largest to approach close to earth, was becoming visible. For the members of Heaven's Gate, who always rose before dawn to scan the heavens for a sign, a message on the Internet that a large body had been spotted hidden behind the comet became a marker from Ti for the arrival of a spacecraft from "the Level Above Human to take us home." On the day after the spring equinox and at the comet's closest approach, 21 women and 18 men, whose ages ranged from 26 to 72, began committing suicide in an amazingly meticulous fashion over a three-day period. Two members stayed alive to explain to the world the rationale behind the deaths but killed themselves a month later.

No other millennial group has so vast an amount of source material available about it. Heaven's Gate has a good scholarly study of its origins and easy access to its literature and web page. Because of its uniqueness and the availability of information, an account of Heaven's Gate's beliefs and practices provides valuable insight into how a cult can bring its members to that state of mind necessary to kill themselves. Do's web page suggests that he incorporated more Christian millennialism into his beliefs after 1975. According to Do's beliefs, the true kingdom of God exists in the most distant heavens as a place without time: It is the "headquarters" for many alien races and the human. Some of those races, the Luciferians, thousands of years ago rebelled against God. Instead of destroying them, God has allowed them to influence humans because of free will. Earth is God's garden where souls are grown, and at the end of every age a Representative takes on a "human vehicle" and comes to earth to harvest souls for the kingdom of heaven. Christ was the previous Representative, who serves as "Heaven's Gate" for anyone who wants to go to heaven, while Antichrist has opposed his efforts. Do and Ti, the current Representatives, took on their human containers in 1975, so while the bodies were Applewhite and Nettles, their minds were Do and Ti. For 20 years Do conducted a classroom for those who wanted to learn the Process for membership in "My Father's House." Now in 1997 the time for the "rendezvous in the clouds" was at hand. That only a few people were part of Heaven's Gate indicated how "full of weeds the garden is." God has decided to spade it under and recycle the world. Heaven's Gate members would not endure this tribulation, but in order to avoid it and rise to meet the spaceship, they had to "leave their containers" behind. Do presented suicide as the release of the spirit from the body to fulfill an interstellar destiny.

While Do's beliefs provided the rationale for collective suicide, it requires more than an ideology to motivate people to take their own lives; Heaven's Gate's lifestyle was equally important. New members were thrown into a very different world that banned the use of alcohol, coffee, drugs, and tobacco. They took new names, usually a single word such as Steel. They had no control over their own time; when they were sent out from the group on a task, they had to check in every 12 minutes. They had identical haircuts and wore the same asexual clothing. In death too all were the same—identical new running shoes, a five-dollar bill and a quarter in their pockets, and a diamond-shaped purple cloth covering them. In regard to sex, not only was celibacy enforced, but several male members, including Do, were castrated to control their sex drive: "There are eunuchs who have made themselves eunuchs for the sake of the kingdom of heaven" (Matt. 19:12). All of these aspects helped to create a sense of shedding the old self and becoming a new person. When a group does this together, it creates a group cohesion, a bonding with other members that can become extremely powerful. The military has known this for a long time, and most everything Heaven's Gate did, except with regard to sex, is done to new recruits in boot camp. There the result, if done right, is the formation of soldiers ready to fall on a grenade for the platoon or go on a suicide mission if ordered. In the case of Heaven's Gate, it formed people who would commit collective suicide at the leader's command. Heaven's Gate serves as the extreme example of both the extent to which its leader went to create group cohesion and the end to which he applied it. It also is an excellent example of the effectiveness of that process shared by every cult. The more it is present, the more likely it is that the cult members will remain together in the face of persecution and take part in violence and even collective suicide.

Among the many other UFO cults, the largest at the present time is Universal Articulate Interdimensional Understanding of Science (Unarius) based in southern California. Its Unarius Academy of Science is well funded by wealthy donors and has a mailing list of 90,000 names. It was founded in 1954 by Ernest and Ruth Norman, both now deceased. They believed that they lived many previous lives and included Jesus and Mary among those they had been. Ruth claimed also to have been the model for the "Mona Lisa." The heart of Unarius belief is that the earth is one of 33 planets with human life in a interplanetary confederacy. Humans on the other planets are more evolved than on earth, which has a dismal 150,000-year history in the war between darkness and light. That war pervades the universe, but the other humans have been more successful in fighting for the light. The first nuclear explosions signaled that humans on earth were in trouble, and their problems would spread to the other planets if left unchecked. The Normans believed that in 2001 spacecraft from the constellation Pleiades will land on Atlantis, which will rise from the sea, to bring earth into higher consciousness and lead it into the new age of logic, reason, and love. They predicted a landing for 1976 and explained the prophecy's failure by arguing that a hostile environment then meant humans were not ready to receive space visitors. It is the same explanation that the Unarius Academy puts forward when asked what if the spaceships fail to come in 2001, but it seems inconsistent with the claim that the Space Brothers are coming because humanity is in trouble.

Unarius is not another Heaven's Gate, since from what is known about it, it seems improbable that its members would commit either violence or mass suicide. Unarius has none of the key elements crucial for group solidarity: It lacks a communal lifestyle, name changing, a uniform mode of dress, a sense of persecution, and the theory that members will enter the New Kingdom as a group. Based on the available information, few of the current millennial groups show such signs. Even Christian Identity, for all of the bluster of its members, is not likely to resort soon to violence, in part because the authorities are certain to handle them with kid gloves for the next few years, but also because the members are widely dispersed, making it difficult to take any collective action.

One recent group that appeared to authorities to be potentially suicidal was the God's Salvation Church, which originated in Taiwan as Chen Tao. Non-ming Chen, a sociologist, founded it in 1993. Chen believes in reincarnation and has declared that he had been Christ's father. His beliefs draw from Buddhism and Taoism, but his eschatology comes more from Christianity and UFO lore. According to Chen, the world has endured four major nuclear tribulations in the distant past. They happen when human devils acting in concert with King Satan overwhelm the earth and drain so much "light energy" from it that natural and man-made disasters erupt. The possibly final one was to occur in 1999, when both great floods and nuclear war would devastate earth and kill three-fourths of humanity before 2000. God would preserve the United States to provide a refuge for "high spiritual light energy" persons (the saints), who would escape the tribulation in spaceships. Chen as the leader of God's Salvation Church would assemble those people somewhere in America. If a large enough number gathered, their collective light energy might be sufficient to overcome the devils and prevent earth's destruction. Otherwise Chen would lead them to heaven.

In 1995 Chen and 140 followers immigrated to San Diego, where he gained a few converts. In December 1997, they came to the attention of authorities investigating a Taiwanese woman's claim that Chen Tao had kidnapped her daughter. While returning the girl to her mother, they learned that the group was going to Garland ("God's Land") Texas, where Christ would come down in a spaceship to pick the members up. Authorities also found backpacks with matching white clothing and sneakers for the members to take to their heavenly rendezvous, raising fears that the group was another Heaven's Gate. The 160 members of the church, dressed in white and wearing sunglasses and white cowboy hats, reached Garland in early 1998. Chen proclaimed that God would appear on television on March 25 to announce his return, and then six days later he would assume a body identical to Chen's, performing three miracles to prove his divinity. God failed to appear on TV that day. Chen's response to the failure of his prediction, far from being suicidal or violent, is unique in millennialism. Although he said that his own faith was unshaken, he asked others to stop believing: "Since God's appearance on television has not been realized, you can take what we have preached as nonsense. I would rather you don't believe what I say anymore."[6] On March 31 Chen gathered some forty remaining members and asked how many intended to stay with him. All present raised their hands. He also offered to allow them to stone him as a false prophet, an offer they refused. He soon predicted God's coming to occur in late 1999 in Lockport, New York. Thirty members moved there with him.

Chen Tao was one of the rather few cults that targeted the year 2000 for the endtime. UFO groups saw greater significance in that date than did Christian ones, which remain largely faithful to the injunction that only the Father knows the day and the hour. The seers from Nostradamus, whose 450-year-old prediction called for the King of Terror to descend from the sky in July 1999, to Jeanne Dixon, who confidently placed the endtime in 2000, were more inclined to see that millennial year as significant. Edward Cayce, an American seer who died in 1945, prophesied a series of ever greater natural catastrophes caused by the tilting of the earth's axis prior to the Second Coming in 2000. The prophecy of St. Malachy, a twelfth-century Irish monk, predicting that there would be 120 more popes, places the present pope as the third from the last. It has long been assumed that his final pope, Peter II, would reign in 2000 and inaugurate the Millennium, but the length of several reigns in the twentieth century has pushed his last pope past 2000. Another prediction noted the alignment of all the other planets on the sun's far side from the earth on June 5, 2000, which was to cause catastrophic shifting of the earth's crust. The weekly tabloids were full of predictions for the Second Coming and the end of time for 2000, but true millennialists, who mostly operate on a different calendar, gave little credence to that date.

Then there was the Y2K computer problem. It hardly qualified as a millennial event, but some described it in apocalyptic terms as the event that would prove to be the undoing of the modern technological society. Others saw it as forcing humanity to recognize its hubris in its desire to play God with computers, gene splicing, and other recent developments in science and technology, and turn back to religion. In a videotape entitled "A Christian's Guide to the Millennium Bug," Jerry Falwell proclaimed that any catastrophe wrought by the computer glitch might be God's work to spark a great religious revival that could lead to Christ's return in 2000.[7]

The fact that rather few Christian millennialists looked to the coming of the year 2000 as a significant event in God's calendar does not mean that it would be free of millennial eruptions. For many already in an apocalyptic state of mind, the lure of seeing the millennium's turn as God's choice for doomsday was too powerful to resist. In October 1998, for example, a group in Colorado, the Concerned Christians, disappeared from Denver shortly before the presumed time for the beginning of the tribulation, in which the city would be destroyed. Their leader Kim Miller allegedly claims that he is one of the two witnesses of Revelation; he would be killed in Jerusalem in late 1999 and after three days be raised from the dead. The cult was found in Israel in early 1999 and expelled, but that did not seem to have broken the members' faith in Miller.

The uneventful coming of the year 2000 seems to have played a major role in causing the destruction of the Movement for the Restoration of the Ten Commandments of God in Uganda in March 2000, another mass suicide associated with millennialism. Although information about the group's motivation remains sketchy, it appears that the failure of a prediction that the end of the world would occur at the stroke of midnight on December 31, 1999, was the primary cause. The nominal leader was Joseph Kibwetere, a Catholic lay teacher of religion, who left his position in 1991 when he met Credonia Mwerinde. She was a young woman with a reputation for sexual promiscuity when she began to have visions from the Virgin Mary in 1988. They began to attract a following, including a Catholic priest, Dominic Kataribado, who also had an important role in the group's leadership as it organized itself into the Movement for the Restoration of the Ten Commandments in 1994.

As membership grew, mostly from among Ugandan Catholics, a commune was established at Kanungu, Uganda.

As the name implies, the Movement emphasized a strict keeping of the Commandments, especially those against adultery and taking the Lord's name in vain. Since speaking was deemed a major cause of breaking both commandments, commune members were prohibited from talking to each other or to outsiders; they developed an elaborate sign language for communication. They handed over their property to the leaders and labored long hours in the commune's fields. The sexes were strictly segregated, and children taken from their parents. The members wore distinctive clothes and lived a regimented life completely isolated from relatives and neighbors. While the members ate meager amounts of monotonous food, the leaders had their own dining room.

In 1996 the Movement produced a pamphlet for proselytizing entitled "A Timely Message from Heaven: The End of the Present Times."[8] It predicted a dreadful series of calamities before the endtime if people did not obey the Ten Commandments, but it did not set a time for them to happen. It did prophesy the destruction of the world by "hurricanes of fire" that would reach inside of buildings and spare no one. In 1999 Kibwetere began to proclaim the endtime would occur at the turn of the millennium. The Movement began to sell off its property and goods in anticipation of it. When nothing happened on January 1, some members apparently lost faith and began to demand the return of the money they had given over to the cult. It is possible too that Kibwetere had died by the end of 1999, because Mwerinde emerged as the leader, although some of those who had contact with the cult before then identified her as the principal leader from the first who used Kibwetere as a figurehead. She set March 17 as the date of the end, and about 540 members including many children assembled in their church, nailed the doors shut, and touched off a mixture of gasoline, sulfuric acid, and insecticide that in seconds killed everyone inside while barely damaging the building. How many of those inside willing were part of a ritual suicide is impossible to say, since there were no survivors. That question became far more difficult to answer when Ugandan authorities uncovered several mass graves of cult members who had been clearly murdered up to six weeks earlier. The supposition is that they were dissidents who were demanding the return of their money, while those who died in the fire were the true be-lievers. The authorities, who early on placed the total number of dead at over 1,000, issued a report in July, 2000, setting it at 780, making the cult less deadly than Jonestown.[9] Whether the leaders died in the fire or es-caped with the cult's funds remains a mystery. If Mwerinde were truly the leader, it would make the Movement unique among millennial cults by having a female leader who engaged in violence.

The events in Uganda help to demonstrate that longing for the end-time is far too deeply ingrained in Christianity and Western Civilization, and indeed all of human culture, for it to disappear after 2000 has come and gone. It provides an answer to several of the most deeply seated human anxieties: It helps to make sense of the evil that seems to pervade the world and promises that a perfect society without evil is close at hand. It explains why "good people" have to suffer persecution and the malice of the wicked. It overcomes not only the fear of death and anni-hilation but also of aging, since the usual millennial promise is that the saints will live forever in a perfect world with bodies in their ideal youthful condition. By incorporating the millennial promise so deeply in its theology, Christianity ensures that millennial cults will appear and disappear as long as it endures. We can expect that historians at the next turn of the millennium will need to add many more chapters to update this book.

NOTES

CHAPTER I

1. W. Stark, *Sociology of Religion* (New York, 1970).
2. F. Manuel, *The Prophets of Paris* (New York, 1962), p. 6.

CHAPTER II

1. F. Grant, *An Introduction to New Testament Thought* (New York, 1950), p. 303.
2. L. Festinger, et al., *When Prophecy Fails* (Minneapolis, 1956). But, see chapter XV, n. 2, for a criticism of the book's methodology.

CHAPTER III

1. A. Collins, "The Early Christian Apocalypses," in *Apocalypse: Morphology of a Genre,* J. Collins, ed. (Missoula, Mont., 1979), pp. 61–121.
2. P. Fredricksen, "Tyconius and Augustine on the Apocalypse," in *The Apocalypse in the Middle Ages,* R. Emmerson and B. McGinn, eds. (Ithaca, N. Y., 1992), pp. 20–37.
3. Lactantius, *Divine Institutes,* Book VII; in *Apocalyptic Spirituality,* B. McGinn, trans. (New York, 1979), p, 73.
4. Fredricksen, "Tyconius and Augustine," p. 21.

CHAPTER IV

1. Translated in B. McGinn, *Visions of the End: Apocalyptic Traditions in the Middle Ages* (New York, 1979), p. 75

2. Ibid., p. 81.
3. Quoted in H. Focillon, *The Year 1000,* F. Wieck, trans. (New York, 1969), p. 65.
4. T. Head and R. Landes, eds., *The Peace of God: Social Violence and Religious Response in France around the Year 1000* (Ithaca, N. Y., 1992), pp. 11–12.
5. A. Silver, *A History of Messianic Speculation in Israel, from the First through the Seventeenth Centuries* (Boston, 1959), pp. 68–69.
6. D. Cohn-Sherbook, *The Jewish Messiah* (Edinburgh, 1997), pp. 106–7.

CHAPTER V

1. Quoted in McGinn, *Visions of the End,* p. 137.
2. *The Divine Comedy of Dante Alighierei,* R. Durling, trans. (Oxford, 1996), p. 435.
3. Quoted in H. Kaminsky, *History of the Hussite Revolution* (Berkeley, 1967), p. 347.

CHAPTER VI

1. Quoted in A. Mendel, *Vision and Violence* (Ann Arbor, 1992), p. 67.

CHAPTER VII

1. Phrase from *The Cause of God* (1659), quoted in J. McGregor, ed., *Radical Religion in the English Revolution* (Oxford, 1984), p. 170.
2. Quoted in A. Mann, *Millennium Prophecies* (Rockport, Mass., 1993), p. 81.
3. Quoted in E. Voegelin, *The New Science of Politics* (Chicago, 1952), p. 115.

CHAPTER VIII

1. Quoted in P. Watts, "Prophecy and Discovery: On the Spiritual Origins of Christopher Columbus's 'Enterprise of the Indies,'" *American Historical Review,* 90 (1985), p. 73.
2. M. Wigglesworth, *The day of doom; or A description of the great and last judgment. With a short discourse about eternity* (London, 1673).

3. Quoted in P. Boyer, *When Time Shall Be No More* (Cambridge, Mass., 1992), p. 74.
4. Quoted in J. Davidson, *The Logic of Millennial Thought* (New Haven, 1977), p. 223.

CHAPTER IX

1. Quoted in J. Talmon, *The Origins of Totalitarian Democracy* (London, 1970), p. 187.
2. Ibid., p. 195.
3. Quoted in K. Kumar, *Utopianism* (Minneapolis, 1991), p. 60.
4. Quoted in V. Geoghegan, *Utopianism and Marxism* (London, 1987), p. 24.
5. Ibid. p. 62.

CHAPTER X

1. Quoted in M. St. Clair, *Millenarian Movements in Historical Context* (London, 1992), p. 316.

CHAPTER XI

1. Quoted in J. Mooney, *The Ghost-dance Religion and the Sioux Outbreak* (Washington, 1896), p. 32.
2. Quoted in R. Utley, *Last Days of the Sioux Nation* (New Haven, Conn., 1963), p. 89.
3. R. Levine, *Vale of Tears: Revisiting the Canudos Massacre in Northeastern Brazil, 1893–97* (Berkeley, 1992), p. 227.

CHAPTER XII

1. J. Winter, *Sites of Memory, Sites of Mourning* (Cambridge, 1995), p. 139–40.
2. Ibid., p. 191.
3. T. S. Eliot, *Collected Poems 1909–1962* (New York, 1963), p. 82.
4. W. Yeats, *The Poems,* R. Finneran, ed. (New York, 1989), p. 187.
5. Quoted in M. Penton, *Apocalypse Delayed* (Toronto, 1985), p. 45.
6. Quoted in O. Friedrich, *The End of the World: A History* (New York, 1986), p. 221.

7. J. Reed, *Ten Days that Shook the World* (New York, 1960). I wish to thank my colleague William Ochsenwald for bringing this source to my attention.

8. Quoted in R. Ellis, *The Dark Side of the Left: Illiberal Egalitarianism in America* (Lawrence, Kans., 1998), p. 102.

9. G. Melton, ed., *Encyclopedia of American Religions,* 5th ed. (Detroit, 1996), p. 520.

10. Quoted in P. Johnson, *Modern Times* (New York, 1983), p. 150.

11. Quoted in R. Brenner, *The Faith and Doubt of Holocaust Survivors* (New York, 1980), p. 158.

CHAPTER XIII

1. L. Giovannitti and F. Freed, *The decision to drop the bomb* (New York, 1965), p. 197. The actual text in the Bhagavad-Gita is somewhat different but equally appropriate: Krishna is asked who he is, "devouring the worlds with flaming mouths and your terrible fires scorch the entire universe. " He replies, "I am time grown old, creating world destruction, set in motion to annihilate the worlds. " From *The Bhagavad-Gita,* B. Miller, trans. (New York, 1986), p. 103.

2. Quoted in S. Zimdars-Swartz, *Encountering Mary* (Princeton, 1991), p. 199.

3. Statistics from W. Christian, "Religious Apparitions and the Cold War in Southern Europe," in *Religion, Power and Protest in Local Communities,* E. Wolf, ed. (Berlin, 1984), 239–66.

4. Quoted in R. Brenner, *The Faith and Doubt of Holocaust Survivors,* p. 143.

5. J. Katz, "Israel and the Messiah," in *Essential Papers on Messianic Movements and Personalities in Jewish History* (New York, 1992), p. 475.

6. J. Walvoord, *The Church in Prophecy* (Grand Rapids, Mich., 1964), p. 171.

7. Quoted in L. Barrett, *The Rastafarians* (Boston, 1977), p. 81.

8. G. Ragni and J. Rado, *Hair: The American Tribal Love-Rock Musical* (New York, 1969).

9. J. Boulware, "A Devil of a Time," *The Washington Post,* August 30, 1998, F1.

CHAPTER XIV

1. T. Reiterman, *Raven: The Untold Story of the Rev. Jim Jones and His People* (New York, 1982), pp. 176–77.

2. J. Mills, *Six years with God: Life inside Reverend Jim Jones' Peoples Temple* (New York, 1979), p. 122.

3. Quoted in G. Halsell, *Prophecy and Politics: Militant Evangelists on the Road to Nuclear War* (Westport, Conn., 1986), pp. 45, 48. It should be noted that Reagan did not use the phrase "evil empire" for the Soviet Union, a term loaded with millennial connotations; he called it the "focus of evil in the world," a phrase more neutral in millennial implications.

4. Quoted in S. O'Leary and M. McFarland, "The Political Use of Mythic Discourse: Prophetic Interpretation in Pat Robertson's Presidential Campaign," *Quarterly Journal of Speech,* 75 (Summer, 1989), 439. Second quote from Robertson, *The Secret Kingdom* (Nashville, 1982), p. 216.

5. Quoted in Halsell, *Prophecy and Politics,* p. 39.

6. A. Mojtabai, *Blessed Assurance: At Home with the Bomb in Amarillo, Texas* (Albuquerque, N. Mex., 1986).

7. Quoted in M. Barkun, *Religion and the Racist Right* (Chapel Hill, 1994), p. 68.

8. L. Sargent, ed., *Extremism in America: A Reader* (New York, 1995), p. 334.

9. D. Reavis, *Ashes of Waco* (New York, 1995), pp. 23–24.

10. S. Wright, ed., *Armageddon in Waco* (Chicago, 1995), p. 127.

CHAPTER XV

1. Aum Shinrikyo, the homicidal Japanese cult that killed dozens in a gas attack in a Tokyo subway in 1995, took its eschatology mostly from Buddhism and Hinduism. It did draw on Revelation for symbols and prophecy, but an explanation of its beliefs is beyond the scope of this book.

2. L. Festinger, et al., *When Prophecy Fails.* Filled with insights into a cult's workings, the study proposed to show what happens upon the failure of an endtime prediction. The authors' often-cited conclusion is that many of the discomfited, rather than losing faith, redouble their efforts to convert others, reconvincing themselves of the truth of their message if they can convince others. The argument is supported by several cases in the history of millennialism, but a problem of the study is that in order to complete their research the several authors and research assistants had to remain active in the UFO cult after the prediction's failure. They made up a large portion of the adults (about 15 real members) who remained involved after the discomfiture. Whether or not their presence was crucial in keeping the others involved, the possibility that it was creates a problem for the book's thesis.

3. According to J. Melton, *The Encyclopedia of American Religion,* 3rd. ed. (Detroit, 1989), pp. 677–78, the real name of the woman (now deceased)

was Dorothy Martin. She lived in Peru for five years after this episode and upon her return established the Association of Sananda and Sanat Kumara, a new age group that emphasizes the channeling of the Masters.

4. R. Balch, "Bo and Peep" A Case Study of the Origins of Messianic Leadership," in *Millennialism and Charisma* R. Wallis, ed. (Belfast, 1982), pp. 13–72. Also, R. Balch, "Waiting for the Ships: Disillusionment and the Revitalization of Faith in Bo and Peep's UFO cult," in *The Gods Have Landed: New Religions from Other Worlds,* J. Lewis, ed. (Albany, N. Y., 1995), pp. 137–66.

5. Quoted in Balch, "'When the Light Goes Out, Darkness Comes': A Study of Defection from a Totalistic Cult," in *Religious Movements: Genesis, Exodus and Numbers,* R. Stark, ed. (New York, 1985), p. 25.

6. Web page: http://www. trancenet. org/groups/gsc/news. shtml

7. *The Roanoke Times,* November 27, 1998, B7.

8. Web page: http://www.rickross.com/reference/tencommandments/tencommandments61.html

9. Web page: http://www.rickross.com/reference/tencommandments/tencommandments109.html

PRINCIPAL SOURCES

B OOKS AND ARTICLES ON MILLENNIALISM and millennial groups abound. The following is a list of the sources that I found especially useful for this book. Most are readily accessible in large public libraries. Works cited in the notes are not repeated.

GENERAL STUDIES

M. Barkun. *Disaster and the Millennium*. New Haven, Conn., 1974.

M. Barkun. ed. *Millennialism and Violence*. London, 1996.

N. Campion. *The Great Year: Astrology, Millenarianism and History in the Western Tradition*. London, 1994.

J. Collins, B. McGinn, and S. Stein. *The Encyclopedia of Apocalypticism*. 3 vols. New York, 1998.

N. Cohn. *Cosmos, Chaos and the World to Come*. New Haven, 1993.

N. Cohn. *The Pursuit of the Millennium*. rev. ed. New York, 1970.

M. Eliade. *The Myth of the Eternal Return*. Princeton, N.J., 1971.

L. Froom. *The Prophetic Faith of Our Fathers*. 4 vols. Washington, 1950.

R. Knox. *Enthusiasm: A Chapter in the History of Religion*. Oxford, 1950.

B. McGinn. *Antichrist. Two Thousand Years of the Human Fascination with Evil*. New York, 1994.

S. O'Leary. *Arguing the Apocalypse*. New York, 1994.

T. Olson. *Millennialism, Utopianism, and Progress*. Toronto, 1982.

M. St. Clair. *Millenarian Movements in Historical Context*. New York, 1992.

CHAPTER II

A. Collins. *Crisis and Catharsis: The Power of the Apocalypse*. Philadelphia, 1984.

PRINCIPAL SOURCES | 273

S. Cook. *Prophecy and Apocalypticism: The Postexilic Social Setting.* Minneapolis, 1995.

B. Daley. *The Hope of the Early Church: A Handbook of Patristic Eschatology.* Cambridge, 1990.

P. Fredricksen. *From Jesus to Christ: The Origins of the New Testament Images of Jesus.* New Haven, Conn., 1988

D. Hellholm. *Apocalypticism in the Mediterranean World and the Near East.* Tübingen, 1989.

C. Hill. *Regnorum Caelorum: Patterns of Future Hope in Early Christianity.* Oxford, 1992.

R. Jewett. *The Thessalonian Correspondence: Pauline Rhetoric and Millenarian Piety.* Philadelphia, 1986.

S. Nigosian. *The Zoroastrian Faith, Tradition and Modern Research.* Montreal, 1993.

D. Russell. *The Method and Message of Jewish Apocalyptic.* Philadelphia, 1974.

W. Schmithals. *The Apocalyptic Movement.* Trans. J. Steely. Nashville, 1975.

L. Thompson. *The Book of Revelation: Apocalypse and Empire.* New York, 1990.

J. VanderKam. *The Dead Sea Scrolls Today.* Grand Rapids, 1994.

CHAPTER III

P. Brown. *Religion and Society in the Age of Saint Augustine.* New York, 1972.

W. Bousset. *The Antichrist Legend.* Trans. A. Keane. London, 1896.

R. Emmerson and B. McGinn. eds. *The Apocalypse in the Middle Ages.* Ithaca, N. Y., 1992.

W. Frend. *The Donatist Church: A Movement of Protest in Roman North Africa.* Oxford, 1971.

K. Steinhausen, *The Apocalypse Commentary of Tyconius: A History of its Reception and Influence.* New York, 1987.

B. Warfield. *Studies in Tertullian and Augustine.* Westport, Conn., 1970.

CHAPTER IV

A. Anderson. *Alexander's Gate, Gog and Magog, and the Enclosed Nations.* Cambridge, Mass., 1932.

R. Landes. *Relics, Apocalypse, and the Deceits of History: Ademar of Chabannes, 989–1034.* Cambridge, Mass., 1995.

G. Teres. "Time Computations and Dionysius Exiguus." *Journal for the History of Astronomy.* 15 (1984), 177–88.

W. Verbeke et al. eds. *The Use and Abuse of Eschatology in the Middle Ages*. Leuven, 1988.

CHAPTER V

D. Burr. *Olivi's Peaceable Kingdom: A Reading of the Apocalypse Commentary*. Philadelphia, 1993.
F. Heymann. *John Zizka and the Hussite Revolution*. Princeton, N.J., 1955.
G. Leff. *Heresy in the Later Middle Ages*. 2 vols. Manchester, 1967.
B. McGinn. *The Calabrian Abbot: Joachim of Fiore in the History of Western Thought*. New York, 1985.
M. Reeves. *The Influence of Prophecy in the Later Middle Ages*. Oxford, 1969.
A. Williams. ed. *Prophecy and Millenarianism: Essays in Honor of Majorie Reeves*. Essex, 1980.

CHAPTER VI

I. Backus. "The Church Fathers and the Canonicity of the Apocalypse in the Sixteenth Century." *The Sixteenth Century Journal*. 29 (1998), 651–666.
R. Barnes. *Prophecy and Gnosis: Apocalypticism in the Wake of the Lutheran Reformation*. Stanford, Calif., 1988.
D. Crouzet. *Les Guerriers de Dieu*. Paris, 1990.
W. Klaassen. *Living at the End of the Ages: Apocalyptic Expectation in the Radical Reformation*. Lantham, Md., 1992.
D. Weinstein. *Savonarola and Florence: Prophecy and Patriotism in the Renaissance*. Princeton, N.J., 1970.
G. Williams. *The Radical Reformation*. Kirksville, Mo., 1995

CHAPTER VII

S. Bolshakoff. *Russian Nonconformity: The Story of "Unofficial" Religion in Russia*. Philadelphia, 1950.
R. Crummey. *The Old Believers and the World of Anti-Christ*. Madison, Wis., 1970.
K. Firth. *The Apocalyptic Tradition in Reformation Britain, 1530–1645*. Oxford, 1979.
C. Hill. *Antichrist in Seventeenth-Century England*. Oxford, 1971.
P. Rogers. *The Fifth Monarchy Men*. London, 1966.
G. Scholem. *Sabbatai Sevi: The Mystical Messiah*. Princeton, N.J., 1975.
K. Thomas. *Religion and the Decline of Magic*. London, 1971.

P. Toon. ed. *Puritans, the Millennium and the Future of Israel: Puritan Eschatology 1600 to 1660.* Cambridge, 1970.

Chapter VIII

R. Bloch. *Visionary Republic: Millennial Themes in American Thought, 1756–1800.* New York, 1985.

R. Middlekauff. *The Mathers: Three Generations of Puritan Intellectuals.* New York, 1971.

J. Phelan. *The Millennial Kingdom of the Franciscans in the New World.* Berkeley, 1970.

E. Tuveson. *Redeemer Nation: the Idea of America's Millennial Role.* Chicago, 1968.

Chapter IX

C. Garrett. *Respectable Folly: Millenarians and the French Revolution in France and England.* Baltimore, 1975.

F. Manuel and F. Manuel. *Utopian Thought in the Western World.* Cambridge, Mass., 1979.

E. Tuveson. *Millennium and Utopia: A study in the Background of the Idea of Progress.* Gloucester, Mass., 1972.

N. Wachtel. *The Vision of the Vanquished.* New York, 1977.

Chapter X

M. Barkun. *Crucible of the Millennium: The Burned-Over District of New York in the 1840s.* Syracuse, N. Y., 1986.

W. Hinds. *American Communities and Co-operative Colonies.* Philadelphia, 1975.

M. Holloway. *Heavens on Earth: Utopian Communities in America 1680–1880.* New York, 1966.

S. Klaw. *Without Sin: The Life and Death of the Oneida Community.* New York, 1993.

I. Mandelkar. *Religion, Society and Utopia in Nineteenth-Century America.* Amherst, Mass., 1984.

R. Numbers and J. Bulter. eds. *The Disappointed: Millerism and Millenarianism in the Nineteenth Century.* Bloomington, Ind., 1987.

D. Pitzer. ed. *America's Communal Utopias.* Chapel Hill, 1997.

K. Rexroth. *Communalism: from its origins to the twentieth century.* New York, 1974.

D. Rowe. *Thunder and Trumpets: Millerites and Dissenting Religion in Upstate New York, 1800–1850.* Chico, Calif., 1985.

CHAPTER XI

E. Clark. *The Small Sects in America.* New York, 1949.

R. Fogarty. *The Righteous Remnant: The House of David.* Kent, Ohio, 1981.

G. Larson. *Prelude to the Kingdom: Mormon Desert Conquest, a Chapter in American Cooperative Experience.* Westport, Conn., 1978.

M. Penton. *Apocalypse Delayed: The Story of the Jehovah's Witnesses.* Toronto, 1985.

E. Sandeen. *The Roots of Fundamentalism: British and American Millenarianism 1800- 1930.* Chicago, 1970.

S. Thrupp. ed. *Millennial Dreams in Action.* New York, 1970.

T. Weber. *Living in the Shadow of the Second Coming: American Premillennialism 1875–1925.* Oxford, 1979.

CHAPTER XII

M. Adas. *Prophets of Rebellion: Millenarian Protest Movements against the European Colonial Order.* Chapel Hill, 1979.

K. Burridge. *New Heaven, New Earth: A Study of Millenarian Activities.* Oxford, 1980.

W. Wagar. *Terminal Visions: The Literature of Last Things.* Bloomington, Ind., 1982.

L. Zamora. ed. *The Apocalyptic Vision in America: Interdisciplinary Essays on Myth and Culture.* Bowling Green, Ohio, 1982.

S. Zimdars-Swartz. *Encountering Mary.* Princeton, N.J., 1991.

CHAPTER XIII

J. Hall. *Gone from the Promised Land: Jonestown in American Cultural History.* London, 1987.

T. Kselman and S. Avella. "Marian Piety and the Cold War in the United States." *Catholic Historical Review.* 72 (1986), 403–424.

V. Lanternari. *The Religions of the Oppressed: A Study of Modern Messianic Cults.* Trans. L Sergio. New York, 1963.

J. Melton. *Encyclopedic Handbook of Cults in America.* New York, 1986.
P. Worsley. *The Trumpet Shall Sound: A Study of "Cargo" Cults in Melanesia.* New York, 1968.
S. Weart. *Nuclear Fear.* Cambridge, Mass., 1988.

CHAPTER XIV

M. Barkun. *Religion and the Racist Right.* Chapel Hill, 1994.
M. Cuneo. *The Smoke of Satan.* New York, 1997.
D. Wojcik. *The End of the World As We Know It: Faith, Fatalism, and Apocalypse in America.* New York, 1997.

CHAPTER XV

R. Abanes. *End-time Visions: The Road to Armageddon?* New York, 1998.
A. Heard. *Apocalypse Pretty Soon.* New York, 1999.
C. Strozier and M. Flynn. eds. *The Year 2000: Essays on the End.* New York, 1997.

USEFUL WEB SITES

www.washingtonpost.com/wp-srv/national/longterm/cult/front.htm
www.mille.org/indexA.html (Center for Millennial Studies)
www.softdisk.com/comp/dan/davidian.html ("A Brief Stop at Mt. Carmel")
www.marianland.com/thirdsec.html ("Third Secret of Fatima")
www.yahweh.com/index.shtml ("House of Yahweh")
www.trancenet.org/links/cults.shtml (Links to sites on cults)
www.watchman.org/chentao.htm (Site on Chen Tao)
www.signministries.org (Extensive glossary of millennial terms)
www.mayhem.net/Crime/cults1.html (Violent cults)
www.enteraConn.com/~jwalz/Eliade/eschat.html (Mircea Eliade on eschatology)
www.millennianet.com/atpro4se/ (Christian prophecy)
www.trancenet.org/heavensgate/ (Mirror site of the original Heaven's Gate web page)
www.wesley.nnc.edu/noncanon.htm (Noncanonical apocalypses)
odin.community.net/~timlig/expo.html (Site on Emmanuel Swedenborg)

INDEX